ELECTROCARDIOGRAPHY
Basic Concepts and Clinical Application

ELECTROCARDIOGRAPHY
Basic Concepts and Clinical Application

Mark E. Silverman, M.D.

Professor of Medicine (Cardiology)
Department of Medicine
Emory University School of Medicine
Chief of Cardiology, Piedmont Hospital
Atlanta, Georgia

Robert J. Myerburg, M.D.

Professor of Medicine and Physiology
Director, Division of Cardiology
University of Miami Medical Center
Miami, Florida

J. Willis Hurst, M.D.

Candler Professor of Medicine (Cardiology)
Chairman, Department of Medicine
Emory University School of Medicine
Chief of Medicine and Cardiology
Emory University Hospital
Chief of Medicine, Grady Memorial Hospital
Chief of the Medical Section
Emory University Clinic
Atlanta, Georgia

McGraw-Hill Book Company

New York St. Louis San Francisco Auckland Bogotá Guatemala Hamburg Johannesburg
Lisbon London Madrid Mexico Montreal New Delhi Panama Paris
San Juan São Paulo Singapore Sydney
Tokyo Toronto

ELECTROCARDIOGRAPHY Basic Concepts and
Clinical Application

Copyright © 1983 by McGraw-Hill, Inc. All rights reserved. Printed in the United States of America. Except as permitted under the United States Copyright Act of 1976, no part of this publication may be reproduced or distributed in any form or by any means, or stored in a data base or retrieval system, without the prior written permission of the publisher.

234567890HALHAL898765

ISBN 0-07-057483-9

This book was set in Times Roman by General Graphic Services, Inc.;
the editors were Joseph J. Brehm and Steven Tenney; the production supervisor was Avé McCracken; the designer was Bob Gumbs.
Halliday Lithograph Corporation was printer and binder.

Library of Congress Cataloging in Publication Data

Silverman, Mark E.
  Electrocardiography, basic concepts and clinical application.

  1. Electrocardiography. 2. Heart—Diseases—Diagnosis.
I. Myerburg, Robert J. II. Hurst, J. Willis (John Willis), date. III. Title. [DNLM: 1. Electro-cardiography. WG 140 S587e]
RC683.5.E5S486 1983   616.1'207547   83-755
ISBN 0-07-057483-9

Dr. Robert P. Grant—Teaching

This book is based on the concepts of Dr. Robert P. Grant—a unique individual who influenced a vast number of medical students, house officers, and colleagues with his brilliant, creative mind and his warm, kind personality.

Photographs of Dr. Robert P. Grant made at Emory University in 1954 by Dr. Leslie French of Hyattsville, Maryland. Dr. Grant developed the spatial vector method of analyzing electrocardiograms while he was a member of the Department of Medicine of Emory University School of Medicine (1947–1950).

Contents

Preface *xv*

Part **One** **Basic Concepts of Electrocardiography**

    Introduction *3*

        Pattern Recognition *3*
        Vector Method *3*

1 **Basic Electrophysiology of the Heart** *5*

    Cellular Electrophysiology *5*
    Sequence of Depolarization and Repolarization *8*

2 **The Spatial Vector Concept and Its Clinical Application** *13*

    The Vector Concept *13*
    The Electrocardiographic Lead System *16*

        The Frontal Plane Leads *20*
        The Precordial Plane Leads *27*

    Summary of the Procedure Used to Determine the Spatial Direction of Electrical Forces Illustrated as Vectors *31*

3 **The Interpretation of the Electrocardiogram** *41*

    Terminology of Electrocardiographic Deflections *41*

        P Wave *41*
        QRS Complex *41*

          Q Wave, R Wave, S Wave *41*

        T Wave *43*

U Wave *43*
Further Terminology *43*

Electrocardiographic Measurements of Electrocardiographic Deflections *43*

Measurement of Heart Rate *43*
Measurement of Electrocardiographic Intervals *43*

PR Interval, QRS Interval, QT Interval 45

Electrical Axis *45*

An Approach to the Interpretation of the Electrocardiogram *46*
Important Considerations in the Interpretation of the Electrocardiogram *48*

Constitutional and Physiologic Influences 48
Technical Considerations 48
Statistical Considerations 50

Inadequate Sample Size, Composition of the Sample, Adequate Statistical Evaluation 51

Confirmation of Electrocardiographic Criteria 52

Part **Two** The Normal Electrocardiogram

4 The Normal Atrial and Ventricular Electrocardiogram *57*

The P Wave *57*
The QRS Complex *58*

The Initial 0.01 s Vector 58
The Initial 0.04 s Vector 61
The Terminal 0.02 s Vector 63
The Mean QRS Vector 63

The ST Segment *65*
The T Wave *65*
The U Wave *67*
The QRS-T Angle *67*
The Normal Preadult Electrocardiogram *69*

Part **Three** The Abnormal Electrocardiogram

Introduction *83*

Section **A** Altered Anatomic or Electrophysiologic Disturbances

5 The Abnormal Atrial Electrocardiogram *85*

Right Atrial Abnormality 86
    Electrocardiographic Criteria for Right Atrial Abnormality 86
    List of Criteria 86
Left Atrial Abnormality 87
    Electrocardiographic Criteria for Left Atrial Abnormality 87
    List of Criteria 87
Right and Left Atrial Abnormality 87
    Important Considerations 87

6 Ventricular Hypertrophy 89

Left Ventricular Hypertrophy 89
    Electrocardiographic Criteria for Left Ventricular Hypertrophy 89
    List of Criteria 89
    Important Considerations 99
Right Ventricular Hypertrophy 100
    Electrocardiographic Criteria for Right Ventricular Hypertrophy 100
    List of Criteria 100
    Important Considerations 104

7 Ventricular Conduction Defects 105

Left Bundle Branch Block 105
    Electrocardiographic Criteria for Left Bundle Branch Block 105
    List of Criteria 105
    Important Considerations 107
Right Bundle Branch Block 113
    Electrocardiographic Criteria for Right Bundle Branch Block 113
    List of Criteria 113
    Important Considerations 115
Nonspecific Intraventricular Block 117

SI, SII, SIII Pattern   *117*
The Concept of Fascicular Block   *119*

   Left Anterior Fascicular Block   *121*

      Electrocardiographic Criteria for Left Anterior Fascicular Block   *121*

         List of Criteria   *121*

   Left Posterior Fascicular Block   *123*

      Electrocardiographic Criteria for Left Posterior Fascicular Block   *125*

         List of Criteria   *125*

   Combinations of Fascicular Block   *125*

      List of Combinations   *127*

   Important Considerations   *127*

8 Preexcitation Syndromes   *131*

      Electrocardiographic Criteria for Preexcitation   *133*

         List of Criteria   *133*

   Important Considerations   *136*

Section B Acquired Diseases That Effect the Electrocardiogram

9 Coronary Artery Disease   *139*

   Myocardial Infarction   *139*

      Electrocardiographic Criteria for the Diagnosis of Myocardial Infarction   *140*

         List of Criteria   *140*

      Definition of an Abnormal Q Wave   *143*
      Important Considerations   *149*
   Extent of the Infarction   *151*
   Site of the Infarction   *153*

      Anterior Infarction   *155*
      Inferior Infarction   *157*
      Posterior Infarction   *159*
      Apical Infarction   *161*
      Subendocardial Infarction   *163*
      Subepicardial Infarction   *163*
      Right Ventricular Infarction   *163*
      Atrial Infarction   *165*

Estimating the Age of the Infarction 165

Myocardial Ischemia *169*

Electrocardiographic Mimics of Myocardial Infarction or Ischemia 173

List of Mimics 173

10 Lung Disease *183*

Chronic Obstructive Lung Disease *183*

Electrocardiographic Criteria for Chronic Obstructive Lung Disease *183*

List of Criteria *183*

Important Considerations 185

Pulmonary Embolus *187*

Electrocardiographic Criteria for Acute Pulmonary Embolus *187*

List of Criteria *187*

Important Considerations 189

Left Pneumothorax *190*

Electrocardiographic Criteria for Left Pneumothorax *190*

List of Criteria *190*

11 Pericarditis *191*

Acute Pericarditis *191*

Electrocardiographic Criteria for Acute Pericarditis *191*

List of Criteria *191*

Important Considerations 195

Chronic Pericarditis *195*

Electrocardiographic Findings for Chronic Pericarditis *195*

List of Criteria *195*

Pericardial Effusion *196*

Electrocardiographic Criteria for Pericardial Effusion *196*

List of Criteria *196*

12 Cardiomyopathy *197*

Idiopathic, Dilated Cardiomyopathy *197*
Hypertrophic Cardiomyopathy *199*
Myocarditis *199*
Hypertension *200*
Infiltrative Cardiomyopathy *200*

13 Aortic and Mitral Valvular Heart Disease *201*

Aortic Stenosis *201*
Aortic Regurgitation *203*
Mitral Stenosis *203*
Mitral Regurgitation *205*
Important Considerations *206*

14 Congenital Heart Disease *207*

Atrial Septal Defects *207*

  Important Considerations *209*

Ventricular Septal Defect *211*

  Important Considerations *213*

Patent Ductus Arteriosus *213*
Pulmonic Stenosis *215*

  Important Considerations *217*

Tetralogy of Fallot *217*

  Important Considerations *217*

Coarctation of the Aorta *219*
Ebstein's Anomaly *219*
Dextrocardia with Situs Inversus *220*

  Important Considerations *220*

15 Miscellaneous Electrocardiographic Abnormalities *221*

Electrolyte Abnormalities *221*

  Hyperkalemia *221*

    Important Considerations *222*

  Hypokalemia *223*

    Important Considerations *224*

  Hypercalcemia *225*

    Important Considerations *225*

Hypocalcemia 225
   Important Considerations 225
Other Electrolytes 225
Central Nervous System Disorders 225
   Important Considerations 226
Digitalis 227
   Digitalis Effect 227
      Important Considerations 227
   Digitalis-Induced Arrhythmias 229
      Important Considerations 229

16 Summary *237*

Part **Four** Cardiac Arrhythmias

17 Introduction to Arrhythmias *241*
   Physiology of Cardiac Impulse Formation and Conduction 241
   The Sequence of Cardiac Excitation 242
   General Mechanisms of Arrhythmias 244
   Electrocardiographic Lead Selection and Length of Tracing 244
   General Versus Specific Diagnoses 245

18 The AV Diagram *247*
   The AV Diagram 247

      Rate *249*
      The *A* Level *249*
      The *V* Level *250*
      The *AV* Level *254*

19 Variations in Sinus Node Rhythms and Atrial Arrhythmias *257*
   Sinus Arrhythmia and Wandering Pacemaker 257
   Sinus Bradycardia 258
   Sinus Tachycardia 259
   Paroxysmal Supraventricular Tachycardia 259
   Ectopic Atrial Tachycardia 264
   Atrial Flutter 264
   Atrial Fibrillation 265
   Atrial Premature Complexes 269

20 AV Junctional Rhythm Disturbances *273*

AV Junctional Pacemaker Function 273
Junctional Escape Complexes 273
Premature Junctional Complexes 274
Junctional Tachycardia 277
AV Dissociation 278

21 Ventricular Arrhythmias *281*

Ventricular Pacemaker Function 281
Ventricular Escape Complexes 281
Premature Ventricular Complexes 281
Differentiation of Premature Ventricular Complexes from Premature Supraventricular Complexes with Aberrant Ventricular Conduction 282
Ventricular Tachycardia and Ventricular Flutter 287
Ventricular Fibrillation 288

22 The Differential Diagnosis of a Tachycardia *291*

Differentiation between Supraventricular and Ventricular Tachycardias 291
Differentiation of the Various Supraventricular Tachycardias 296

23 Abnormalities of Conduction and Heart Block *299*

First-Degree AV Block 300
Second-Degree AV Block 300
Complete AV Block 302
Sinoatrial (SA) Block 302
Special Terms Used to Describe Block 306

24 Arrhythmic Patterns Due to Various Interacting Mechanisms *309*

Group Beating 309
The Parasystoles 315
Fusion Complexes 318
Reciprocal Rhythm 318

Appendix *319*

References *323*

Glossary *331*

Index *337*

Preface

The cardiac evaluation is considered incomplete without an electrocardiogram. Unfortunately, there has been a decline in the skills of electrocardiographic interpretation by many physicians. This is probably due to several reasons: the introduction of exciting new diagnostic methods in all areas of medicine; a decreased emphasis on teaching electrocardiography to students and house staff; an increased reliance upon computer-assisted interpretation; and a dependence upon cardiologists and coronary-care nurses to provide the interpretation.

Despite this neglect, the importance of the electrocardiogram in detecting cardiac disease and arrhythmias remains undiminished. Electrocardiography has never been easy to learn, requiring a personal commitment and discipline to puzzle out many tracings in solitude before a firm grasp of the subject can occur. To ease this intellectual labor, a form of instruction has developed that requires only the pattern recognition of certain obvious electrocardiographic patterns of heart disease. This approach is somewhat akin to learning the snow-plow method of skiing—the novice is able to stand up immediately and ski gentle inclines without too much trouble—and has proved useful in quickly introducing coronary-care personnel and students to electrocardiography. It does not, however, provide the ability to make skillful turns on the more demanding contours of difficult electrocardiograms.

Electrocardiography: Basic Concepts and Clinical Application uses the spatial vector method initially introduced in 1949 by Robert Grant, M.D., at Emory University School of Medicine, as a way to begin and build skills of interpretation. Specific diagnostic criteria and a discussion of the frailties of these criteria are included to emphasize that the vector approach is practical and effective in the daily interpretation of the electrocardiogram. It is not intended to be a quick read for those who wish to dip only a tentative toe into the shallow depths of electrocardiography. The material is presented in a straightforward, didactic way so that the diligent learner will soon be able to interpret correctly both simple and more complex tracings with confidence based upon an understanding of basic principles. The more experienced clinician can use this book to enhance skills and extend knowledge acquired previously.

The text is divided into four major Parts. In Parts One and Two, basic concepts of electrocardiography and the vector approach are introduced. Conventional electrocardiographic terminology and measurements are provided followed by an approach that is useful in interpreting the electrocardiogram. A chapter on important considerations examines constitutional, physiologic, and technical influences on the electrocardiogram and emphasizes statistical concepts that are essential to understand in the interpretation of any biologic test. The normal electrocardiogram is then analyzed using the vector approach to understand the genesis of the twelve-lead (scalar) electrocardiogram. Abnormalities of the electrocardiogram are discussed in Part Three in terms of altered anatomic or electrophysiologic disturbances and electrocardiographic clues that may lead to an etiologic diagnosis.

Part Four of the book presents the electrocardiographic analysis of cardiac arrhythmias utilizing the AV diagram or ladder as developed by Sir Thomas Lewis in the early 20th century. The approach to interpreting cardiac arrhythmias should not be memorized any more than that of the atrial and ventricular electrocardiogram. The use of the AV diagram as a method of teaching allows a more basic understanding of arrhythmias and can be taught to the beginner as well as utilized by the expert in the analysis of complex arrhythmias.

Like any clinical test, the value of the final electrocardiographic interpretation will depend upon the correct application of certain established diagnostic criteria, an appreciation of the capabilities and limitations of these criteria, and the astute incorporation of the results into an overall assessment of the patient.

We are grateful to the following people who were instrumental in the development of the book:

Our Wives: Diana, Wilhemina, and Nelie for their love, support, and tolerance.

Our Teachers: Especially Robert Grant, Henry Marriott, and Joseph Ryan.

Our Secretaries: Carol Miller, Pat Kirby, Cathy Jones, and Thelma Gottlieb whose forbearance and deciphering skills made the task easier.

The Medical Illustrations Department of Emory University: Patsy Bryan and David Murphy (for this edition) and Grover Hogan, Kathleen Mackay Powell, Patsy Bryan, Joe Jackson, Bob Beveridge, Eddie Jackson, and McClaren Johnson (for prior editions) for their artistic talent.

The Publisher: McGraw-Hill, especially Robert McGraw, Joseph Brehm, and Steven Tenney for their guidance.

The Word Processor: For saving arduous hours of proffreading.

Many of the illustrations and some of the material in the first part of this book were initially published in 1952 as the *Atlas of Spatial Vector Electrocardiography* coauthored by J. Willis Hurst, M.D., and Grattan Woodson, M.D. Revisions of the book, including a new section on cardiac arrhythmias, were published in 1968 and again in 1973 as *Introduction to Electrocardiography* by J. Willis Hurst, M.D., and Robert J. Myerburg, M.D. Parts One, Two, and Three of the present book are otherwise new (except for a revision of the spatial vector concept); Part Four has been modified in order to update terminology and introduce concepts based on an appreciation of recent electrophysiologic studies.

Mark E. Silverman
Robert J. Myerburg
J. Willis Hurst

Part One
Basic Concepts of Electrocardiography

Introduction

The electrocardiogram (ECG) is an amplified, timed recording of the magnitude and direction of bioelectrical forces generated by the depolarization and repolarization of myocardial cells during each cardiac cycle. Since its initial development and clinical application by Waller, Einthoven, and others in the late nineteenth and early twentieth century, two methods of interpretation have been found useful:

Pattern Recognition

This commonly practiced method requires memorizing the normal contour that is anticipated for each of the 12 leads and the type of alteration that can occur with various constitutional, biologic, and pathogenic influences. Since the range of normal is quite inclusive and there are many diseases that can affect the heart, this approach is burdened by extensive memorization. In addition, it does not stem from electrophysiologic principles and therefore does not provide a sound framework for comprehending difficult tracings.

Vector Method

In this method the interpreter applies electrophysiologic principles to understand the direction and magnitude of the normal electrical forces. The electrocardiogram is mentally visualized and then analyzed in terms of abnormalities of these forces. After the basic vector concepts are comprehended, simple and more complex tracings should be understandable without the necessity of memorizing the many variables inherent in the pattern method. This book uses the vector method to teach the analysis of the electrocardiogram.

Chapter 1
Basic Electrophysiology of the Heart

Cellular Electrophysiology

A simplified explanation of cellular electrophysiology will provide the necessary background for the concept of electrical vectors. At rest the interior of the cell contains a high potassium and low sodium concentration; the reverse is true outside the confines of the cellular membrane (Fig. 1–1). During this resting state the cellular membrane prevents sodium ions from crossing but is permeable to the movement of potassium ions. Since the potassium ions carry a positive charge out of the cell, leaving relatively more negative charges inside, an electrical (potential) difference is created between the inside and the outside of the cell. This potential difference, measuring about 90 mV, is known as the *membrane resting potential*. The cell may be conceptualized as a double line of positive and negative charges separated by the cellular membrane (Fig. 1–1). Each facing pair of positive and negative charges is termed a *dipole*. In the resting state, when there is no movement of sodium ions across the membrane, the cell is considered to be *polarized* (charged). *Depolarization* occurs when the cell membrane is stimulated electrically and becomes permeable to an influx of sodium ions resulting in a rapid change in the potential difference across the cellular membrane from −90 mV to +20 mV (Fig. 1–2). Restoration of the electrical charges to the original resting state of −90 mV is the process of *repolarization*.

As sodium ions rush into the cell, a series of elec-

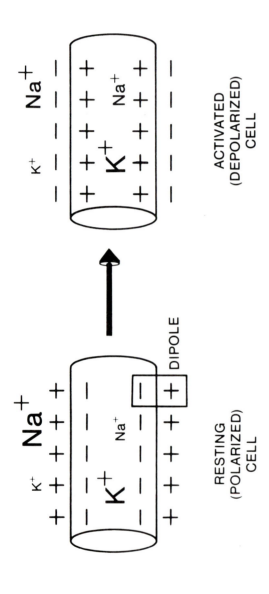

FIG. 1–1. Conceptualized myocardial cell at rest (left) and during the activated state (right). The change in sodium (Na+) and potassium (K+) concentration with depolarization is shown together with the reversal in electrical charge across the cellular membrane. An electrical dipole is outlined.

trical changes occurs in which the surface of the cell becomes electrically negative while the interior becomes positive (Fig. 1-1). This activity is followed by a complex sequence of movement of other ions, including potassium, calcium, and chloride, which cause a series of electrical changes ultimately leading to complete repolarization. The electrophysiologic curve of these changes is known as the *transmembrane action potential* (Fig. 1-2). Five phases can be identified. *Phase 0* is the phase of depolarization in which a stimulus allows positive sodium ions to rush into the cell. The transmembrane potential rapidly climbs from its resting level of -90 mV, and, at the critical threshold potential level of approximately -60 mV, an abrupt, all-or-none excitation occurs causing the action potential to overshoot to $+20$ mV. If a threshold potential

tassium continues to move outward. When the membrane resting potential of −90 mV has been restored, the cell is again fully polarized and is in the *phase 4* "resting state." In terms of the electrocardiogram, which represents the summed action potentials of all of the cells, the QRS complex coincides with phase 0, the ST segment with phase 2, the T wave with phase 3, and the isoelectric baseline with phase 4.

Sinus node pacemaker cells differ from other myocardial cells because they have a lower (less negative) resting membrane potential, a slowly rising phase 4 which can spontaneously reach threshold potential and trigger depolarization, a more slowly rising phase 0, and a rounded, slowly falling curve of repolarization which cannot be separated into phases 1, 2, or 3.

Once threshold is reached, a current is propagated from one dipole to the next as a wave front of depolarization spreads along the axis of the cell and to adjoining cells. As this occurs, the cell becomes partitioned into a positive (as yet unactivated) pole and a negative (depolarized) region with an intense electrical field extending around each of the positive and negative poles in all directions (Fig. 1–3). The *transitional region* separating the two fields is at zero potential, neither positive nor negative, and is always perpendicular to the direction of the electrical current.

Einthoven considered that the entire heart acted as a single dipole source from which an electrical field originates. There is debate as to whether this simplified

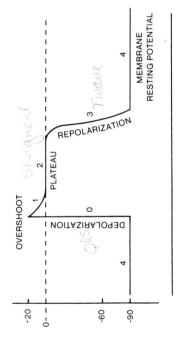

FIG. 1–2. A monophasic action potential curve illustrating the four phases of depolarization and repolarization of a resting myocardial cell is shown. The curve plots millivolts on the ordinate against time on the abscissa.

of −60 mV is not reached because of a weak stimulus, an action potential does not occur. *Phase 1*, mediated primarily by the movement of potassium and chloride ions, is an early brief phase of repolarization from +20 mV back to a level of near 0 mV. *Phase 2* is known as the plateau phase since the potential difference remains level or very slow repolarization occurs. This phase is produced largely by an inward calcium movement tending to counterbalance an outward potassium flow. This well-developed, lengthy phase 2 provides the long refractory period of myocardial tissue which is uniquely different from other muscle or nerve tissue. During the rapid repolarization period of *phase 3*, po-

7

from their origin, they diminish in electrical potential. As mentioned earlier, a transitional plane of zero potential is always perpendicular to the direction of this electrical force. These positive and negative electrical fields and the zero potential plane reach out through the conducting medium of the tissues of the chest to intersect the surface of the body where they can be detected by the leads of the electrocardiographic machine. During each cardiac cycle many electrical forces are generated as electricity spreads throughout the heart. Since these forces vary in direction and magnitude, the orientation of the positive and negative fields and zero potential plane will change. Each electrocardiographic lead from its fixed position registers these movements to provide a graphic display of the course of the electricity relative to that lead.

Sequence of Depolarization and Repolarization

The cardiac cycle is normally initiated by the spontaneous electrical depolarization of sinus node pacemaker cells. These cells are located at the junction of the superior vena cava with the right atrium and right atrial appendage (Fig. 1–5A). Electricity spreads from this area to the atrioventricular (AV) node apparently by several preferential conduction pathways in the interatrial septum and by Bachmann's bundle linking the

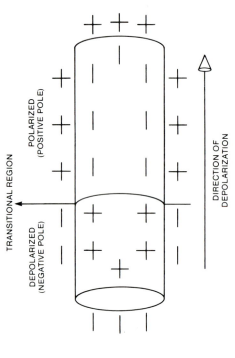

FIG. 1–3. A conceptualized myocardial cell showing depolarization spreading from left to right. The cell is divided into a depolarized region and a polarized region. A transitional region, with its plane always perpendicular to the direction of depolarization, separates the two poles and will move to the right as more of the cell becomes depolarized.

model is appropriate for all conditions; however, the single dipole theory does provide a useful concept for purposes of discussion. The single dipole field is viewed as emanating from the center of the chest as a three-dimensional field with a series of shells of positive and negative equipotential forces around each pole (Fig. 1–4). As these forces extend farther and farther away

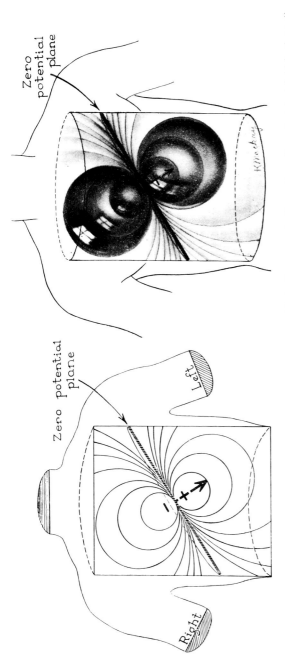

FIG. 1-4. (A) A frontal plane view of an electrical field. The origin of the electrical force is located at the center of the cylinder. Note the plane of zero potential separating the positive and negative halves of the electrical field. The plane of zero potential is perpendicular to the direction of electrical force. The rings represent lines of equipotentiality. For simplicity only three rings are shown. This schematic illustration is not intended to show all the details of an electrical field.

(B) A diagrammatic illustration of an electrical field in three-dimensional space. The lines of equipotential are illustrated as shells. For simplicity only three shells are completed. The plane of zero potential is perpendicular to the direction of electrical force and extends in all directions to intersect the surface of the cylinder.

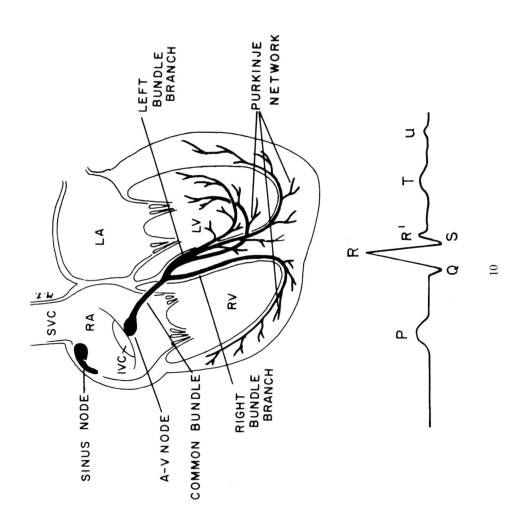

FIG. 1–5. (A) Diagrammatic representation of the heart. The impulse-forming and conducting system is shown. (B) The lettered deflections of an electrocardiogram.

the ventricular septum into at least two and possibly three major divisions (fascicles). At the level of the two papillary muscles of the left ventricle, the left bundle branch arborizes into a complex subendocardial network of Purkinje fibers. The middle third of the left side of the ventricular septum is the first area to be excited. Depolarization then spreads from the endocardium to the epicardium of the two ventricles, moving upward from the apical to the basilar regions of the ventricles. The *QRS complex* is produced by the spread of electricity through the ventricular myocardium (Fig. 1–5B). Following ventricular depolarization, there is a brief period of minimal electrical activity corresponding to the *ST segment* of the electrocardiogram. This period is terminated by ventricular repolarization proceeding from epicardium to endocardium, apex to base, inscribing the *T wave* on the electrocardiogram. The *U wave*, a low-amplitude deflection of uncertain significance, follows the T wave (Fig. 1–5B).

two atria. As the wave of depolarization heads toward the AV node, there is concentric depolarization of the atrial myocardium. The *P wave* on the electrocardiogram is the electrocardiographic representation of the sum of this atrial depolarization (Fig. 1–5B). The AV node, located in the lower right atrium between the coronary sinus and the septal tricuspid leaflet, delays the electrical impulse before the impulse travels through the bundle of His to the ventricular conducting system (Fig. 1–5A). The PR interval measures the time that the impulse takes to travel between the sinus node and the inception of the bundle branches. This period includes the delay in the AV node.

The two bundle branches originate at the top of the muscular ventricular septum (Fig. 1–5A). The right bundle branch is slender and courses over the right side of the ventricular septum to the anterior papillary muscle of the right ventricle where it divides into a Purkinje network of specialized conducting fibers. The left bundle branch divides widely over the left side of

Chapter 2

The Spatial Vector Concept and Its Clinical Application

The Vector Concept

Any force that has magnitude and direction can be considered to be a vector and may be graphically represented as an arrow. The point of the arrowhead indicates the direction of the vector while the length of the shaft corresponds to the magnitude of the force (Fig. 2–1). The individual cell described previously can be viewed as a vector of electrical force always directed toward the positive aspect of the cell (Fig. 1–3).

At any given moment during the spread of depolarization, there are many instantaneous vectors, each with its own magnitude and direction (Figs. 2–2A and B). Since the electrocardiogram is recorded at a distance from the heart, the leads perceive mainly the vectorial sum of these individual vectors (Figs. 2–2B and C). Each vectorial sum is known as the *instantaneous resultant vector*, and its direction and magnitude determine the deflection of the electrocardiogram at that moment. As the process of depolarization spreads from the sinus node throughout the conducting pathways, the atrial and ventricular myocardium are depolarized in a sequential manner. A number of instantaneous resultant vectors are therefore generated at successive instants. Since the origins of the individual vectors are electrically relatively equidistant from

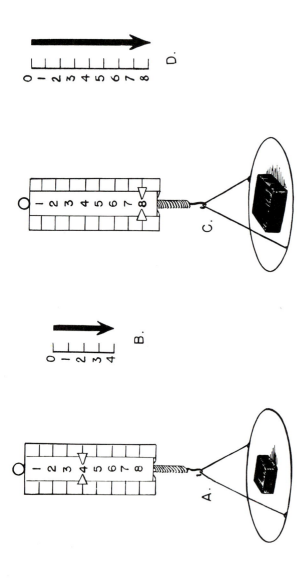

Fig. 2–1. Mechanical force represented as a vector.
(A) Scales with a 4-lb weight.
(B) Arrow divided into four units directed downward.
(C) Scales with an 8-lb weight.
(D) Arrow divided into eight units directed downward.

the recording electrodes, these instantaneous vectors can be treated as if they arise from a common origin at the relative zero point of the electrical field (Fig. 2–2B).

The summation of all of these instantaneous vectors can be derived and is known as the *mean QRS vector*. This is illustrated schematically by the seven vectors shown in Fig. 2–2. Each of the seven vectors represents magnitude and direction at successive instants, and each one is also the summation of an infinite number of vectors generated from all points being excited at that given instant.

If a line is drawn connecting the termini of all the instantaneous vectors, a "loop" will be formed which reflects the change in magnitude and direction of vectors from instant to instant in a single cardiac cycle (Fig. 2–2C). When all of these instantaneous vectors are added together, the resultant vector is the mean QRS vector (Fig. 2–2D). The mean QRS vector represents the average direction and magnitude of all of the instantaneous QRS vectors. A mean vector can be determined for atrial depolarization, ventricular depolarization, and ventricular repolarization. By understanding the normal direction and magnitude of the instantaneous vectors and the mean vectors, and the relationship of each to the other, one can analyze and interpret the electrocardiogram.

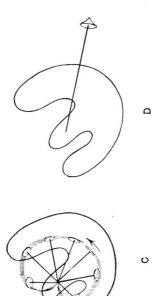

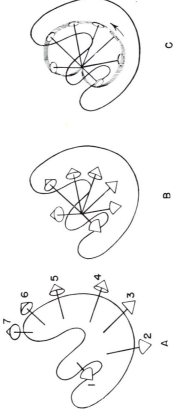

FIG. 2–2. Diagram illustrating depolarization of the ventricular musculature as viewed in space.

(A) The numbered arrows indicate the sequence in which electrical forces are generated during a single QRS cycle as drawn in three-dimensional space (i.e., vector no. 1 not only is directed to the right and downward but also is directed slightly anteriorly, and vector no. 7 is directed upward and posteriorly).

(B) The spatial instantaneous forces, or vectors, are illustrated as if all forces arise at a common origin.

(C) A line drawn through the termini of the spatial instantaneous vectors produces the spatial QRS loop.

(D) The mean spatial QRS vector is the net effective (resultant) vector of all the spatial instantaneous vectors.

15

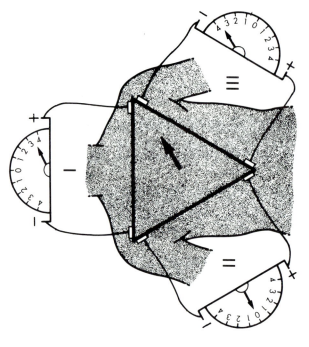

FIG. 2-3. The electrocardiographic lead system. Bipolar frontal leads I, II, and III are presented. An arrow, representing an electrical vector, emanates from the heart and points to the left shoulder. The positive and negative pole of each lead axis connects to a galvanometer. The galvanometer registers a deflection according to the magnitude and direction of the electrical vector as perceived by each lead. Since the vector is perpendicular to lead II, the galvanometer reads 0.

The Electrocardiographic Lead System

Electricity generated by the heart is detected by metallic plates or suction cups, called electrodes, that are covered by conducting paste or saline pads and affixed to designated locations on the body surface. Each lead consists of two poles connected to a sensitive recording galvanometer, the basic component of the electrocardiographic machine (Fig. 2-3). The imaginary line between the two poles of each lead is known as the lead axis. Twelve leads, six in the frontal plane and six in the horizontal plane, are routinely recorded. A switch box in the machine allows the operator to switch quickly from one lead to the next.

When the electrical force is directed toward the positive pole of the galvanometer, the recording stylus is displaced above the baseline; a negative deflection indicates that the electrical force is oriented away from the positive pole (Fig. 2-3). No displacement occurs when the electrical forces are perpendicular, neither positive nor negative, in respect to the two poles of that particular lead, or when the heart is electrically silent. This baseline position is called the *isoelectric line*.

This important principle of projection of the electrical forces on the lead axis can be illustrated by the following example.

In Fig. 2-4 a rod, representing an electrical force, is placed between a light source and a screen which

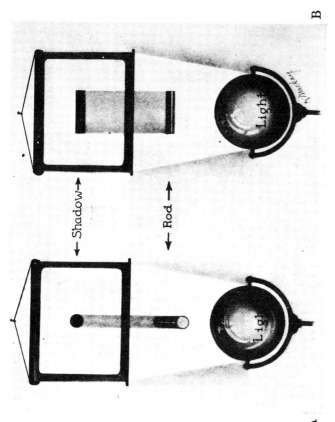

FIG. 2–4. Diagram illustrating the principle of projection of a shadow utilizing a light source, rod, and screen. The screen is analogous to a lead axis and the rod corresponds to a vector.
(A) The rod is perpendicular to the screen and the shadow cast by the light is very small.
(B) The rod is parallel with the screen and the resultant shadow cast by the light is quite large. This experiment can be performed using a pencil placed near the screen and the light source placed at a distance to demonstrate how an electrical vector can influence a lead depending on whether it is closer to the perpendicular or the parallel to that lead.

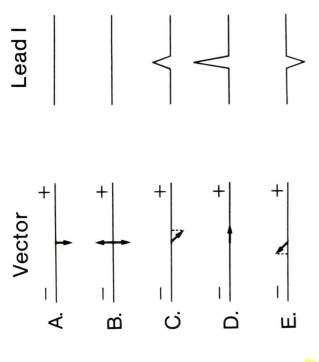

FIG. 2–5. (A–E) An electrical force, illustrated as a vector, is shown as it is perceived by lead I. The corresponding electrocardiographic deflection is shown on the right. Figures A and B show that a force perpendicular to lead I results in a zero net deflection. Figure C and D demonstrate that a positive deflection will be produced if the vector is oriented toward the positive pole of lead I. The greatest positive deflection is produced by the vector in Fig. D which is parallel to lead I. In Fig. E the vector is oriented toward the negative pole of lead I and the resultant electrocardiographic deflection is negative.

corresponds to a lead axis. When the light is turned on, a shadow is projected on the screen. The shadow cast on the screen will be smallest when the rod is perpendicular to the screen and largest when the rod is parallel with the screen (Fig. 2–4). There is an important similarity between this simple example and the projection of an electrical force on a lead axis. In Fig. 2–5 a vector, representing an electrical force, is drawn perpendicular to a lead axis and no net deflection is obtained; when the vector is parallel to the lead axis, its largest deflection will be recorded (Fig. 2–5D). If the vector is located somewhere between these two extremes, the magnitude of the deflection will be determined by how much the vector projects upon the lead axis. This is determined by drawing a line from the end of the vector perpendicular to the lead axis (Figs. 2–5C and E).

The diagrams shown in Figs. 2–4 and 2–5 illustrate a very basic and important principle of the vector method: the closer an electrical force is directed to the perpendicular of a particular lead, the smaller the net (sum of positive and negative) deflection. A zero net deflection means that the force is exactly perpendicular to that lead. Conversely, when an electrical force is directed parallel with a given lead axis, the largest deflection will be recorded in that lead. In Fig. 2–6 a vector, representing an electrical force, is directed slightly downward and to the left, perpendicular to the lead III axis. Accordingly, the smallest frontal lead

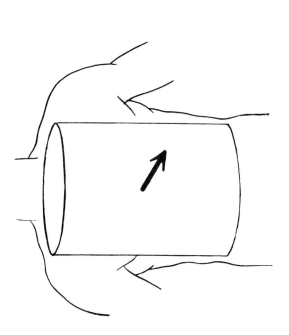
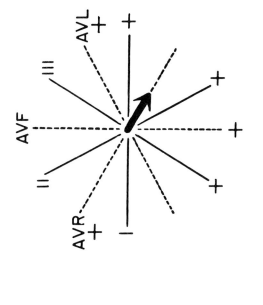
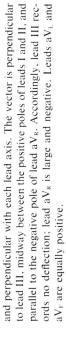

FIG. 2-6. (A) An electrical force represented by a vector located in the center of the chest.
(B) The hexaxial reference system superimposed on an electrical vector. The degree of positivity or negativity of the frontal lead can be determined by drawing a line from the tip of the arrow head to and perpendicular with each lead axis. The vector is perpendicular to lead III, midway between the positive poles of leads I and II, and parallel to the negative pole of lead aV_R. Accordingly, lead III records no deflection; lead aV_R is large and negative. Leads aV_L and aV_F are equally positive.

19

The Frontal (Limb, Extremity) Plane Leads

The leads attached to the four extremities can reveal the direction—right, left, superior, or inferior—and the magnitude of electricity in the frontal plane and therefore are referred to as *frontal leads* (Fig. 2–9). Frontal leads I, II, and III are *bipolar*, each lead consisting of a positive and a negative pole. Because the amplitude of the electrical forces diminishes in proportion to the square of the distance from the heart, electrodes placed anywhere on the extremities are considered to be remote from the heart. For convenience the frontal leads are positioned on the wrists and ankles but are essentially sensing electricity from the vantage point of the shoulders and groin. Lead I measures the potential difference between the left and right shoulder; lead II between the groin and right shoulder; and lead III between the groin and left shoulder (Fig. 2–9A). The lead attached to the right leg serves solely as a ground wire. Einthoven arbitrarily assigned the positive terminals to be the left arm (shoulder) for lead I, the left leg (groin) for lead II, and the left leg (groin) for lead III. He also assumed that these leads are electrically equidistant from the heart and form the sides of an equilateral triangle surrounding the heart in the form of an upside-down pyramid (Fig. 2–9A). Although this is not strictly true, Einthoven's triangle has proven to be a clinically useful concept. The sides of the triangle can

deflection will be recorded in lead III. Stated another way, when the smallest lead deflection is found in lead III, the vector representing that deflection must be relatively perpendicular to lead III. In Fig. 2–7 a vector, representing an electrical force, is directed downward and to the left, parallel with lead II. The largest frontal lead deflection will then be found in lead II. When the largest frontal lead deflection is found in lead II, the vector representing that deflection must therefore be relatively parallel to lead II.

The last two diagrams also illustrate that the axis of lead I is perpendicular to lead aV_F, lead II is perpendicular to lead aV_L, and lead III is perpendicular to lead aV_R. In Fig. 2–6 the largest deflection of the unipolar frontal leads will be recorded in lead aV_R and, since the force is directed away from the positive electrode, the deflection will be negative. In Fig. 2–7 the largest deflection is in lead II. Since the axis of lead aV_L is perpendicular to the axis of lead II, lead aV_L is minimally influenced by the electrical force.

The moment-to-moment variation of the instantaneous QRS electrical forces can now be shown by drawing lines from the termini of these vectors to and perpendicular with a given lead axis to demonstrate how an electrocardiographic deflection is actually produced. Figure 2–8B illustrates how leads I, II, aV_R, and aV_F are derived from the six instantaneous vectors shown in Fig. 2–8A.

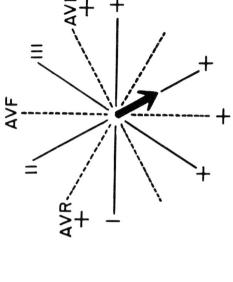

Fig. 2-7. (A) An electrical force represented by a vector located in the center of the chest.
(B) The hexaxial reference system superimposed on the vector. Lead II records the largest deflection because the vector is parallel to the positive pole of that lead. Leads I and III are equally positive. Lead aV_L is not influenced by the electrical force because the vector is perpendicular to it. Lead aV_R is negative and aV_F is similar in size but positive.

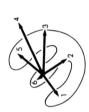
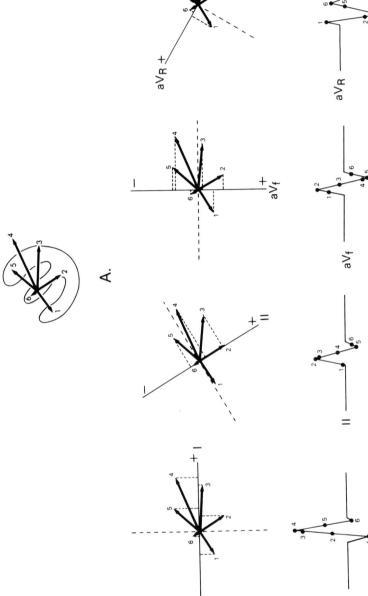

FIG. 2–8. (A) Diagram showing six consecutive vectors emanating from a common origin. (B–E) Leads I, II, aV$_f$, and aV$_R$ are drawn to illustrate how each perceives the six consecutive vectors as shown in A.

be moved to a common central point and still maintain the same spatial relationship of the leads (Fig. 2–9B). In this more familiar configuration the positive poles of leads I, II, and III are seen to be 60° apart with lead I at 0°, lead II at +60°, and lead III at +120°. The relationship among these three leads can be expressed mathematically as

==lead I deflection + lead III deflection== = lead II deflection

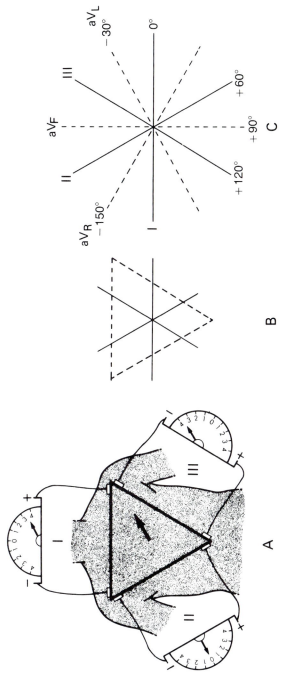

FIG. 2–9. (A) The "electrical" equilateral triangle of Einthoven showing the relationships of the bipolar frontal leads I, II, and III. (B) The triaxial reference system of Bayley is produced when the sides of the Einthoven triangle are translated to a common central point. (C) The hexaxial reference system is produced by combining the triaxial system of Bayley together with the unipolar frontal lead axis.

were originally added to the standard leads I, II, and III because of an erroneous concept that they afforded a special view of the inside of the right ventricle (aV$_R$), inferior surface of the heart (aV$_F$), and the lateral wall of the left ventricle (aV$_L$). Although this concept has been shown to be incorrect, many correlations have been made with these leads and they remain useful. These unipolar frontal leads are 120° apart with the positive pole of aV$_L$ at $-30°$, aV$_F$ at $+90°$, and aV$_R$ at $-150°$ (Fig. 2–9C). The relationship among these three leads can be expressed mathematically as

lead aV$_R$ deflection + lead aV$_L$ deflection
  + lead aV$_F$ deflection = 0

Together with the standard leads I, II, and III, the unipolar frontal leads complete the *hexaxial reference system*. (Fig. 2–9C) It is essential to memorize the exact location by degree of the positive pole of each of these six frontal leads.

Dr. Robert Grant devised the following method of determining the direction of electrical forces in the frontal plane.

With the lead axes and polarity of the hexaxial reference system in mind, the frontal plane direction of the P, QRS, ST, and T vectors of the heart can be determined. This is done quickly and relatively accurately by simple inspection of the six frontal leads. The following discussion will be concerned with only the

The galvanometer measures the *difference* in voltage detected by the two poles of each *bipolar* lead and produces a deflection from the isoelectric line in proportion to the amplitude of this voltage. For example, if the positive electrode of lead I detects a voltage of $+4$ mV while the negative electrode detects -2 mV, the potential difference of $+6$ mV is measured. Since the resultant force at this instant is positive, the stylus is displaced $+6$ mV above the isoelectric line of lead I.

Frontal leads aV$_R$, aV$_L$, and aV$_F$ are *unipolar leads*. With a unipolar lead system, the positive (exploring) electrode detects the voltage from its position at the right shoulder (aV$_R$), left shoulder (aV$_L$), or groin (aV$_F$) (Fig. 2–9C). The opposite pole is produced by interconnecting leads I, II, and III to form a pole with an electrical potential of 0. This pole is also known as the *central* or *indifferent terminal* since it is assumed to be at the origin of the electrical forces within the chest. The galvanometer for a unipolar lead then measures the electrical difference between the positive electrode and zero potential. For example, if the voltage detected at the right shoulder by lead aV$_R$ is -2 mV, then the galvanometer will register the difference between -2 mV and 0 mV, a negative displacement of 2 mV below the isoelectric line at that moment. A resistance is added to augment (therefore the aV$_R$, aV$_L$, aV$_F$) the deflection in these leads. The V, standing for potential, symbolizes the unipolar nature of the lead. These leads mean QRS vector, but similar principles hold in calculating other mean and instantaneous vectors.

The direction of the mean QRS vector is determined as follows: If the total QRS deflection in one lead is found to have as much area above the isoelectric line as below it, or is resultantly zero, the mean QRS vector must be perpendicular to that lead. From the QRS deflections in the other limb leads, it is easy to determine on which side of the lead axis the arrow should be drawn. Note that when mean vectors are being calculated, the total deflection is studied and its enclosed area, not its amplitude alone, is used to determine the relative size of the deflection. In practice, it is perhaps easier to inspect the bipolar frontal leads I, II, and III first, tentatively plot the vector direction, and then correct it by inspecting leads aV_R, aV_L, and aV_F. In Fig. 2–10 the QRS is resultantly zero in lead I and is, therefore, drawn perpendicular to lead I. Since the deflections are equally positive in leads II and III, the vector must be directed inferiorly. A mean vector with this direction has its largest projection on lead aV_F and will record the largest positive deflection in lead aV_F.

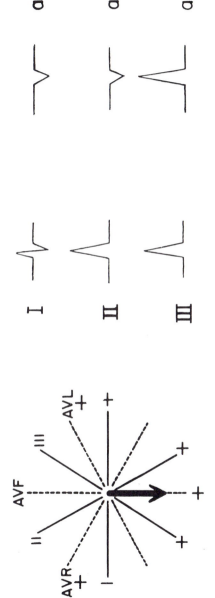

FIG. 2–10. The QRS complex is resultantly zero in lead I and large and equally positive in leads II and III. The mean vector is therefore directed downward and perpendicular to lead I. Leads aV_R and aV_L are equally negative, and lead aV_F is large and positive for a mean vector with this direction.

Its projection on leads aV_R and aV_L is smaller, producing equal but negative deflections in aV_R and aV_L.

If inspection of the three bipolar frontal leads reveals that the resultant QRS complex is conspicuously larger in one lead than in the other two leads, then the mean QRS vector will be relatively parallel to that lead. In Fig. 2–11, the QRS complex is largest in lead II and is directed so that leads I and II are both positive. In this case, lead aV_L is in a critical position. If the vector is perfectly parallel to lead II, lead aV_L should be resultantly zero. Since aV_L is slightly positive, the vector must be adjusted so that it will project a small positive quantity on the lead axis of aV_L.

By using the six frontal lead axes in such a manner, the direction of a vector can be located with an accuracy of about plus or minus 5°. The vector positions lying between those illustrated can be determined by interpolation.

The direction of a vector provides most of the clinical information; the magnitude of the vector does not need to be established in absolute terms. If the QRS complex encompasses a certain area and the T waves contain

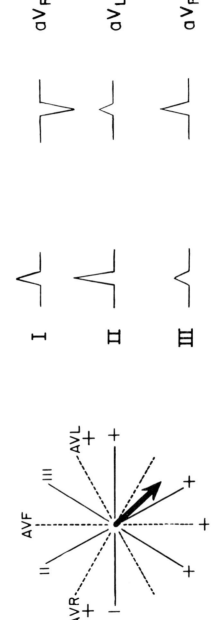

FIG. 2–11. The QRS complex is largest and positive in lead II and smaller but still positive in leads I and III. The mean QRS vector would be tentatively drawn parallel with lead II. Since the QRS complex is resultantly slightly positive in lead aV_L, the mean QRS vector must be rotated slightly to the left.

roughly half that area, it is satisfactory to draw the mean QRS vector twice as long as the mean T vector to indicate their relative magnitude.

The Precordial (Chest, Horizontal) Plane Leads

Information from the horizontal plane—right, left, anterior, and posterior—is provided by *precordial* or *chest* leads that are strung along the chest wall in close proximity to the heart (Fig. 2–12A and B). The six precordial leads are unipolar (V) leads. The positive electrodes of V_1 to V_6 are on the anterior chest wall while the other end of each lead is electrically connected to a central terminal of approximately zero potential, considered to be the center of the chest. Because these V leads are in close proximity to the

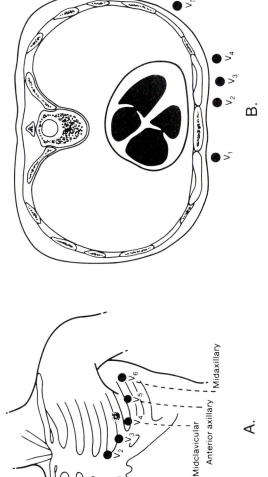

FIG. 2–12. (A) A schematic of the chest wall viewed with the subject in a slight left anterior oblique position. The precordial locations of leads V_1 to V_6 are illustrated. (B) A transverse plane through the chest showing the approximate relationship of the precordial leads to the cardiac chambers.

heart, they are influenced to some extent by the nearby myocardium as well as by the vectors of more distant electrical forces. This is an important difference from the frontal leads which are much farther from the heart and therefore register only vectorial influences.

cm toward the center of the chest at the level of the V_1 and V_2 electrode positions. In reality, the origin of the electrical force is probably not centrally located and varies from subject to subject. For simplicity it is regarded to be at a centrally located fixed point.

Certain aspects of the precordial leads deserve additional comment. The axes of these leads can be visualized by drawing a line from the exploring chest electrode through the origin of the electrical force in the center of the chest to the opposite side of the chest. Since the position of the six axes will vary from subject to subject, depending on chest contour, they do not have a set mathematical relationship with each other as do the frontal lead axes. As with the frontal leads, an electrical force directed toward a V lead will produce a positive deflection on that lead; an electrical force directed away from the V lead will produce a negative deflection on that lead. The axes of V_1 and V_2 are nearly perpendicular to the frontal plane; therefore, an electrical force parallel with the frontal plane will minimally influence the V_1 and V_2 electrodes. The lead axis of V_6, being in the midaxillary line, is almost a frontal plane lead and frequently resembles lead I. The lead axes of V_3, V_4, and V_5 are influenced by frontal plane as well as anteroposteriorly directed forces.

Dr. Robert Grant devised the following method for determining the direction of electrical forces in space.

In Fig. 2–13 the spatial characteristics of the electrical field produced by a vector perpendicular to lead

The V leads, by convention, are located as follows (Fig. 2–12A):

V_1: On the fourth intercostal space just to the right of the sternum
V_2: On the fourth intercostal space just to the left of the sternum
V_3: Midpoint between V_2 and V_4
V_4: On the fifth intercostal space on the midclavicular line
V_5: On the anterior axillary line at same transverse level as V_4
V_6: On the midaxillary line at same transverse level as V_4

On occasion, additional important information is obtained by placing the V lead one interspace above or below the conventional positions or by recording from a more posterior site. In infants and children a V_3R lead is routinely recorded from the right side of the chest in the position corresponding to V_3 on the left side. Other right-sided V leads are occasionally necessary.

The precordial electrode positions are shown on the diagram of the human chest in Fig. 2–12A. The origin of electrical activity is considered to be roughly 2 to 3

III and parallel with the frontal plane is diagrammatically illustrated. When the electrical field is viewed spatially, the zone of zero potential becomes a plane dividing the chest or cylinder into negative and positive halves. It can be seen that the electrodes for leads V_2 through V_6 are recording from the positive zone of the electrical field while the electrode for lead V_1 is recording from the negative zone of the electrical field. The line on the surface where the zero potential plane intersects the surface of the chest (or cylinder) is called the transitional pathway for that vector. Transitional complexes are recorded by those electrodes placed on the transitional pathway (Fig. 2–13). When a mean vector is considered, the transitional pathway is identified by finding the precordial lead where the total deflection is resultantly zero or nearest zero. A complex which is resultantly zero is often equiphasic, enclosing as much area above the line as below; therefore the transitional complex will be the precordial lead that is closest to being equiphasic. The precordial lead with the largest deflection cannot necessarily be considered to be parallel with the mean electrical force, since some of the chest electrodes are nearer the heart than others and may record larger deflections. On the other hand, the precordial electrode which records the transitional pathway record transitional complexes.

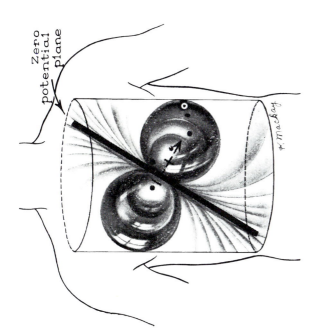

FIG. 2–13. Diagrammatic "spatial view" of an electrical field produced by a force perpendicular to lead III. A cylinder representing the chest is shown. The zero potential plane extends to intersect the surface of the cylinder to produce the transitional pathway. In this case lead V_1 records from the negative portion of the electrical field and leads V_2, V_3, V_4, V_5, and V_6 record from the positive portion of the electrical field. V lead electrodes placed on the transitional pathway record transitional complexes.

tional pathway combined with the frontal plane direction of a vector permits orientation of the vector in space, it is instructive to allow a vector to retain the same frontal plane position but to rotate it anteriorly or posteriorly and identify the area of negativity, positivity, and the plane of zero potential. In Fig. 2–15A and E, a vector is shown drawn perpendicular to lead aV_F and then rotated posteriorly and anteriorly so that the heavy arc of the zero potential plane changes position relative to the precordial leads. Note how the location of the transitional complex would identify the plane of zero potential.

In Fig. 2–15, it should be obvious that the direction of a vector determines the zone of relative positivity and relative negativity and the location of the transitional pathway. Stated in another way, the transitional complex identifies the direction of the vector since that complex is always perpendicular to the precordial vector.

Using the precordial leads to determine the extent to which a vector is anteriorly or posteriorly directed has limitations. If the electrodes are not properly positioned, the transitional pathway may be incorrectly placed. Furthermore, the electrode positions will vary from person to person depending on chest contour, even though the positions have been correctly chosen. If the chest is broad, the electrode positions of V_2, V_3, and V_4 tend to be near the same horizontal line. If the chest is thin and long, these electrode positions tend

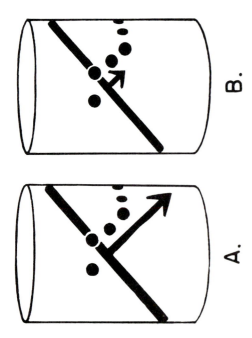

FIG. 2–14. The location of the transitional pathway produced by the large vector in (A) is the same as that produced by the small vector in (B).

complex is on an axis perpendicular to the electrical force since the position of the transitional pathway is determined by the direction of the force and not by its magnitude (Fig. 2–14).

After defining the direction of a vector in the frontal plane as previously described, the next step is to locate the transitional pathway to determine how far anteriorly or posteriorly this vector deviates from the frontal plane. To illustrate how the location of the transito be more vertically placed, one above the other (Fig. 2–16). Therefore, a transitional complex at lead V_4 would indicate a more posteriorly directed vector in a broad-chested person than in a thin-chested person.

Only one size of cylinder will be utilized in the illustrations in the remainder of this book. This is done for the sake of simplicity and at the expense of accuracy since it is virtually impossible to draw an electrical cylinder for every chest. Because of this individual variability, precordial leads cannot define a vector position as accurately as frontal leads. The range of error is probably about 15°. In practice the gross variations in chest size and contour can often be inferred from body weight, height, and other clinical information. The accuracy of interpretation will always be enhanced by knowing these data.

Summary of the Procedure Used to Determine the Spatial Direction of Electrical Forces Illustrated as Vectors *(Fig. 2–17)*

Step 1. Determine the frontal plane direction of the mean P, QRS, and T vectors by inspecting the bipolar frontal leads and then alter their directions to satisfy the unipolar frontal leads. This can be quickly accomplished by recalling that when an electrical force is relatively parallel with a given lead axis, it records its largest deflection on that lead; when an electrical force is relatively perpendicular to a given lead axis, it records its smallest deflection on that lead. The polarity of the leads must be kept in mind.

Step 2. Visualize the mean P, QRS, and T vectors within a cylinder. The frontal plane position as determined in Step 1 is retained and its origin is located in the center of the cylinder.

Step 3. Inspect the unipolar precordial leads and identify the transitional QRS and T complexes. A transitional complex is defined as a deflection which is equally negative and positive or resultantly zero.

Step 4. Orient the QRS vector posteriorly or anteriorly, as necessary, to a point where the zero potential plane of the QRS vector will pass through the electrode position which records the transitional complex. The mean T vector is then treated similarly.

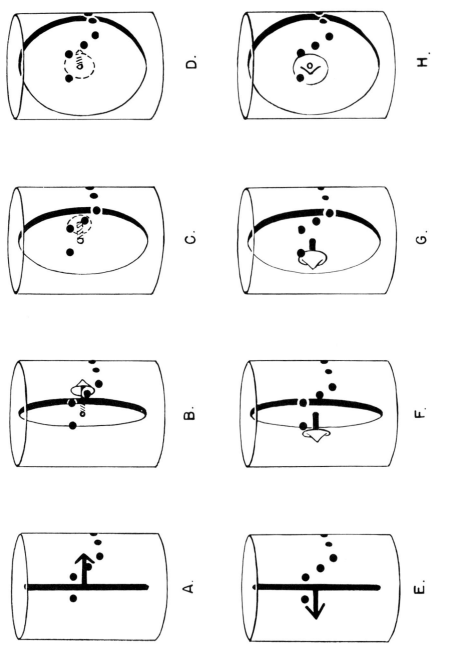

FIG. 2–15. (A) When the vector is directed to the left and is flush with the frontal plane, V_1 will record a negative deflection and V_2, V_3, V_4, V_5, and V_6 will record positive deflections.

(B) When the vector is rotated 10° posteriorly, V_1 will record a negative deflection, V_2 will be resultantly zero, and V_3, V_4, V_5, and V_6 will record positive deflections.

(C) When the vector is rotated 40° posteriorly, V_1, V_2, and V_3 will record negative deflections, V_4 will be resultantly zero, and V_5 and V_6 will record positive deflections.

(D) When the vector is rotated 70° to 80° posteriorly, V_1, V_2, V_3, V_4, and V_5 will record negative deflections, and V_6 will record a positive deflection.

(E) When the vector is directed to the right and is flush with the frontal plane, V_1 will record a positive deflection, and V_2, V_3, V_4, V_5, and V_6 will record negative deflections.

(F) When the vector is rotated 10° anteriorly, V_1 will record a positive deflection, V_2 will be resultantly zero, and V_3, V_4, V_5, and V_6 will record negative deflections.

(G) When the vector is rotated 40° anteriorly, V_1, V_2, and V_3 will record positive deflections, V_4 will be resultantly zero, and V_5 and V_6 will record negative deflections.

(H) When the vector is rotated 70° to 80° anteriorly, V_1, V_2, V_3, V_4, and V_5 will record positive deflections, and V_6 will record a negative deflection.

It is useful, though not routinely necessary, to be able to illustrate the spatial instantaneous vectors by drawing the spatial *QRS loop*. The spatial QRS loop enables one to visualize the change in magnitude and direction of vectors from instant to instant in a single QRS cycle. A simple way to draw the spatial QRS loop is illustrated and described in Fig. 2–18.

It is frequently necessary to calculate a mean vector for the forces generated during the *initial and terminal portions of the QRS*. The method for determining the direction of a mean vector representing the forces generated during the initial 0.01, initial 0.04, and terminal 0.02 s is described and illustrated in Fig. 2–19.

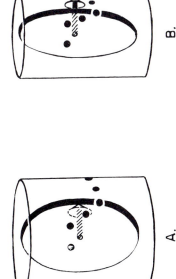

FIG. 2–16. (A) A cylinder representing a large, broad-chested subject. (B) A cylinder representing a thin, long-chested subject. The transitional pathway passes through electrode position V_4 in each instance but the vector is rotated more posteriorly in (A) than in (B).

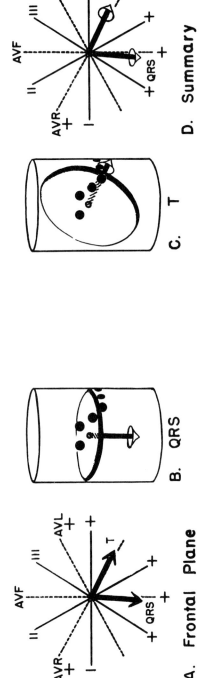

FIG. 2–17. An electrocardiogram is shown with the QRS and T deflections represented below by mean spatial vectors.

(A) The frontal plane projection of the mean spatial QRS and T vectors. The resultant QRS deflection is approximately equal in leads II and III and is slightly negative in lead I. The largest deflection in the unipolar frontal leads is in lead aV_F and the deflection is positive. These QRS characteristics can be represented by a mean QRS vector directed relatively parallel to lead aV_F but rotated to the right just enough for a small negative quantity to be projected on lead I. The T wave is largest and positive in lead I and smallest in lead III. When a long strip of lead III is studied, the T wave is seen to vary with respiration, but is most often slightly negative. These T-wave characteristics can be represented by a mean vector directed just to the left of a perpendicular to lead III. The largest negative deflection will therefore be recorded in lead aV_R.

(B) The mean spatial QRS vector oriented in the cylindrical replica of the chest. The QRS vector must be rotated 20° posteriorly because the transitional pathway passes between electrode positions V_3 and V_4.

(C) The mean spatial T vector oriented in the cylindrical replica of the chest. The mean T vector must be rotated 50° posteriorly because the transitional pathway passes between electrode positions V_4 and V_5.

(D) Final summary figure illustrating the mean spatial QRS and T vectors. The rim of the arrow tip is oriented spatially so that it parallels the transitional pathway of that particular vector and produces a three-dimensional effect.

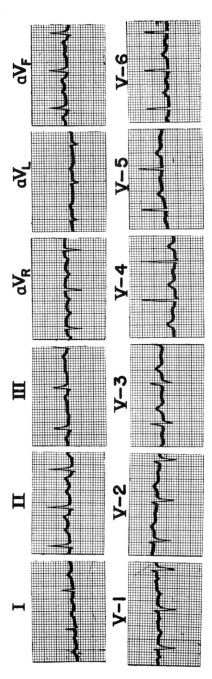

FIG. 2-18. Part I A normal electrocardiogram.

Part II How to construct the QRS loop. In this illustration the tracing shown in Part I is used as an example.

(A) The frontal plane projection of the mean spatial QRS vector is established first. In this case the QRS deflection is largest and positive in lead II and slightly negative in lead aV_L. The mean QRS vector will therefore be directed just to the right of the positive limb of lead II. A simple, rough outline of the QRS loop is drawn to satisfy the deflection recorded from the lead axis located nearest to the mean QRS vector. In this case a simple loop is drawn to satisfy the lead II deflection. Accordingly, a small initial portion of the loop (less than 0.02 s) must project a small negative quantity on lead II and the remaining portion (0.06 s) must project large positive quantities on lead II.

(B) The simple QRS loop constructed in (A) is altered to satisfy the three bipolar frontal leads. In this case lead III must have a small initial negative deflection and the remaining portion of the QRS deflection must be positive. The simple outline drawn in (A) is satisfactory in regard to lead III. The loop must be altered so that an initial small negative deflection can be recorded in lead I. The initial negative deflection is so small in lead I that it is hardly visible. It must be present, however, since the initial negative deflection in lead II is larger than the initial negative deflection in lead III, and the deflection magnitude of lead II must equal the deflection magnitude of lead III plus the magnitude of lead I. The terminal 0.02 s of the QRS complex is slightly negative in lead I, and the loop must be altered so that this can occur.

(C) The loop constructed to satisfy the deflections of the bipolar frontal leads is altered to satisfy the unipolar frontal leads. In this case the QRS loop shown in (B) is satisfactory in regard to leads aV_R and aV_F but is not satisfactory for lead aV_L. The loop must be altered so that an initial small positive deflection followed by a larger negative deflection can be recorded in lead aV_L.

(D) The transverse plane projection of the mean spatial QRS vector is established next. The transverse plane can be visualized by facing the subject and inspecting the QRS loop from above. Note in (A) the dotted line is drawn perpendicular to lead I through the arrow tip of the mean QRS vector. This line is continued downward

(Legend for Fig. 2-18 continued on page 38)

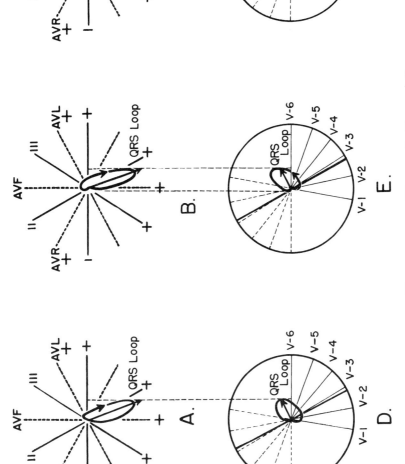

(Legend for Fig. 2–18 continued from page 36) in the drawing to intersect the V_6 axis of (D) and therefore indicates how much of the mean spatial QRS vector can be seen from above. The precordial lead recording the transitional QRS complex is identified next. The mean QRS vector is directed perpendicular to the lead axis which records the transitional QRS complex. In this case, the deflection recorded at electrode position V_3 is almost transitional but is resultantly slightly positive. Accordingly, the lead axis from which a perfect transitional complex would be recorded will be located approximately as indicated by the heavy line shown in (D), (E), and (F). (Note that the complex recorded at V_2 is resultantly more negative than the complex recorded at V_3 is resultantly positive. Therefore an electrode placed nearer V_3 than V_2 would record a transitional complex.) The mean QRS vector is directed perpendicular to the heavy lead axis line and extends to intersect the dotted line which represents the extent to which the vector can be seen from above. A simple outline of the QRS loop is then drawn to encompass the mean QRS vector and should roughly satisfy the lead recording the precordial transitional QRS complex.

(E) The transverse QRS loop constructed in (D) is now altered to satisfy the deflections recorded at electrode positions V_1, V_2, and V_3. Two dotted lines are shown drawn perpendicular to lead I in (B) and continued downward to intersect the axis of lead V_6 in (E). The transverse QRS loop must lie within the two dotted lines since it cannot extend a greater distance to the right or left. In this case the deflection in lead V_1 has a small initial positive deflection and a larger negative deflection. Accordingly, the initial portion of the loop must be directed toward the V_1 electrode while the remaining portion of the loop must be negative to lead V_1. The same situation exists regarding the deflection recorded in V_2. The loop must be drawn so that lead V_3 can record a complex which is nearly transitional but resultantly slightly positive.

(F) The transverse QRS loop constructed in (E) is next altered to satisfy the deflections recorded at electrode positions V_4, V_5, and V_6. In this case the loop must be changed so that lead V_4 can record a small initial negative deflection of 0.01 s duration followed by a large positive deflection of 0.04 s duration which is followed by a small terminal negative deflection of 0.03 s duration. Since lead V_5 records barely visible and brief initial and terminal negative deflections, the loop must be altered to allow this. The QRS duration in V_6 appears narrow because the initial and terminal instantaneous forces are approximately perpendicular to the lead axis of V_6.

FIG. 2–19. The initial 0.01 s, 0.04 s, mean QRS, and terminal 0.02 s vectors are drawn in the frontal and precordial planes for the electrocardiogram at the top. The initial 0.01s vector is very small and is difficult to place in the frontal plane. Since leads III and aV_R are both positive, it is probably located about +120°. In the precordial plane it must be anterior and near the perpendicular to lead V_5, since a small negative deflection is first seen in V_6.

The initial 0.04 s vector is resultantly positive in leads I, II, and aV_L and slightly resultantly negative in lead III. Therefore the initial 0.04 s vector must be slightly to the left of the perpendicular to lead III and closest to lead I, which is the most positive lead. In the precordial plane the mean initial 0.04 s vector is negative in V_1 to V_2 and positive in V_3 to V_6. It is therefore directed slightly posteriorly (about 15 to 20°).

The mean QRS vector is largest in lead I but must be located slightly to the right of V_1 since lead aV_F is resultantly slightly positive. In the precordial plane the mean QRS vector is posterior and perpendicular to the V_3 transitional lead. The terminal forces are negative in leads II and aV_F and must be just to the left of the positive pole of aV_L. Since the terminal 0.02 s vector is negative in V_1 to V_5 and positive in V_6, it must be approximately 70 to 80° posteriorly.

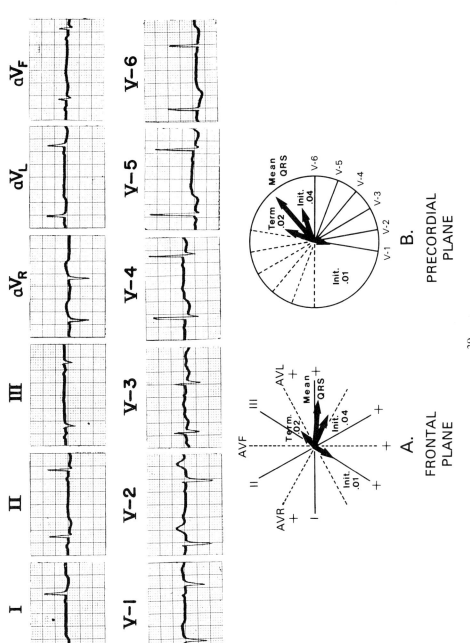

Chapter 3
The Interpretation of the Electrocardiogram

Before the electrocardiogram can be interpreted, various measurements must be made. In this section the accepted terminology of the various waves and intervals and the ground rules for determining the standard measurements will be mentioned. A useful approach to each tracing that ensures an orderly, complete evaluation is provided followed by important considerations that must be taken into account in the interpretation of the electrocardiogram.

Terminology of Electrocardiographic Deflections

The series of electrocardiographic deflections are arbitrarily designated as follows (Fig. 3–1):

P Wave
The P wave is the first deflection of the cardiac cycle, reflecting atrial activation from either a sinus or ectopic atrial impulse. Depending on the lead, the P wave may be positive (above the baseline), negative (below the baseline), or diphasic.

QRS Complex
Ventricular depolarization is represented as the QRS complex. The complex is labeled according to the following agreed-upon characteristics.

Q Wave The Q wave is a negative deflection at the onset of the QRS complex.

R Wave The R wave is the first upward deflection

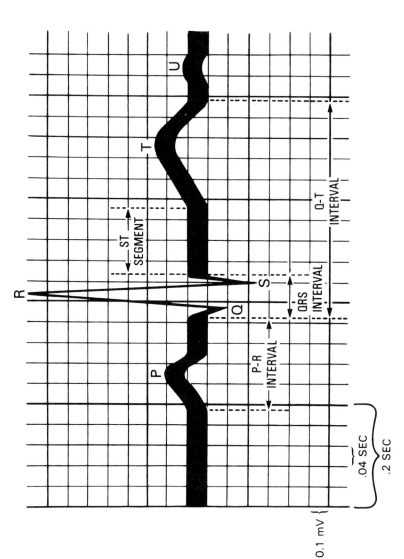

FIG. 3–1. Diagram of the electrocardiogram illustrating the designation of deflections and the duration of the intervals for one cardiac cycle on the standard grid format used for measuring the amplitude of deflections and the duration of the intervals. The paper speed is 25 mm/sec.

1 mm apart. Bolder horizontal and vertical stripes appear after every fifth small square. Voltage is measured in terms of millimeters of vertical displacement above the top or bottom border of the isoelectric line. All electrocardiograms are standardized so that 1 millivolt (mV) of electrical force will cause a 10-mm vertical displacement of the recording stylus. Therefore each vertical mm equals 0.1 mV.

Time is measured along the horizontal axis. At a standard recording speed of 25 mm/s, each faint vertical line is 0.04 s apart and each bold vertical stripe is 5×0.04 s or 0.2 s apart. One minute of recording will span 300 (60 s/0.02 s) major squares.

Measurement of Heart Rate (Fig. 3–2)

The quickest method of determining an approximate heart rate is to count the number of major (5 mm) squares between consecutive QRS complexes (R to R interval) and divide this number into 300. By this simple calculation, a heart rate of 300 per minute is present when QRS complexes are one square apart, 150 per minute when two squares apart, 100 per minute when three, etc. If the complexes are separated by a fraction more than a whole number, an appropriate adjustment is made: 3½ squares is halfway between 100 and 75 and therefore the heart rate is 88 per minute.

Measurement of Electrocardiographic Intervals

The electrocardiographic intervals should be measured in whichever lead, frontal or precordial, that displays whether or not a Q wave is present. A second positive deflection, if present, is called an R' wave.

S Wave An S wave is the first downward deflection below the isoelectric line after an R wave. A second S wave would be S'.

T Wave

The T wave, the deflection due to ventricular repolarization, follows the QRS complex. It may be positive, negative, or diphasic, depending on the lead.

U Wave

The U wave is a low-amplitude deflection that may follow the T wave.

Further Terminology

A *monophasic* QRS complex consists of a single R (positive) wave or a QS (negative) complex. Any complex is said to be *bi-* or *diphasic* when there is a deflection that is partly above and partly below the isoelectric line. A *triphasic* complex means that the QRS complex has an RSR' configuration. Capital letters—Q, R, and S—are used when the individual deflections equal or exceed 5 mm. Lowercase letters—q, r, s—are applied to individual deflections below 5 mm.

Electrocardiographic Measurements of Electrocardiographic Deflections (Fig. 3–1)

A standard electrocardiogram is crosshatched into squares of faint vertical and horizontal lines which are

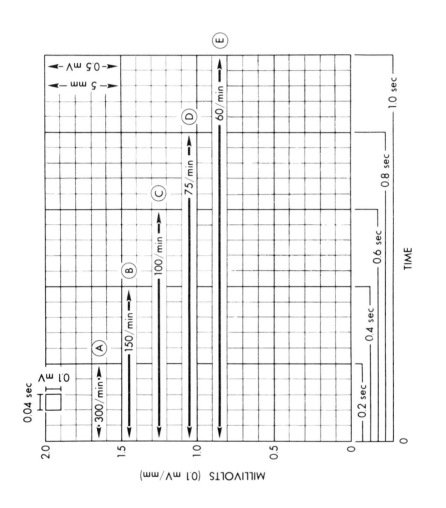

FIG. 3–2. Rate-interval relationship. Standard time calibration is 1 mm = 0.04 s and 5 mm = 0.20 s. Standard voltage is 0.1 mV/mm. A repetitive event occurring every 5 mm (0.20 s) (A) on the time axis is occurring at 300 per minute. A repetitive event occurring every 10 mm (0.40 s) (B) is occurring at 150 per minute. C, D, and E indicate that repetitive events at 0.60, 0.80, and 1.00 s are occurring at rates of 100, 75, and 60 per minute, respectively.

[From R. J. Myerburg in Petersdorf et al. (eds.), *Harrison's Principles of Internal Medicine*, 10th ed., chapter 249, McGraw-Hill, New York, 1982.]

the longest interval and in which the onset and termination can be accurately delineated. The chosen lead may be different for each interval.

The following intervals are routinely measured (Fig. 3–1):

PR Interval The PR interval is measured from the beginning of the P wave to the beginning (Q or R wave) of the QRS complex (Fig. 3–1). The normal range for the adult can vary from 0.12 to 0.20 s. The interval is usually shorter with faster heart rates and in children (Appendix, Table 1). A small percentage of normal people will have a PR interval greater than 0.20 s.

QRS Interval The duration of the QRS interval is measured from the onset (Q or R wave) to the end of the QRS complex (Fig. 3–1). The lead with the widest QRS complex is selected for the measurement. The normal QRS interval in the adult is 0.06 to 0.10 s. Children have a narrower QRS duration.

QT Interval This interval is measured from the onset of the QRS interval to the termination of the T wave (Fig. 3–1). A lead with a well-defined T wave, usually a mid-precordial lead, is often selected. This interval spans total ventricular depolarization and repolarization and varies with heart rate, age, sex, and autonomic influences. Normal values corrected for heart rate and sex are given in the Appendix (Table 2). The QT interval can be corrected for heart rate by dividing it by the square root of the RR interval. This is referred to as the QT_c; the upper limit of normal is 0.43 s.

Electrical Axis

By the method outlined earlier, the spatial orientation of the mean QRS and T vectors in the frontal plane are determined and placed on the hexaxial reference system. The normal mean QRS axis for the adult should fall between $-30°$ and $+90°$ (Fig. 3–3). Left axis deviation indicates a mean QRS vector between $-30°$ and $-90°$ while right axis deviation is between $+90°$ and $-150°$. The normal mean T vector is relatively parallel to the QRS vector (Fig. 3–4).

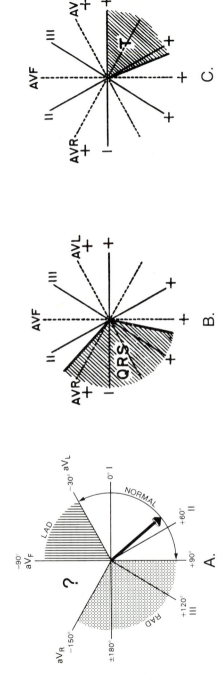

FIG. 3–3. (A) The hexaxial frontal plane reference system illustrating the normal range of the mean QRS axis for adults (arrow), left axis deviation (LAD), and right axis deviation (RAD). The area between −150° and −90° can be considered extreme right axis deviation or extreme left axis deviation.
(B) The mean QRS vector of the newborn can be found within the wide limits of the shaded area shown above.
(C) The mean T vector of the newborn can be found within the wide limits of the shaded area shown above.

An Approach to the Interpretation of the Electrocardiogram

The interpretation of an electrocardiogram should always proceed in a stepwise fashion so that all elements of the tracing are carefully analyzed in a consistent manner. The following sequence is recommended:

Step 1. Measure and record the heart rate and the PR, QRS, and QT intervals. Comment if the heart rate, rhythm, or PR interval are abnormal.

Step 2. Draw or mentally place the P-wave vector on the hexaxial reference system. Measure the maximum height and duration of the P wave and inspect the P-wave contour. Comment if the P vector, measurements, or contour are abnormal.

Step 3. Draw or mentally place the initial 0.01 s, initial

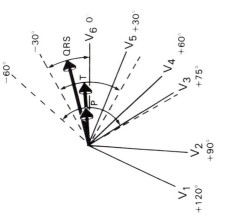

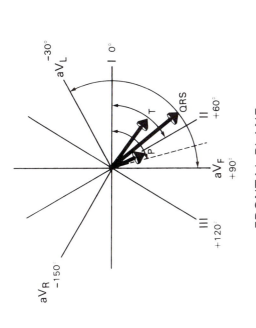

FRONTAL PLANE   PRECORDIAL PLANE

FIG. 3-4. The approximate normal range of the adult mean P, QRS, and T vectors is shown for the frontal and precordial planes. The arrows point to the most common position, and the arcs at the tip of each arrow demonstrate the approximate normal range of each vector.

0.04 s, terminal 0.02 s, and mean QRS vector on the hexaxial reference system. Comment if there is an abnormality of the magnitude or direction of the QRS vectors or the QRS duration.

Step 4. Analyze the ST segment for displacement above or below the isoelectric line. Comment if abnormal.

Step 5. Draw or mentally place the T-wave vector on the hexaxial reference system. Analyze the T-wave height, contour, and vector. Comment if abnormal.

Step 6. Comment on the QRS-T angle and QT_c if abnormal.

Step 7. Comment on the U wave if abnormal.

Important Considerations in the Interpretation of the Electrocardiogram

The electrocardiogram is a highly complex measurement that is influenced by an interaction of biologic and technical factors as well as by various diseases. Truly normal values for each age group, sex, body weight, chest size, and numerous other variables that can significantly affect the electrocardiogram have never been derived. Differentiation between normal and abnormal is therefore fraught with difficulty; an interpretation, by necessity, must often be imprecise or preceded by words of caution such as "probably," "possible," "nonspecific," "cannot rule out," "suggests." The interpreter must also appreciate the statistical meaning of sensitivity, specificity, and predictive value. In addition, a "normal" resting electrocardiogram does not certify that the *heart* is normal. Severe cardiac disease, particularly of the coronary arteries, may be present without any discernible alterations of the normal electrical forces and intervals. In this section various considerations that must be taken into account when interpreting the resting electrocardiogram will be discussed.

Constitutional and Physiologic Influences

The electrocardiogram is influenced by a number of constitutional and physiologic influences that must be considered when a recording is interpreted. Constitutional variables include age, sex, body weight, body height, chest configuration, anatomic position of the heart, and race. Age is the single most important biologic variable. With increasing age the R- and S-wave amplitudes decrease, the mean QRS axis shifts leftward, and the PR interval increases. Compared with men, women below age 60 have smaller-amplitude R, S, and T waves and a decreased initial septal force. In addition, the QRS, PR, and QT intervals are shorter, and the ST segment vector may be more superiorly-posteriorly directed. Obesity is associated with a horizontal mean QRS vector and a decreased amplitude of the R and T wave while a slender person tends to have a more vertical mean QRS axis. The anatomic position of the heart in the chest closely correlates with the mean QRS axis in the frontal plane. Blacks have a shorter QRS interval, larger QRS amplitude, and a more posterior T vector than whites.

Heart rate, QRS, ST, and T vectors, and amplitudes of various waves are significantly influenced by systemic blood pressure, intracardiac pressures, hematocrit values, heart size, electrolytes, body temperature, exercise conditioning, hyperventilation, emotions, high altitude, recent food ingestion, smoking, and probably many other physiologic variables.

Technical Considerations

Technical considerations include position of the precordial leads relative to the anatomic position of the heart, width of the sternum, fidelity of the ECG machine, conducting medium used under the electrodes, observer variability, error of measurement, baseline variation, and normal day-to-day variation. These technical problems are a source of great concern, for they potentially contribute a significant variability to each tracing. The relation of the traditional precordial leads to the anatomic position of the heart will obviously vary considerably, depending on the chest configuration. Electrocardiographic machines vary in their proficiency in responding faithfully to small deflections or to rapid rates of deflection—diagnostic Q waves that are apparent when recorded on one machine may be slurred into the R wave by another machine; ST segment depression in the precordial leads may reflect a problem with frequency response and not ischemia. Corroded or unkempt electrodes, the incorrect use of alcohol rather than saline pads, and imperfect contact of the electrode with the skin may affect voltage.

Disagreement in the interpretation of the same ECG among experienced observers is common. The discrepancies can be quite significant, averaging about 30 percent. The same observer may offer a different opinion on the same ECG on repeat interpretation. Different observers often disagree on the measurements of intervals and amplitudes. This error of measurement adds to the difficulties of human interpretation of the ECG.

The computer has been called upon to improve the diagnostic accuracy of interpretation. The computer is superior to human interpretation in measurements of intervals, amplitudes, and axis; is more consistent in its application of criteria; has reduced technical errors in recording, mounting, and reporting; and provides a cost saving when applied to large populations. Problems remain with interpreting arrhythmias and certain types of abnormalities; comparing old and current tracings; reading technically poor tracings; and incorporating clinical information into the final interpretation. Nevertheless, computer interpretation with physician over-read has current approval and promises added precision and improved criteria of interpretation.

A day-to-day variation of the normal ECG has been documented. Even when scrupulous attention is given to placing chest leads in the identical position by marking the chest, there is a substantial fluctuation in the QRS and T amplitude and mean QRS axis. This is most marked for small deflections such as q waves and r-wave amplitude. Time measurements are only minimally affected. The variation is exaggerated when technicians are not using lead placement markers. These day-to-day changes explain, at least in part, why an ECG will easily meet criteria for left ventricular hypertrophy on one day but not on the next or be diagnostic of inferior infarction on one occasion but show small initial r waves in the same inferior leads on a subsequent tracing.

Statistical Considerations

The contribution of any diagnostic test is highly dependent on its ability to discover a high percentage of the patients with the disorder while excluding those without it. This is commonly expressed in terms of sensitivity, specificity, and predictive accuracy. An understanding of these terms is essential in order to appreciate the capabilities and limitations of the resting electrocardiogram.

The *sensitivity* of a test is defined as the probability of a positive result for a disease if all the patients have the disease. This may be restated as

$$\text{Sensitivity (\%)} = \frac{TP}{TP + FN} \times 100$$

where TP = true positives (number of patients being tested who meet the normal for the condition being tested who meet the criterion) and FN = false negatives (number of patients abnormal for the condition being tested who do not meet the criterion). Therefore, a test which correctly detects all the patients with the disease has a sensitivity of 100 percent.

The *specificity* of a test is defined as the probability of a negative result for a disease if none of the patients has the disease. This may be restated as

$$\text{Specificity} = \frac{TN}{TN + FP} \times 100$$

where TN = true negatives (number of patients without the condition being tested who do not meet the criterion) and FP = false positives (number of patients without the condition being tested who do meet the criterion). Therefore, a test with a specificity of 100 percent detects only the patients with the disease.

The *predictive accuracy* is the percentage of positive results that are truly positive, or

$$\text{Predictive accuracy} = \frac{TP}{TP + FP} \times 100$$

where TP = true positives (number of patients abnormal for the condition being tested who meet the criterion) and FP = false positives (number of patients without the condition being tested who do meet the criterion).

The value of a test is highly dependent on the prevalence of the disease in the study population. Bayes' theorem incorporates the prevalence of the disease in the study population into the analysis and allows the interpreter to predict more accurately the chance of disease being present given a positive or negative test. The essence of the Bayes theorem is that the number of false-positive results will increase as the prevalence of the disease decreases; the predictive accuracy is correspondingly lower. As the prevalence of the disease increases, the predictive accuracy will be higher.

These considerations are illustrated by the following example:[1]

Assume that the ECG criteria for left ventricular hypertrophy have both a specificity and a sensitivity of 95 percent and that 1000 patients are tested from a population in which 90 percent have left ventricular hypertrophy. Since the test has a sensitivity of 95 percent, then 855 (900 × 95 percent) would be true positives. If the specificity is 95 percent, 5 of the 100 patients without left ventricular hypertrophy will be false positives. Since a total of 855 of the 860 patients actually have left ventricular hypertrophy, there is a predictive accuracy of 99.4 percent. If, however, the prevalance of left ventricular hypertrophy in the 1000 patients is only 2 percent, then 20 patients would have left ventricular hypertrophy and 980 would not. This time 19 of 20 will be true positives and 49 of 980 will be false positives. The predictive accuracy, based on 19 true positives out of 68 with a positive test result, is now only 28 percent. In actuality, the sensitivity for commonly used precordial plane criteria for left ventricular hypertrophy is about 55 percent and the specificity is around 89 percent. Again, assuming a population of 1000 patients and a prevalence of 2 percent, a predictive accuracy of only 9.3 percent is obtainable.

This concept of predictive accuracy dependent on disease prevalence has important implications on the reading of electrocardiograms by interpreters who are unfamiliar with the patient. If the population of tracings includes a high percentage of normal tracings—routine preoperative tracings, yearly screening tracings in an asymptomatic population, insurance testing, etc.—the likelihood of a false-positive diagnosis of left ventricular hypertrophy, ST-T abnormality, old myocardial infarction, etc., will be significantly increased. Criteria derived from an older, abnormal population should not be applied indiscriminately to a group with a low prevalence of disease—the tracing should not be overinterpreted. On the other hand, the same criteria can be more rigorously used when the tracings are from a known population with a high incidence of disease, such as a coronary care unit.

The accuracy of electrocardiographic criteria, particularly the differentiation between normal and abnormal, has been extensively studied by Simonson. In his many articles, which are fundamental to understanding the limitations of the ECG, he stresses the following problems:

Inadequate Sample Size Because of the significant effect of constitutional factors—age, sex, race, weight, chest configuration—and unknown factors, a large population sample is necessary to arrive at meaningful conclusions. Simonson estimates a minimal sample size

---

[1] Adapted from D. R. Redwood, J. S. Borer, and S. E. Epstein: Whither the ST segment during exercise? *Circulation* 1976; 54:703. Used by permission of the authors and the American Heart Association, Inc.

of 1000 men and women and a desirable sample size of 1800 is necessary to determine normal limits for various subgroups. This figure contrasts with the sample size of 100 to 200 used in many studies.

Composition of the Sample An ideal sample would be truly representative of the average, healthy population. This requires fastidious screening to eliminate any disorder that may conceivably influence the electrocardiogram. Common pitfalls include the use of hospitalized patients, patients who have died with "normal" hearts, or a group preselected in some way, such as medical students, people who answer an advertisement to have a free electrocardiogram, etc. This concern has plagued many studies and is a major reason why the results of one study cannot be compared with or added to those of another study.

Adequate Statistical Evaluation Studies that compile values for a "normal population" and use the extreme values as the limits of normal include many false normals. This error increases as the sample enlarges. Unfortunately, this was the method used by many early studies that are now the basis for current criteria. A more acceptable method for achieving a statistically sound boundary of normal is to determine a percentile distribution and establish a cutoff point at both ends of the normal distribution. A frequently used cutoff is 2.5 percent at each end so that 95 percent of the normal population is included in the limits. This approach still strands 2.5 percent of the normal subjects below and 2.5 percent above the normal limits. Multivariate analysis, aided by a computer, greatly strengthens the validity of this approach.

Confirmation of Electrocardiographic Criteria

Electrocardiographic criteria are only as reliable as the standard against which they are verified. Standards have changed, however, as new techniques have become available. Early studies used clinical criteria such as "disorders capable of producing strain on the left or right side of the heart," "chest pain thought to result from angina pectoris," and "chest x-ray evidence of cardiac chamber enlargement" for comparison. Each of these approaches is seriously flawed since none is subject to precise measurement and pathologic authentication. For example, as many as 20 percent of patients who have chest discomfort confidently diagnosed as angina pectoris have been found to have normal coronary arteries at angiography. Yet many of our current standards have been predicated on these precarious clinical criteria. At first glance, autopsy confirmation would seem to be the desirable standard. Autopsy information, although of great importance, suffers several limitations. It cannot reveal physiologic influences, such as intraluminal pressure, heart rate, and blood pressure, that may influence the electrocardiogram in the living individual. Nor is the tension and thickness of the postmortem myocardial wall the same as that in a living individual. Autopsy technique differs greatly from study to study—the septum may or may not be included as part of the left heart; the epicardial fat may or may not be removed; the measurements of thickness may be taken in different places. Since the autopsy population is highly selected for advanced disease, autopsy data provide highly skewed information and endow the electrocardiogram with an exaggerated precision.

Newer diagnostic techniques, such as intracardiac pressure and electrophysiologic measurements; coronary and ventricular angiography; echocardiography; radioisotopic scans; myocardial biopsy; and a more sophisticated understanding of epidemiologic approaches, statistical methods, and computer science have provided a better definition of normal values and enhanced electrocardiographic correlations.

Part Two
The Normal Electrocardiogram

Chapter 4

The Normal Atrial and Ventricular Electrocardiogram

Now that the basic concepts of electrocardiography and the vector method have been introduced, the electrocardiogram can be analyzed in terms of normal and abnormal vectors (Figs. 3–4, 4–2 to 4–12). In this chapter the *normal* electrical forces that determine the different electrocardiographic deflections will be discussed and placed in the context of the 12-lead scalar electrocardiogram. Normal values and the range of normal will be emphasized.

The P Wave

The normal, sinus-initiated P wave is a composite of vectors resulting from the depolarization of the left and right atrium. It is useful to visualize the vector of the first and last half of the P vector to determine the normality of right and left atrial depolarization (see Chapter 5). The resultant mean P vector is oriented inferiorly and leftward and is either flush with the frontal plane or slightly anterior. In the frontal plane the normal mean P vector may be from $0°$ to $+75°$ and most commonly is near $+60°$. When this P vector is drawn onto the hexaxial reference system (Fig. 3–4), the P wave will be positive in leads I, II, and aV_F and inverted in aV_R. Lead II usually registers the largest P wave while leads aV_L and III may be positive, negative, or diphasic depending on the proximity of the P vector to that lead. Since the mean P vector is directed ways. The P wave may remain normal despite considerable heart disease or may display a peculiar configuration without any obvious reason.

The QRS Complex

Ventricular depolarization normally lasts 0.10 s or less and can be analyzed in terms of four vectors—an initial, small 0.01 s vector, an initial major 0.04 s vector, a terminal 0.02 s vector, and the mean QRS vector (Fig. 2–19). The spatial orientation of these four vectors is determined by the anatomic spread of the electrical impulse, each representing the sum of many simultaneous vectors. Because many of the simultaneous forces are pointing in opposite directions and therefore nullify each other, the QRS complex really represents only about 10 percent of the actual electricity that is generated by the ventricular myocardium.

In the following discussion the four normal QRS vectors will be more fully described. By understanding these vectors, the normal QRS complex and its variations for each frontal and precordial lead can be easily comprehended.

The Initial 0.01 s Vector *(Fig. 4–2)*

Ventricular depolarization commences on the left side of the middle third of the ventricular septum. Excitation then travels across the septum from the left to the

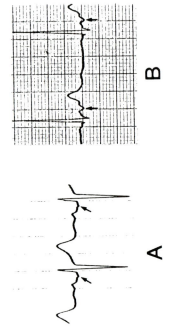

FIG. 4–1. (A), (B) Two examples of atrial repolarization (Ta) (arrows). In A the Ta is seen in the PR segment, while B shows the Ta in the ST segment.

leftward and slightly posteriorly, the P wave is often diphasic or negative in V_1 and sometimes V_2. The P wave is always upright from V_3 to V_6 in adults (Fig. 3–4). Minor notching of the dome of the P wave is not uncommon, reflecting the different vectors of right and left atrial depolarization.

From beginning to end the P wave may have a normal duration up to 0.11 s, while its amplitude should not exceed 2.5 mm. A small negative deflection of atrial repolarization, the Ta wave, though usually not apparent, may occasionally be seen within the PR or ST segment (Fig. 4–1A and B). The contour, height, and duration of the P wave may vary from one tracing to the next in the same individual, depending on heart rate and influences affecting the atrial conducting path-

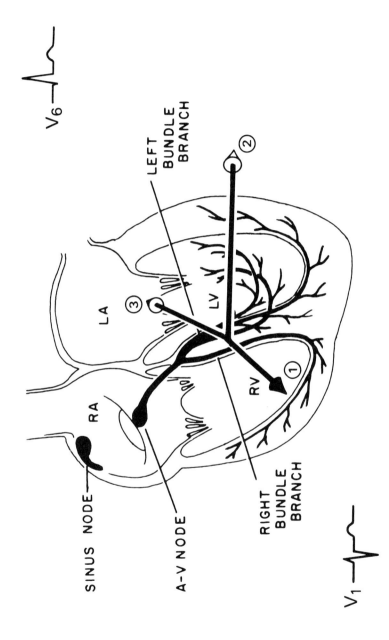

FIG. 4–2. Schematic drawing of the heart and conducting system. The normal 0.01 s vector (1), 0.04 s vector (2), and terminal 0.02 s vector (3) are shown superimposed on the drawing. Leads V_1 and V_6, as determined by these vectors, are illustrated.

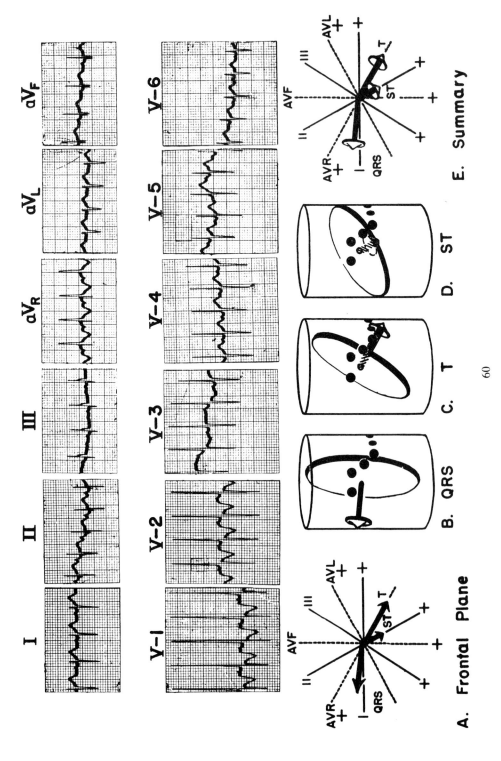

FIG. 4–3. The electrocardiogram of a 2-day-old infant.

(A) The frontal plane projection of the mean spatial QRS, ST, and T vectors. The QRS complex is largest and negative in lead I and resultantly slightly negative in lead aV_F. QRS complexes of this nature can be represented by a mean vector directed relatively parallel with the lead I axis. The mean QRS vector must be directed about 10° above the lead I axis since it projects a small negative quantity onto the lead aV_F axis. The resultant negativity of the QRS in leads I and II indicate that the vector points to the right rather than to the left. The T wave is smallest in lead III, upright in leads II and III, and deeply inverted in lead aV_R. Accordingly, the mean T vector is perpendicular to lead III and is directed downward and to the left. The ST segment deviation appears largest and positive in lead II and therefore the ST vector is parallel with lead II.

(B) The mean spatial QRS vector oriented in the cylindrical replica of the chest. The QRS must be rotated 40° anteriorly so that the transitional pathway will pass between electrode positions V_3 and V_4. Note the diphasic precordial complexes.

(C) The mean spatial T vector oriented in the cylindrical replica of the chest. The T vector must be rotated 20° posteriorly so that the transitional pathway will pass through electrode position V_4.

(D) The mean spatial ST vector oriented in the cylindrical replica of the chest. The ST vector must be rotated 30° posteriorly so that the transitional pathway will pass between electrode positions V_3 and V_4. (The ST segment is definitely negative in V_1, V_2, and V_3 and, when studied in a long strip of electrocardiogram, is very slightly positive in V_4, V_5, and V_6. The ST positivity is slight in V_4, V_5, and V_6, because these leads record near the transitional pathway and are recording from a greater distance than electrodes placed at V_1, V_2, and V_3.)

(E) Final summary figure illustrating a spatial QRS-T angle of 150°. The mean ST vector is nearly parallel with the mean T vector.

right side. Since the septum is anatomically aligned about 45° to the left of the midline, the direction of this septal force is anterior and usually rightward in the general direction of the positive poles of V_1 and V_2 and away from V_5 and V_6. A small r wave, varying from minuscule to several millimeters will be inscribed in V_1 and V_2 while V_4, V_5, and V_6 will often record a small *septal* q wave.

In the frontal plane this initial 0.01 s vector may be superior or inferior. If the septal force is superior, normal brief q waves will be recorded in inferior leads II, III, and aV_F and an r wave in leads I and aV_L. When the septal force is inferiorly directed, the inferior leads display an r wave while q waves may be seen in leads I and aV_L. The finding of a q wave of less than 0.03 s in duration and 1 to 3 mm in depth (less than 25 percent of the following R wave) in a limb lead can therefore be a perfectly normal consequence of septal depolarization. On occasion an even broader q wave is found in lead III or aV_L in normal individuals.

The Initial 0.04 s Vector *(Fig. 4–2)*

By 0.04 s the septum and part of the apical and anterior wall of the right ventricle have depolarized. The thick left ventricular wall is stimulated next, producing a major vector which always points inferiorly, leftward, and posteriorly. Simultaneous right ventricular forces are essentially dwarfed by the magnitude of these left

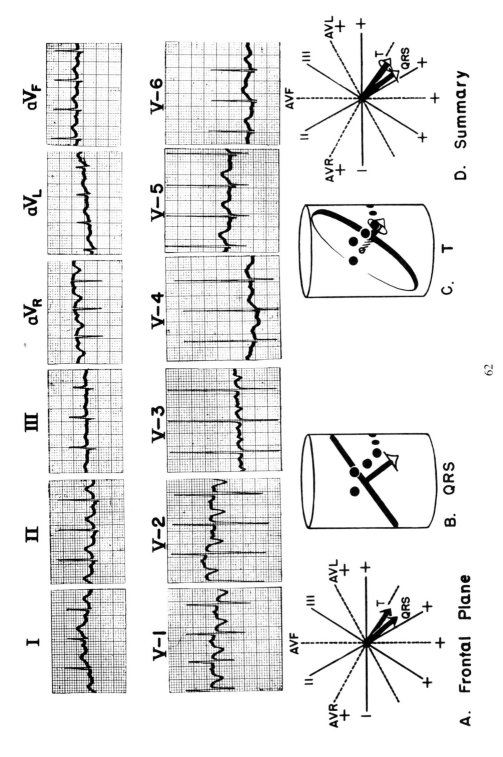

FIG. 4–4. The electrocardiogram of a normal child, age 2.
(A) The frontal plane projection of the mean QRS and T vectors. The QRS complex is largest and positive in lead II and slightly positive in leads III and aV_L. QRS complexes of this nature can be represented by a mean vector directed just to the left of the positive limb of lead II. The T wave is largest in lead II, large and negative in lead aV_R, and slightly positive in lead III. Such T waves can be represented by a mean vector directed just to the right of a perpendicular to lead III.
(B) The mean spatial QRS vector oriented in a cylindrical replica of the chest. Note that the QRS complex in V_1 varies with the respiratory cycle and that some of the complexes are transitional while others are negative. The transitional pathway is, therefore, slightly different with each phase of respiration. Since V_3, V_4, V_5, and V_6 are definitely positive, it is reasonable to place the transitional pathway so that the mean QRS is flush with the frontal plane. A vector so located would represent an average vector position for all phases of respiration.
(C) The mean spatial T vector oriented in a cylindrical replica of the chest. The T vector is rotated 20° posteriorly because the transitional pathway passes through electrode position V_3.
(D) Final summary figure illustrating a spatial QRS-T angle of 20°.

ventricular forces. In the frontal plane the 0.04 s vector is between leads I and aV_F, resulting in an R wave in leads I, II, and aV_F, and away from aV_R which records an S wave. Since leads aV_L and III are near the perpendicular to this force, an R or an S wave may be seen. The posterior-leftward direction is responsible for the increasing amplitude of the R wave in V_2 to V_5 and the S wave in V_1 to V_2 in the precordial plane. In children and young adults it may be very large, exceeding 30 mm in some people. With increasing age a smaller vector should be expected.

The Terminal 0.02 s Vector *(Fig. 4–2)*

The final area of the ventricles to depolarize is the posterolateral and basilar wall of the left ventricle and the infundibular area of the right ventricle. This terminal vector is small and oriented posteriorly, superiorly, and to the left or right. This vector contributes to the R wave of leads I, aV_L, and V_6 and the S wave of V_1. If it is rightward, a normal r' wave may be displayed in aV_R and V_1 and an s wave in V_6.

The Mean QRS Vector *(Fig. 3–4)*

The mean QRS vector is the summation of all electrical forces generated during ventricular depolarization. This vector is determined mainly by the 0.04 s vector and is oriented leftward, inferiorly, and slightly posteriorly. Depending upon age, body build, anatomic position of the heart, and other factors, the normal mean QRS vector may be between −30° and +90° in the frontal plane (or slightly rightward of +90° in young adults and children). In the precordial plane the mean QRS vector can be from 0° to −30° (average −15°).

63

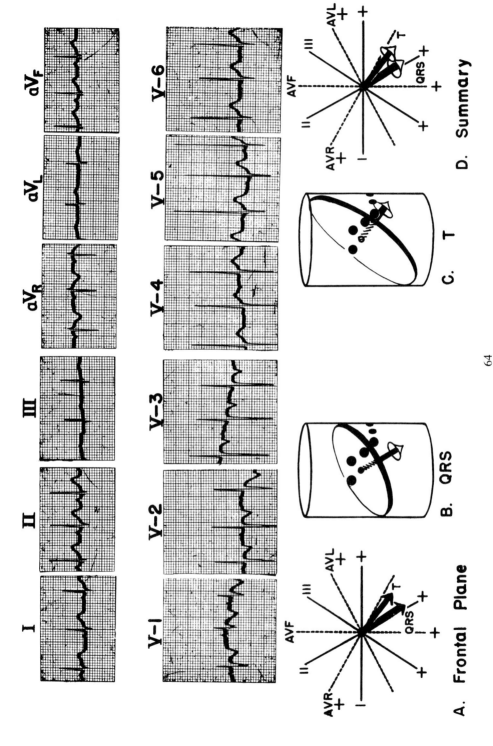

FIG. 4–5. The electrocardiogram of a normal child, age 3½, illustrating a posteriorly directed T vector.

(A) The frontal plane projection of the mean QRS and T vectors. The QRS complex is largest and positive in lead II and slightly positive in lead aV_L. QRS complexes of this nature can be represented by a mean vector directed just to the left of the positive limb of the lead II axis. In the bipolar frontal leads, the T wave is smallest and positive in lead III and, in the unipolar frontal leads, the T wave is largest and negative in lead aV_R. Under these circumstances the mean T vector will be directed just to the right of the negative limb of lead aV_R.

(B), (C) The mean spatial QRS and T vector oriented in cylindrical replicas of the chest. Both the QRS and T vectors are rotated approximately 30° posteriorly because their transitional pathways pass between electrode positions V_3 and V_4.

(D) Final summary figure illustrating a spatial QRS-T angle of 20°.

The ST Segment (Fig. 3–1)

The ST segment joins the end of the QRS complex, *the J point*, to the beginning of the T wave. Though usually isoelectric, as compared to the TP or PR segment for baseline reference, an ST vector pointing anteriorly, inferiorly, and leftward, parallel to the T vector, may occur in some normal, usually young individuals (Fig. 4–11). An ST segment elevation of 1 to 4 mm in leads I, II, and V_4 to V_6 can be observed for this reason. This ST elevation, known as an *early repolarization pattern*, usually begins with a fishhooklike deformity followed by a concave ST segment and a prominent T wave (Fig. 4–11—lead V_4). Leads V_1 and V_2 may show a slanting, slightly elevated ST segment into a prominent T wave in some normal individuals. On occasion the T wave may be inverted. ST-segment depression exceeding 0.5 mm in any lead is always abnormal. The duration of the ST segment is not considered to be helpful, and therefore it is not measured.

The T Wave

The repolarization of the ventricles inscribes a T wave with a mean vector that is inferior, leftward, and near the horizontal (Fig. 3–4). The mean T vector may vary from 0° to +60° in the frontal plane and −30° to +30° in the horizontal plane. In the normal adult the mean spatial T vector is usually located within 60° of the mean spatial QRS vector. It lies to the right of a markedly leftward mean spatial QRS vector and to the left of a vertical mean spatial QRS vector. The mean T vector is always anterior to the mean QRS vector. Since this vector is roughly parallel to the mean QRS vector, the T wave is usually above the baseline in leads with a positive QRS and below the baseline where the QRS is predominately negative. In the frontal plane the T wave is always upright in leads I, II, and usually aV_F, inverted in aV_R, and either slightly positive, diphasic, flat, or inverted in leads III and aV_L. Precordial leads V_2 to V_6 are always upright in the adult while V_1

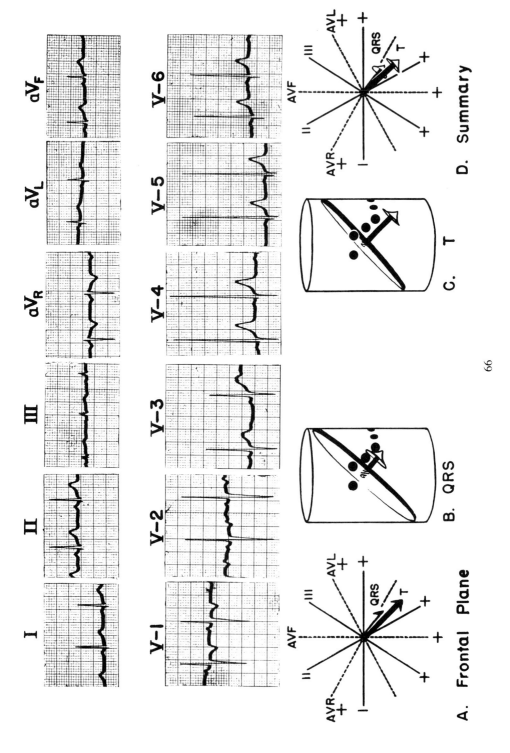

FIG. 4–6. The electrocardiogram of a normal child, age 6.

(A) The frontal plane projection of the mean QRS and T vectors. The QRS complex is small but positive in lead III in the bipolar frontal leads and large and negative in lead aV_R in the unipolar frontal leads. QRS complexes of this nature can be represented by a mean vector directed just to the right of a perpendicular to the lead III axis. The T wave is largest and positive in lead II but slightly positive in lead aV_L. T waves of this nature can be represented by a mean vector directed just to the left of the lead II axis.

(B) The mean spatial QRS vector oriented in the cylindrical replica of the chest. The QRS vector must be rotated approximately 15° posteriorly because the transitional pathway passes between the electrode positions V_2 and V_3.

(C) The mean spatial T vector oriented in the cylindrical replica of the chest. The T vector must be rotated approximately 10° posteriorly because the transitional pathway passes between the electrode positions V_2 and V_3.

(D) Final summary figure illustrating a spatial QRS-T angle of 5°. Note the multiphasic T waves in lead V_2. These peculiar waves are produced because electrode position V_2 is recording very near the transitional pathway for the T wave. Under such circumstances some of the instantaneous T vectors project positive quantities in that lead while other instantaneous T vectors, located only a few degrees away, project negative quantities. In this case the early instantaneous T vectors are directed more posteriorly than the terminal instantaneous T vectors, producing a negative deflection during the early part of the T wave and a positive deflection during the last part of the T wave. The multiphasic contour is not seen in the other precordial T waves because all the instantaneous T vectors project either positive quantities or negative quantities on the other precordial lead axes.

may show an inverted, flat, or upright T wave. Generally the amplitude of the T wave does not exceed 6 mm in the limb leads. In the precordial leads V_2 to V_4, the T wave, particularly in young males, may be considerably higher. The duration of the T wave is not measured.

The U Wave (Fig. 3–1)

The normal U-wave amplitude is between 5 and 25 percent of the neighboring T wave. In general it is less than 1 mm in amplitude, highest at low heart rates, and barely detectable at rates above 90 per minute. If present, it is normally positive in all leads with a positive T wave as well as leads III and V_1.

The QRS-T Angle (Fig. 3–4)

The angle subtended by the mean QRS and mean T vectors, known as *the QRS-T angle*, provides useful information concerning the relationship between the forces of repolarization and depolarization. In the frontal plane the QRS-T angle should not diverge by more than 60°.

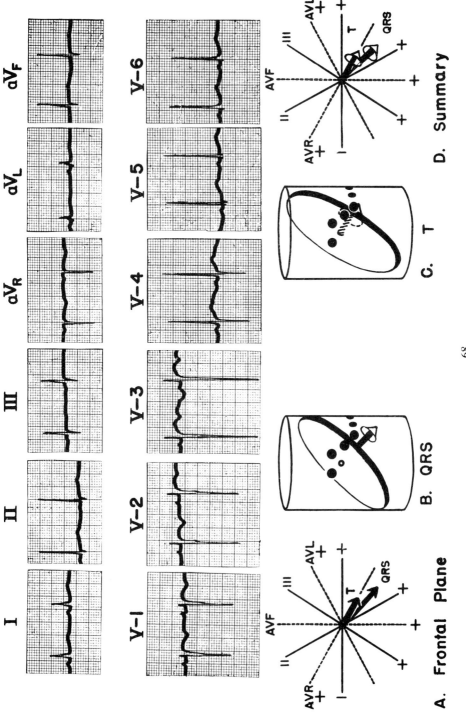

FIG. 4–7. The electrocardiogram of a normal child, age 12, illustrating a posteriorly directed T vector. (Such a T vector position may occasionally be seen in a normal adult.)

(A) The frontal plane projection of the mean QRS and T vectors. Note that the QRS is largest and positive in lead II and slightly positive in lead III and aV$_R$. QRS complexes with such characteristics can be represented by a mean vector directed to the left of the lead II axis and to the right of a perpendicular to lead III. The T wave is flat in lead III and can be represented by a mean vector directed perpendicular to lead III. It is drawn to the left because the T wave is upright in leads I and II.

(B), (C) The mean spatial QRS and T vectors oriented in cylindrical replicas of the chest. The QRS and T vector must be rotated about 35° posteriorly so that the transitional pathway for both will pass between the electrode positions V$_3$ and V$_4$.

(D) Final summary figure illustrating a spatial QRS-T angle of 15°.

The Normal Preadult Electrocardiogram

So far we have been discussing the normal adult electrocardiogram. There are, however, normal evolutionary changes that occur from the newborn period to adult life that must be taken into account (Figs. 4–3 to 4–8). At birth the right ventricular forces predominate over left ventricular forces. Therefore, the mean QRS spatial vector is to the right of and usually parallel to the frontal plane or slightly anterior (Figs. 3–3B and C). The initial and terminal forces are often oppositely directed, giving rise to diphasic precordial QRS complexes and a broad transition zone. The mean T vector is leftward and posterior but may rotate considerably in early life. Between the newborn period and young adulthood, the mean QRS will rotate leftward toward lead II and tilt slightly posteriorly. The T vector also rotates in a similar frontal direction but may remain posterior. This posterior T vector produces inverted T waves in the V$_1$ to V$_4$ leads which is referred to as *retention of the juvenile pattern* (Fig. 4–7). This may last into the third decade of life. During the teenage years it is not uncommon to see the mean QRS vector rotate to the right and become more vertical than before. The posterior direction of the mean QRS which is established in early life persists.

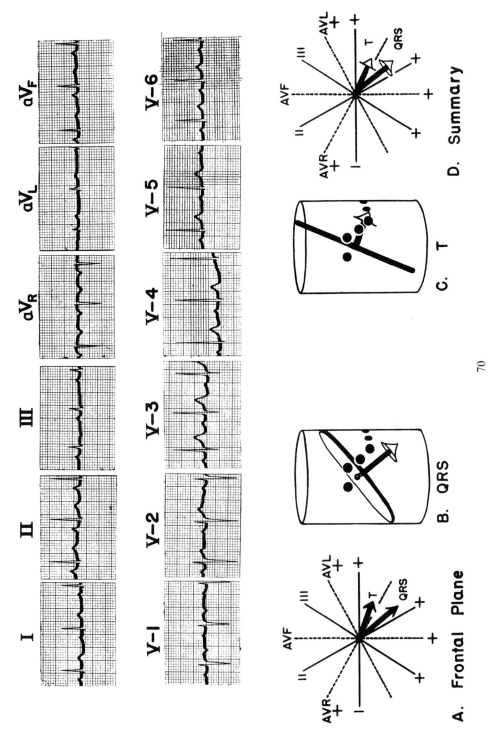

FIG. 4–8. The electrocardiogram of a normal youth, age 18.

(A) The frontal plane projection of the mean QRS and T vectors. The QRS complex is largest in lead II and slightly positive in lead aV_L. These findings indicate that the mean QRS vector is just to the left of the lead II axis. The T wave is smallest but slightly negative in lead III and positive in lead aV_F. The mean T vector is therefore to the left of a line perpendicular to lead III.

(B) The mean spatial QRS vector oriented in the cylindrical replica of the chest. The QRS vector is rotated approximately 15° posteriorly because the transitional pathway passes between the V_2 and V_3 electrode positions.

(C) The mean spatial T vector oriented in the cylindrical replica of the chest. The T vector is flush with the frontal plane because the transitional pathway for the T wave passes between the V_1 and V_2 electrode position.

(D) Final summary figure illustrating a spatial QRS-T angle of 25°.

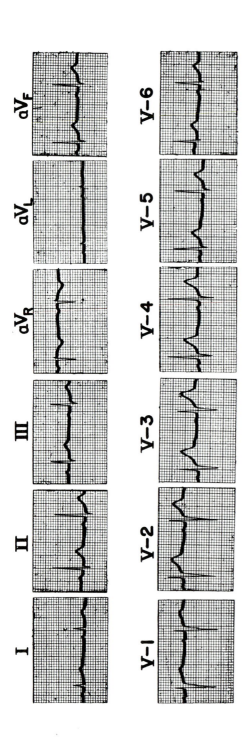
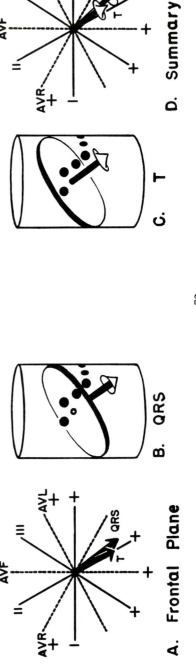

FIG. 4-9. The electrocardiogram of a normal adult, age 40, illustrating a mean QRS vector in the intermediate position.

(A) The frontal plane projection of the mean spatial QRS and T vectors. The QRS complex is resultantly largest in lead II and slightly positive in lead aV_L. requiring that the mean QRS vector be drawn just to the left of the lead II axis. A QRS vector so directed is said to be in an intermediate zone. The T wave is largest in lead II and slightly positive in lead aV_L. The T wave, represented as a vector, is located just to the left of the lead II axis.

(B) The mean spatial QRS vector oriented in the cylindrical replica of the chest. The mean QRS vector is rotated approximately 80° posteriorly because the transitional pathway passes between electrode positions V_3 and V_4.

(C) The mean spatial T vector oriented in the cylindrical replica of the chest. The mean T vector is rotated at least 15° anteriorly because the V_1 electrode position records from the positive portion of the electrical field. When all the precordial T waves are upright, it may be necessary to obtain leads to the right of the usual precordial lead positions in order to localize a vector position precisely. Since the T wave in lead V_1 is smaller than the T wave in lead V_6, one can assume that lead V_1 was recording nearer the transitional pathway of the mean T vector than was lead V_6. Accordingly, it is likely that the mean T vector is only slightly anteriorly directed.

(D) Final summary figure illustrating a spatial QRS-T angle of 45°.

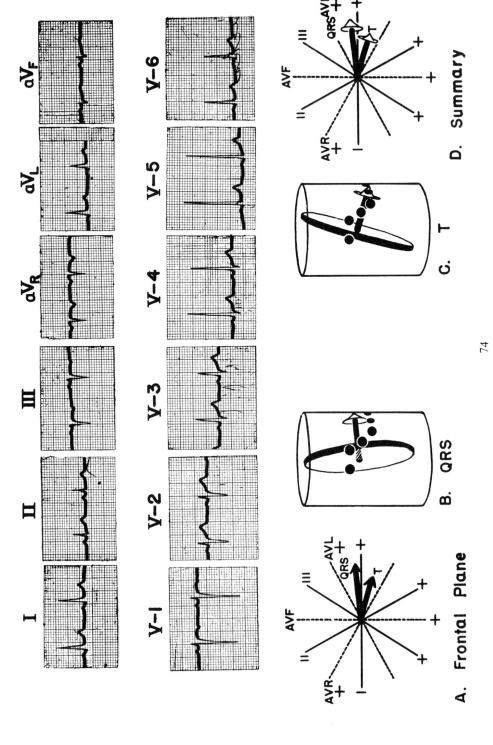

FIG. 4–10. The electrocardiogram of a normal adult, age 51, illustrating a mean QRS vector in the horizontal position.

(A) The frontal plane projection of the mean spatial QRS and T vectors. The QRS is largest in lead I and slightly negative in lead aV$_F$. These findings place the mean QRS vector slightly to the left of the lead I axis. Note that the QRS vector is pointing relatively far to the left. The T wave is largest in lead I, slightly negative in lead III, and slightly positive in lead aV$_F$. These T-wave characteristics illustrated as a vector are shown.

(B) The mean spatial QRS vector oriented in the cylindrical replica of the chest. The mean QRS vector is rotated approximately 20° posteriorly because the transitional pathway passes between electrode positions V$_2$ and V$_3$.

(C) The mean spatial T vector oriented in the cylindrical replica of the chest. The mean T vector is rotated approximately 5° anteriorly because its transitional pathway passes between electrode positions V$_1$ and V$_2$.

(D) Final summary figure illustrating a spatial QRS-T angle of 25°.

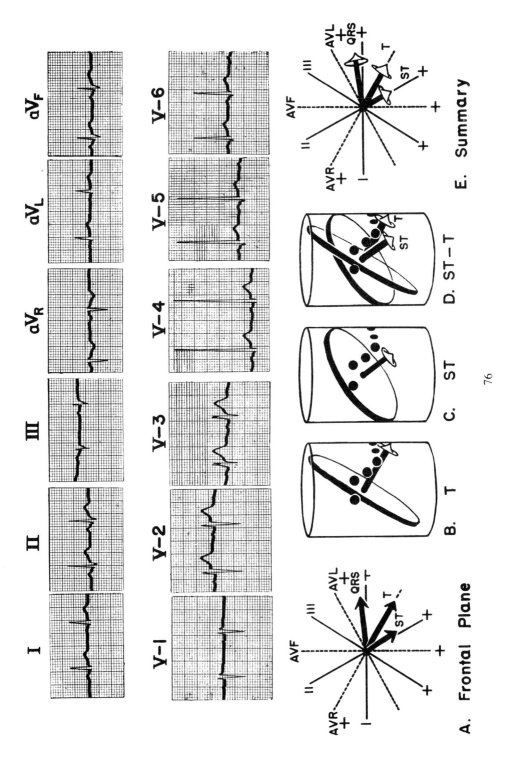

Fig. 4-11. The electrocardiogram of a normal adult, age 27, illustrating the normal ST segment vector (early repolarization pattern).

(A) The frontal plane projection of the mean spatial QRS, ST, and T vectors. The mean QRS vector is almost parallel with lead I since it is resultantly largest in lead I. The QRS is slightly negative in lead aV$_F$, and therefore the QRS vector must be rotated slightly to the left of the positive limb of lead I. The mean T vector is perpendicular to lead III because the T wave is flat in lead III. The ST vector is almost parallel to lead II since the ST segment deviation is greatest in lead II. It is actually located slightly to the left of such a position because the ST segment is slightly elevated in lead aV$_L$.

(B) The mean spatial T vector oriented in the cylindrical replica of the chest. The mean T vector is rotated about 10° anteriorly because V$_1$ records from the transitional pathway.

(C) The mean spatial ST vector oriented in the cylindrical replica of the chest. The ST vector is directed a few more degrees anteriorly than the T vector since it is more positive in V$_1$.

(D) The mean spatial ST and T vectors superimposed. The mean spatial ST vector is nearly parallel with the mean spatial T vector. If a lead were recorded from the right, lower, anterior part of the chest, a resultantly negative QRS complex associated with an elevated ST segment and inverted T wave would be found. This finding would resemble the pattern of myocardial infarction. However, as will be seen, the vectors of myocardial infarction have altogether different directions from the vectors found in normal persons.

(E) Final summary figure showing relationships of the mean spatial QRS, ST, and T vectors. The spatial QRS-T angle is 40°.

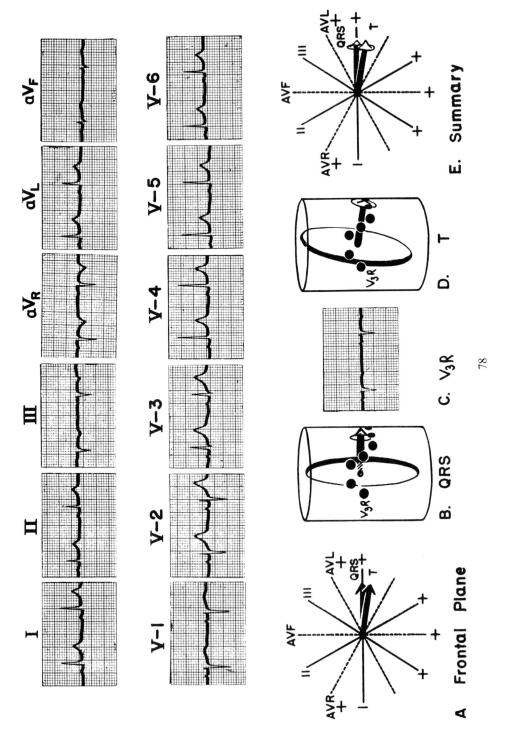

FIG. 4-12. The electrocardiogram of a normal adult, age 70, illustrating the value of additional precordial leads.

(A) The frontal plane projection of the mean spatial QRS and T vectors. The QRS complex is resultantly zero in lead aV_F and is large and positive in lead I. The mean QRS vector is drawn to the left and parallel to lead I. The T wave is largest and positive in lead I and is slightly positive in lead aV_F. These T-wave findings can be represented by a mean T vector 10° to the right of the mean QRS.

(B) The mean spatial QRS vector oriented in the cylindrical replica of the chest. The QRS must be rotated 20° posteriorly because the transitional pathway passes between the electrode positions V_2 and V_3.

(C) Since the T waves are positive in all the routine precordial leads and no "transitional" T wave is present, the degree of anterior T-vector rotation cannot be accurately estimated. An additional chest lead such as V_3 recorded on the right side of the chest (V_3R) may be helpful. The placement of the electrode depends upon the characteristics of the vector under study. (C) shows the deflection recorded from electrode position V_3R.

(D) The mean spatial T vector oriented in the cylindrical replica of the chest. The mean T vector must be rotated 20° anteriorly because the transitional pathway passes between electrode positions V_1 and V_3R.

(E) Final summary figure illustrating a spatial QRS-T angle of 40°. In the elderly person it is not uncommon to see a T vector rotated considerably anteriorly producing a spatial QRS-T angle of 90°.

Part Three
The Abnormal Electrocardiogram

Introduction

Abnormalities of the electrocardiogram occur when the magnitude or direction of instantaneous electrical forces is altered by abnormal anatomy, electrophysiologic disturbances, or various diseases. These abnormal influences on the electrocardiogram are considered in this part and specific criteria are given, where possible, to aid in the diagnosis. At times a specific diagnosis can be made or suggested, particularly if the underlying problem is severe. In many patients, however, the electrocardiogram is nonspecifically changed, and the interpretation must be cautiously stated so that an unwarranted conclusion is not reached.

Section A
Altered Anatomic or Electrophysiologic Disturbances

Chapter 5
The Abnormal Atrial Electrocardiogram

Abnormalities of the P wave have previously been felt to indicate either atrial enlargement or hypertrophy. This interpretation is unsatisfactory for several reasons: The P wave is often normal despite evidence that atrial enlargement is present; the P wave is sometimes abnormal though heart disease is not apparent; the P wave may be intermittently abnormal within the same tracing or on consecutive tracings.

Recent evidence suggests that a disturbance in interatrial conduction may be the major reason for an abnormal P wave. Anatomic or physiologic influences on one or both atria may affect conduction velocity through the atrial conduction pathways or shift the direction of conduction from one pathway to another. These specialized pathways are influenced by the autonomic nervous system, heart rate, intraatrial pressure, atrial size and thickness, and various diseases. Therefore, we prefer to use the noncommital term *atrial abnormality*, rather than atrial enlargement or hypertrophy, when referring to an abnormal P wave. An *interatrial conduction defect* may prove to be a more specific diagnostic term.

Separating a right from a left atrial abnormality is another difficulty that confounds the electrocardiographer. At times a P wave suggests a right atrial abnormality when the heart disease affects primarily the left heart. The converse is also true. Of course, heart disease involving one side of the heart often affects both sides. In addition, the atria share a common septum and internodal conducting pathways. Conclusions about the specific atrium at fault are therefore often erroneous. Nevertheless, criteria have evolved for right and left atrial abnormalities, and it is necessary to know these rules as well as their fallacies.

Right Atrial Abnormality *(Figs. 5–1, 14–3)*

Since the sinus node is located in the upper medial aspect of the right atrium, the right atrial wall is stimulated first and is responsible for the early part of the P wave. The vector of right atrial depolarization is directed inferiorly, anteriorly, and leftward, heading from the sinus node toward the AV node. A right atrial abnormality affects primarily the initial portion of the P wave, shifting the P vector anteriorly and rightward and increasing its magnitude. The total duration of the P wave is not lengthened. The analysis of the P wave for a right atrial abnormality is aided by plotting the P vector for the first half of the P wave.

Electrocardiographic Criteria for Right Atrial Abnormality

A Tall, Peaked P Wave ≥ 2.5 mm and Less Than 0.11 s in Duration in Leads II, III, or aV_F

Initial Deflection in $V_1 \geq 1.5$ mm

A Mean P Vector Shifted Rightward of $+70°$ in the Frontal Plane

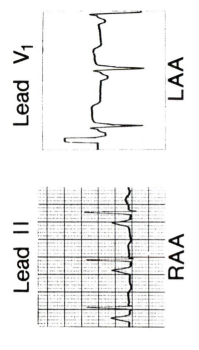

FIG. 5–1. Atrial abnormalities. Tall peaked P wave of right atrial abnormality (RAA) in lead II and terminal negative deflection of left atrial abnormality (LAA) in lead V_1 are shown. Note that the initial P forces are affected with a right atrial abnormality; terminal forces are changed with a left atrial abnormality. This can be determined by visualizing the vectors for the first half and then the second half of the P wave.

Atrial Abnormalities

This pattern may be seen with pulmonary hypertension, chronic or acute lung disease, cor pulmonale, and congenital defects of the pulmonic or tricuspid valves. The term "P pulmonale" was formerly used as a label for this type of P wave; however, this term is no longer acceptable since left atrial problems can produce a similar finding.

Left Atrial Abnormality *(Figs. 5–1, 6–3, 6–4, 12–1)*

Left atrial depolarization occupies the middle and last part of the P wave. The left atrium, which lies posteriorly as well as to the left of the right atrium, has a vector of depolarization directed inferiorly, posteriorly, and to the left. A left atrial abnormality shifts the terminal P vector posteriorly and prolongs the P-wave duration. A vector analysis of the last half of the P wave is helpful in evaluating for a left atrial abnormality.

Electrocardiographic Criteria for Left Atrial Abnormality

A Terminal Negative Deflection of the P Wave in $V_1 \geq 0.04$ s (One Small Square) in Duration and 1 mm (One Small Square) in Depth (Fig. 5–1) This criterion, known as the Morris index, is referred to as a P terminal force ≥ -0.04 mm/s.

A P Wave in Lead II ≥ 0.12 s in Duration

Notching of the P Wave in Any Lead When the Peaks of the Two Notches Are Separated by More Than 0.04s Remember that minor notching is often a normal finding.

Hypertension, mitral valve disease, acute pulmonary edema, and hypertrophic cardiomyopathy are some of the causes of a left atrial abnormality. The term "P mitrale," formerly used as a descriptive term for a left atrial abnormality, has now been abandoned since it may be inaccurate or misleading. The Morris index, which utilizes the P terminal force in V_1, has been found to be the most sensitive and specific guideline for a left atrial abnormality; a P-wave duration ≥ 0.12 s is the second most useful criterion (Table 5–1).

Right and Left Atrial Abnormality *(Figs. 10–2, 13–2)*

Since a number of diseases may affect both atria, a P wave may be seen that reflects criteria for both a right and left atrial abnormality. An example is shown in Fig. 10–2. Note that the initial P forces in V_1 are anterior, producing an early, tall, peaked configuration, while the later forces are large and negative.

Important Considerations

Conclusions based on the analysis of the P wave are sometimes invalid. A normal P wave does not exclude significant atrial disease; an abnormal P wave may be present in an apparently normal heart. When the P wave points to the right atrium, left atrial disease may be the problem and vice versa. Despite this note of caution, the P wave remains a valuable source of information.

Table 5-1

Criteria Used for Left Atrial Abnormality

Criteria	Percent sensitivity	Percent false positive	Percent false negative
P wave ≥ 0.12 (lead II)	62	33	5
Notching (any lead)	64	24	12
P terminal force (V$_1$)	77	12	11

Source: Adapted from B.A. Termini and Y. Lee. Echocardiographic and electrocardiographic criteria for diagnosing left atrial enlargement. *South. Med. J.* 1975: 68:161. Used by permission of the authors and *The Southern Medical Journal*.

Chapter 6
Ventricular Hypertrophy

Left Ventricular Hypertrophy (LVH) (Figs. 6–1 to 6–3)

The left ventricle includes most of the left posterolateral surface of the heart and is situated behind and to the left of the right ventricle. Compared to the right ventricle, the left ventricle is three to four times thicker and supplies approximately 75 percent of the total voltage generated during depolarization of the two ventricles. Because its apex is tilted forward, pointing near the left nipple, the left ventricle also has an inferior surface. Accordingly, the normal left ventricular vector is directed leftward, posteriorly, and slightly inferiorly toward the area of the greatest muscle mass (Fig. 4–2). This corresponds to the initial 0.04 s QRS vector and produces the R wave in leads I and V_4 to V_6 and the S wave in V_1 to V_2. As the left ventricle hypertrophies, the magnitude, but not necessarily the direction, of the 0.04 to 0.06 s vector will change. The electrocardiographic criteria for left ventricular hypertrophy depend primarily on detecting an increase in the magnitude of this force.

Electrocardiographic Criteria for Left Ventricular Hypertrophy

An Increased Magnitude of the Mean Left Ventricular Vector The most commonly used voltage criteria are listed in Table 6–1, along with sensitivity and specificity values as determined at autopsy. Left ventricular hypertrophy can be suggested when any one of the

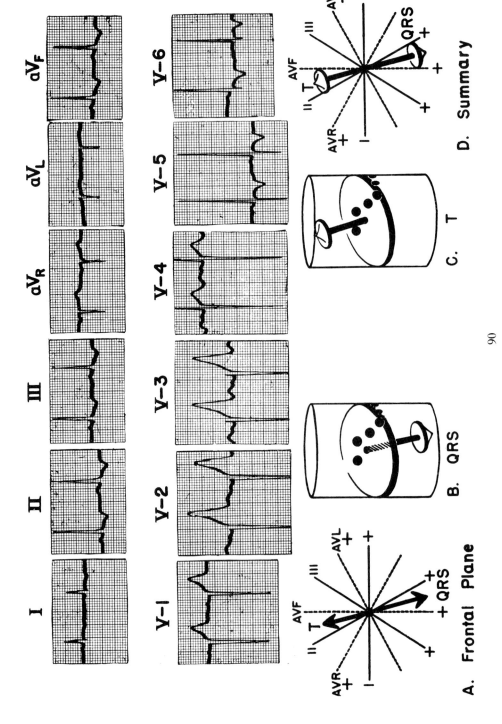

FIG. 6–1. The electrocardiogram of a patient, 32 years of age, with calcific aortic stenosis, illustrating left ventricular hypertrophy.

(A) The QRS complex is largest in lead II, positive in lead I, and negative in lead aV_L. QRS complexes of this nature can be represented by a mean vector directed to the right of the positive limb of lead II. The T wave is slightly negative in lead I, large and negative in leads II, III, and aV_F, and positive in lead aV_L. Accordingly, the mean T vector is directed to the right of the negative limb of lead aV_F but to the left of a perpendicular to lead aV_L.

(B), (C) The spatial orientation of the mean QRS and T vectors. The mean QRS is rotated 50° posteriorly because the transitional pathway passes between the V_4 and V_5 position. The mean T vector is tilted 50° anteriorly because the transitional pathway passes between the V_4 and V_5 position. Note the increased magnitude of the QRS complexes.

(D) Final summary figure showing the spatial arrangement of the vectors. The mean QRS vector is directed downward and posteriorly and the mean T vector is directed to the right and anteriorly. The spatial QRS-T angle is 180°. These findings are characteristic of left ventricular hypertrophy associated with an abnormally wide QRS-T angle. The mean QRS is vertically directed and may be related to the thin, long-chested build of the patient.

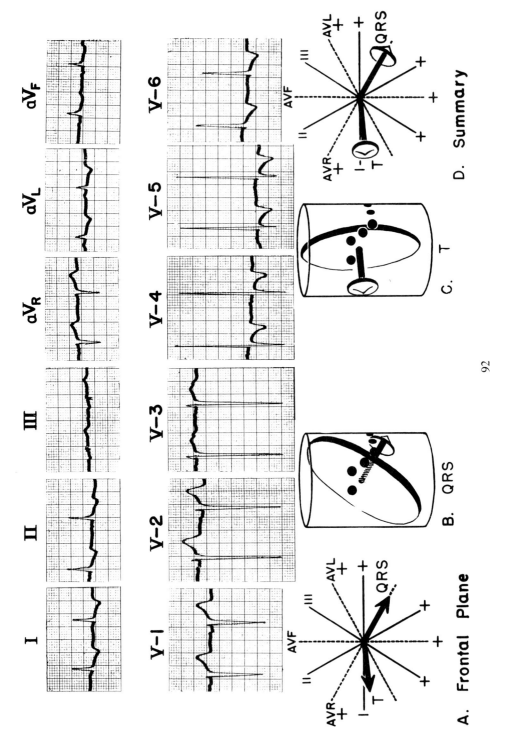

FIG. 6–2. The electrocardiogram of a patient, 51 years of age, with essential hypertension, illustrating left ventricular hypertrophy.

(A) The QRS complex is resultantly zero in lead III and positive in leads I and II. The mean QRS vector is therefore directed perpendicular to lead III. The T wave is large and negative in lead I and slightly positive in lead aV_F. The mean T vector is therefore directed relatively parallel with the negative limb of the lead I axis but must project a small positive quantity on lead aV_F.

(B). (C) The spatial orientation of the mean QRS and T vectors. The mean QRS vector is rotated 30° posteriorly because the transitional pathway passes between V_3 and V_4. The mean T vector is tilted 30° anteriorly because the transitional pathway passes between V_3 and V_4.

(D) Final summary figure showing the spatial arrangement of the vectors. The QRS voltage is large. The mean QRS vector is directed to the left and posteriorly and the mean T vector is directed to the right and anteriorly. Because the QRS and T vectors are directed in such a manner, the QRS complex is upright in lead I and V_6, and the T wave is inverted in lead I and V_6. This "pattern" has been recognized for years as indicating left ventricular hypertrophy. The spatial QRS-T angle is 150°. This patient was on digitalis but its effect is masked because of the ST and T changes of left ventricular hypertrophy.

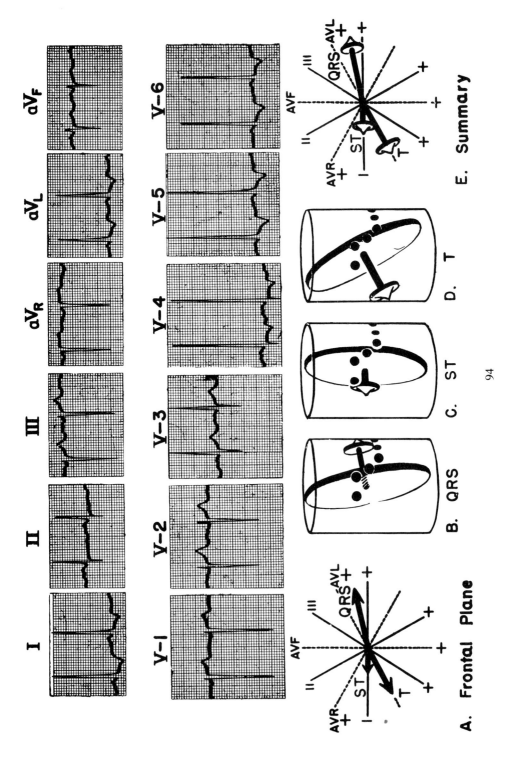

FIG. 6–3. The electrocardiogram of a patient, 61 years of age, with essential hypertension, illustrating left ventricular hypertrophy.

(A) The QRS complex is large and positive in lead I, resultantly positive in lead II, and resultantly negative in lead aV_F. The mean QRS vector is therefore directed relatively parallel with the positive limb of lead I and slightly superiorly in order to project a slightly negative quantity on lead aV_F. The T wave is large and negative in lead I and flat in lead II. The mean T vector is therefore directed perpendicular to lead II. The ST segment displacement is greatest in lead I and least in lead aV_F. Accordingly, the mean ST vector is directed parallel with the negative limb of lead I.

(B), (C), (D) The spatial orientation of the mean QRS, ST, and T vectors. The mean QRS vector is directed 20° posteriorly because the transitional pathway passes between V_2 and V_3. The mean ST vector is directed 30° anteriorly because the transitional pathway passes between V_3 and V_4. The mean T vector is directed 30° anteriorly because the transitional pathway passes between V_3 and V_4. Note that the mean spatial ST vector is relatively parallel with the mean spatial T vector.

(E) Final summary figure showing the spatial arrangement of the vectors. The mean QRS vector is directed to the left and posteriorly and the mean T vector is directed to the right and anteriorly. The QRS voltage is increased and the spatial QRS-T angle is 175°. The mean ST vector is relatively parallel to the mean T vector and represents forces of repolarization.

Table 6–1. Criteria Used for Left Ventricular Hyperthrophy

	Sensitivity,%	Specificity,%
A Limb Lead Criteria		
RI + SIII > 25 mm	10.6	100
RaV_L > 11 mm	10.6	100
RaV_F > 20 mm	1.3	99.5
B Precordial Lead Criteria		
$SV_1 + RV_5$ or $RV_6 > 35$ mm	42.5	95
SV_1 or $V_2 + RV_5$ or $RV_6 > 35$ mm	55.6	88.5
$SV_1 + RV_5$ or $RV_6 > 30$ mm	55.6	89.5
Greatest R + greatest S > 45 mm	45	89.5
RV_5 or $RV_6 > 26$ mm	25	98.5
Supportive Criteria		
Ventricular activation time ≥ 0.05 s in V_5 or V_6		
ST-T opposite the QRS (patient not on digitalis)		
LAD: − 30°		
C Point Score System of Romhilt and Estes*	54	97
1. Amplitude (any of the following, 3 points):		
a. Largest R or S wave in the limb leads ≥ 20 mm		
b. S wave in V_1 or $V_2 ≥ 30$ mm		
c. R wave in V_5 or $V_6 ≥ 30$ mm		
2. ST-T segment changes (typical pattern of left ventricular strain with the ST-T segment vector shifted in direction opposite to the mean QRS vector)		
a. Without digitalis (3 points)		
b. With digitalis (1 points)		
3. Left atrial involvement (3 points): terminal negativity of the P wave in V_1 is 1 mm or more in depth with a duration of 0.04 s or more		
4. Left axis deviation: − 30° or more (2 points)		
5. QRS duration ≥ 0.09 s (1 point)		
6. Intrinsicoid deflection in $V_5 V_6 = 0.05$ s (1 point)		

*Left ventricular hyperthrophy: 5 points.
Probable left ventricular hyperthrophy: 4 points.

Source: Adapted from D. W. Romhilt, K. E. Bove, and R. J. Norris: A critical appraisal of the electrocardiographic criteria for the diagnosis of left ventricular hyperthroph. *Circulation* 1969; 40:185. Used by permission of the authors and the American Heart Association, Inc.

Table 6–2
Criteria Used for Right Ventricular Hypertrophy

A Precordial Lead Criteria	Sensitivity, %	Specificity, %
R/S ratio $V_1 \geq 1$	6	98
qR in V_1	5	99
$R'V_1 \geq 7$ mm	2	99
$R'V \geq 10.5$ mm	13	94
R/S ratio $V_6 \leq 1$	16	93
Dip in the normally rising R/S curve between any pair of pretransitional leads	28	76

B Limb Lead Criteria	Sensitivity, %	Specificity, %
Right axis deviation $\geq +110°$	12–19	96
SI, II, III pattern	24	87
$RaV_R \geq 5$ mm	0	100

Additional findings

Ventricular activation time ≥ 0.035 s in V_1.
T inversion right precordial leads.
ST depression right precordial leads.
Shortening and notching of SV_1.
QRS may be normal or slightly prolonged.
A right ventricular conduction delay producing an R' may occur.
Small r and deep S may be seen in $V_5 V_6$.

oseptal infarction. The normal q in V_6 also disappears. This is a result of either septal fibrosis or a conduction defect related to left ventricular hypertrophy. On rare occasions, the mean QRS is rotated so posteriorly and superiorly that a QS deflection suggesting an inferior infarction is inscribed in leads II, III, and aV_F.

A Shift in the Position of the Mean Left Ventricular Vector The increased left ventricular mass may shift the mean QRS vector superiorly, posteriorly, and to the left. This results in a leftward shift in the precordial lead transition zone and a superior mean QRS vector in the frontal plane. This may not occur, or the shift of the QRS vector may remain within normal limits. At times a more vertical mean QRS axis related to age or a narrow body build will be present. A mean QRS axis above $-30°$ in the frontal plane is often due to fibrosis of the septum, which causes an anterior fascicular block.

A Prolonged Left Ventricular Activation Time Normally the peak of the R wave in V_5 or V_6 occurs about 0.04 s after the onset of the QRS. With left ventricular hypertrophy, this period of ventricular activation is prolonged, presumably because of an increased left ventricular wall thickness or a conduction delay. The sudden downward deflection that follows the peak of the R wave is known as the *intrinsicoid deflection*; a delay of ventricular activation of 0.05 s or greater is referred to as a *delay in the onset of the intrinsicoid deflection*.

listed criteria is met. These voltage criteria alone are not very useful under age 40, since normal values are quite high in this population, particularly in adolescent boys where very tall R waves of 30 mm or more may be seen. Note that precordial lead criteria are far more sensitive, though less specific, than limb lead criteria.

The precise orientation of the mean left ventricular vector will determine in which plane the increased ventricular voltage is best displayed—a superior vector parallel to the frontal plane will be best seen in leads I and aV_L while, in the more common situation, a posterior vector close to the perpendicular to the frontal plane will enhance the voltage in V_5 to V_6. In addition, the electrocardiogram is more alert to total cardiac mass than wall thickness in diagnosing left ventricular hypertrophy; when the heart is large, the precordial lead sensitivity is 50 to 60 percent, as compared to a 30 to 40 percent sensitivity for small hearts.

Alteration of Initial Septal Forces The increased thickness of the ventricular septum may augment the initial 0.01 to 0.02 s QRS vector. An increased R wave in lead V_1 and a deep Q wave in the inferior and/or lateral leads I, aV_L, and V_6 may reflect this alteration. This increased septal force is characteristic of hypertrophic cardiomyopathy. In acquired left ventricular hypertrophy due to hypertension or aortic valvular disease, the R wave in leads V_1 to V_3 is often small and may be lost entirely, leaving a QS pattern that mimics anter-

Although this delay is fairly characteristic of left ventricular hypertrophy, it is not a major criterion that can be used to support the diagnosis.

At times the total QRS duration is prolonged to 0.11 to 0.12 s. If the initial septal forces are small, it can be difficult or impossible to decide whether left ventricular hypertrophy or a left bundle branch block is the correct diagnosis.

An ST-T Vector Opposite the Mean QRS Vector As left ventricular hypertrophy increases, the ST and T vectors typically shift anteriorly and to the right, away from the QRS vector. ST-segment depression, sometimes quite marked, and T-wave inversion will be seen in leads with a tall R wave; reciprocal ST-segment elevation and prominent upward-slanting T waves will be inscribed in the right precordial leads. This pattern, in which the QRS-T angle is 160 to 180°, resembles ventricular ischemia and has been referred to as "left ventricular strain," a term that is descriptive but physiologically confusing.

A Left Atrial Abnormality A left atrial abnormality is a fairly sensitive, though not specific, finding in left ventricular hypertrophy. Since the abnormal P wave may precede diagnostic QRS voltage changes, it is an excellent early clue to the presence of left ventricular hypertrophy. In patients whose QRS voltage is reduced by lung disease or obesity, a left atrial abnormality may be the major finding.

A Combination of the Above The specificity of the diagnosis of left ventricular hypertrophy is enhanced when more than one of the above criteria is met. For example, the voltage criteria may be of borderline significance or of questionable value because the patient is young. The presence of oppositely directed ST-T changes (in the absence of digitalis or other known causes) or a left atrial abnormality strongly buttresses the diagnosis. The point score system devised by Romhilt and Estes (Table 4) takes into account the relative contributions of each of the criteria for left ventricular hypertrophy. This approach, though 97 percent specific, is still only 54 percent sensitive to the presence of left ventricular hypertrophy.

Important Considerations

• Although the diagnosis of left ventricular hypertrophy might appear rather straightforward on initial analysis, the ability of the electrocardiogram to detect left ventricular hypertrophy accurately is not very satisfactory. This is because the size of the normal 0.04 vector is highly variable and is greatly affected by age, sex, race, body build, breast tissue, skin thickness, and other constitutional factors. The proximity of the precordial electrodes to the heart and the position of the heart relative to the chest wall are important considerations. In addition, heart size, hematocrit, lung disease, pleural and pericardial effusion, heart disease, and heart failure can alter the voltage significantly.

by the clinician who can factor age, body weight, and chest configuration into the final assessment.

Right Ventricular Hypertrophy (RVH)
(Figs. 6–4, 10–2, 14–1 to 14–3)

The right ventricle is an anterior structure, located in the middle of the chest just behind the sternum. The normal right ventricular vector develops in the first 0.03 s of ventricular depolarization and is oriented anteriorly, inferiorly, and to the right. Physiologic hypertrophy of the right ventricle accounts for the anteriorly oriented mean QRS vector of the newborn. In the normal adult, however, the right ventricular wall is thin compared with the left ventricular wall. The right ventricular vector is dominated by the magnitude of the simultaneous 0.02 to 0.04 s left ventricular vector and therefore contributes very little to the resultant mean QRS vector. Considerable right ventricular hypertrophy must develop before electrocardiographic manifestations can be recognized. Criteria for right ventricular hypertrophy in the adult are listed in Table 6-2. These criteria enjoy a relatively high specificity but provide a very low degree of sensitivity.

Electrocardiographic Criteria for Right Ventricular Hypertrophy

An Increased Magnitude of the Right Ventricular Vector With a significant degree of right ventricular

- Significant changes in QRS voltage from day to day in the same lead are common and sometimes very puzzling. On one day voltage criteria for left ventricular hypertrophy are easily met; the next tracing shows normal voltage. This is most commonly seen in the precordial leads and may be attributed to variations of lead placement, body position, or normal day-to-day variations in voltage.
- There is also a difference in the electrocardiographic response to different causes of ventricular hypertrophy and cavity size. For example, aortic regurgitation, which produces a diastolic volume load and a very dilated left ventricle, differs considerably from valvular aortic stenosis, which causes a systolic pressure load and less ventricular dilatation. Criteria for a diastolic volume load and a systolic pressure load are discussed in the section on aortic valvular disease.
- The presence of either a right or left bundle branch block obscures or invalidates voltage criteria for left ventricular hypertrophy because the usual cancellation of oppositely directed right and left ventricular forces that occurs during normal conduction is circumvented.
- The commonly applied criteria for left ventricular hypertrophy are relatively cautious; they apply only to a population above age 40 and can diagnose autopsy-proven left ventricular hypertrophy less than 60 percent of the time. Any liberalization of the criteria will incorporate an unacceptably large number of false positives into the diagnosis. The interpretation is best made

hypertrophy, the mean QRS vector is displaced anteriorly, rightward, and either inferiorly or superiorly. The anterior-rightward shift increases the height of the R or R' wave in V_1, and, in a reciprocal fashion, deepens the S wave of V_6. Specific voltage criteria for right ventricular hypertrophy, as listed in Table 5, include an $RV_1 \geq 7$ mm, an $R'V_1 \geq 10$ mm, and $RaV_R \geq 5$ mm in the absence of a prolonged QRS duration. This increase in the anterior forces will naturally change the ratio of the R-wave amplitude to the S-wave amplitude in the precordial leads—a reversal of the R/S ratio. Right ventricular hypertrophy is suggested when the R/S ratio in V_1 exceeds 1 or the R/S ratio in V_6 is ≤ 1.

Different causes of right ventricular hypertrophy, as well as gradations in the severity of right ventricular hypertrophy, may result in different morphologic patterns in lead V_1. These patterns are sometimes classified as type A, B, and C. In type A right ventricular hypertrophy a large, essentially monophasic R wave is recorded in V_1. An equiphasic RS morphology is considered a type B pattern, while an rS or rSr' configuration defines the type C pattern. In addition to these three patterns, a qR or qRs configuration in V_1 may be seen with severe right ventricular hypertrophy. This pattern, when present, is highly specific for the presence of an abnormal degree of right ventricular hypertrophy in the newborn and infant as well as the adult.

In the frontal plane the inferior or superior rightward vector of right ventricular hypertrophy may increase the R' in a$V_R \geq 5$ mm; produce a deep S wave in leads I, II, and III (*SI, II, III pattern*); and shift the frontal plane mean QRS vector rightward. A right axis greater than $+110°$ is very uncommon over age 30 and, in the absence of a posterior fascicular block or lung disease, should arouse suspicion for right ventricular hypertrophy. A combination of a right axis deviation greater than $+110°$ and a reversed R/S amplitude ratio in V_1 and V_6 is strong evidence for right ventricular hypertrophy. The SI, II, III pattern is not very specific for right ventricular hypertrophy since it may occur in normal subjects or with lung disease.

Prolongation of Right Ventricular Activation Time The normal onset of the intrinsicoid deflection in V_1 occurs within 0.03 s. A ventricular activation time ≥ 0.035 s in V_1 is seen with significant right ventricular hypertrophy.

Displacement of the ST and T Vectors to the Left, Posteriorly, and Either Superiorly or Inferiorly Minor to moderate increases in right ventricular thickness may not modify the normal direction of ventricular repolarization. With advanced degrees of right ventricular hypertrophy, the ST and T vectors may rotate in the same direction away from the right ventricle. ST-segment depression and T-wave inversion in V_1 to V_2 is

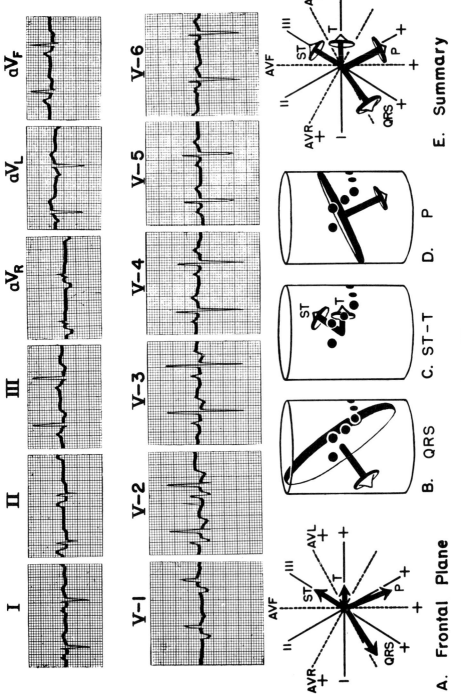

FIG. 6–4. The electrocardiogram of a patient 30 years of age with mitral stenosis, illustrating right ventricular hypertrophy.

(A) The QRS complex is large and positive in lead III and large and negative in lead aV_L. The QRS complex is resultantly slightly positive in lead II. Accordingly, the mean QRS vector is relatively parallel with the negative limb of lead aV_L but is directed so that it projects a small positive quantity on lead II. It is difficult to identify where the ST segment ends and where the T wave begins. The ST segment appears largest and negative in lead III, slightly negative in lead II, and isoelectric in lead aV_R. The mean ST vector is therefore directed parallel to the negative limb of lead III. The T wave is largest and positive in lead I, slightly positive in lead II, and resultantly zero in lead aV_F. The mean T vector is directed relatively parallel with the positive limb of lead I. The P wave is large and positive in lead II and is small and negative in lead aV_L. The mean P vector is therefore directed just to the right of the positive limb of lead II.

(B), (C), (D) The spatial orientation of the mean QRS, ST, T, and P vectors. The mean QRS vector is directed 20° anteriorly because the transitional pathway passes through V_3. The mean ST vector is directed 20° to 30° posteriorly, and the mean T vector is directed 20° posteriorly. The mean P vector is directed 5° posteriorly because the transitional pathway for the mean P vector passes very near V_2. The large P-wave deflections indicate atrial enlargement.

(E) Final summary figure showing the spatial arrangement of the vectors. The mean QRS vector is directed to the right and anteriorly indicating right ventricular hypertrophy. Tremendous P waves, as illustrated in this tracing, usually indicate left atrial enlargement. The rather large ST vector associated with a relatively small T vector and a short QT interval (0.28 s) suggests digitalis effect. Note that an abnormally wide QRS-T angle can be recognized in this case even though digitalis effect is present.

the result. The spatial QRS-T angle is frequently 150 to 180°.

Right Atrial Abnormality The right atrium is necessarily involved in the hemodynamic stresses imposed by right ventricular hypertrophy. Therefore a right atrial abnormality consisting of a tall, peaked P wave, as previously defined, is often present.

Important Considerations

- Physiologic right ventricular hypertrophy of the newborn is almost impossible to distinguish electrocardiographically from a pathologic cause of right ventricular hypertrophy.

- After the newborn period, right ventricular hypertrophy due to congenital heart disease, such as pulmonic stenosis, is much easier to recognize than right ventricular hypertrophy due to acquired disease. This is because the mean QRS begins and remains rightward, and the thickness of the right ventricle may exceed the left ventricle. Acquired right ventricular hypertrophy, as seen with mitral stenosis or left ventricular disease, has to contend with fully developed left ventricular forces as well as left ventricular pathogenic influences on the electrocardiogram. The degree of acquired right ventricular hypertrophy seldom outstrips the left ventricular thickness. In addition, right ventricular hypertrophy in the adult is often due to lung disease, which may greatly reduce the voltage of the precordial leads or alter the mean QRS vector. Other factors, including the duration of the disease, left and right ventricular pressure, pulmonary arterial resistance, and the anatomic position of the heart, will also affect the electrocardiogram.

- Right ventricular hypertrophy may be obscured because of left ventricular hypertrophy, left or right bundle branch block, or anteroseptal myocardial infarction.

- An anteriorly oriented QRS may produce a misleading impression of right ventricular hypertrophy and lead to a false-positive diagnosis. This can occur with normal hearts, right bundle branch block, posterior myocardial infarction, Wolff-Parkinson-White syndrome, dextrocardia, acquired anatomic shifts of the heart, and, rarely, isolated cases of septal hypertrophy.

- Chronic obstructive lung disease, in the absence of right ventricular hypertrophy, can simulate right ventricular hypertrophy by producing a right axis deviation and a reversed R/S ratio in V_5 or V_6. However, the anterior forces are usually reduced, and a prominent R wave is not seen in V_1.

Chapter 7
Ventricular Conduction Defects

The QRS interval of the normal adult electrocardiogram seldom exceeds 0.10 s. When the QRS duration is greater than 0.10 s, ventricular conduction is delayed. The delay may be due to an impairment of conduction over either the right or the left bundle branch—*a bundle branch block*—or to a delay involving part or all of both branches of the ventricular conducting system. A QRS interval between 0.10 and 0.12 s is termed *incomplete*, while an interval of 0.12 s or greater is called a *complete bundle branch block*. An appreciation of conduction defects requires an understanding of the anatomy of the conduction system, the expected sequence of ventricular depolarization, and the direction and magnitude of the forces of ventricular depolarization as presented in Chapters 1 and 4 and Fig. 7-1.

Left Bundle Branch Block *(Figs. 7-2 to 7-6)*

Electrocardiographic Criteria for Left Bundle Branch Block (LBBB)

A Loss of the Normal Initial 0.01 s Septal Vector When a left bundle branch block is present, the normal, initial, left-to-right septal depolarization, attributed to stimulation of the middle third of the left side of the septum by the left bundle, does not occur. Instead, the right side of the septum and the anterior right ventric-

Normal

V₆

LEFT BUNDLE BRANCH

LA

RA

SINUS NODE

A-V NODE

RIGHT BUNDLE BRANCH

RV

LV

V₁

FIG. 7-1. Schematic drawing of heart, conduction system, and leads V_1 and V_6. The normal sequence of conduction is demonstrated. Vector 1, due to initial left-to-right septal depolarization, is directed anteriorly and rightward producing a small r wave in V_1 and a small q wave in V_6. Vector 2, due to left ventricular depolarization, is directed inferiorly, leftward, and posteriorly, producing the deep S wave in V_1 and the tall R wave in V_6. Vector 3 is the terminal 0.02 s vector and is directed posteriorly. This vector may not be apparent on the electrocardiogram or, if oriented rightward, may produce a small r' wave in V_1.

ular wall depolarize before the left ventricle, producing an initial vector which is leftward, inferior, and, depending on the vectorial sum of the septal and right ventricular free wall forces, usually anterior (Fig. 7–3). On occasion this vector may be flush with the frontal plane or posteriorly oriented. The normal *septal q wave in leads I, V_5, and V_6 is therefore lost, and the r wave in V_1 to V_3 is diminished or absent.*

A Posterior Shift and Delay of Mid and Late Left Ventricular Forces During the first 0.04 s of the QRS interval, the right ventricle and septum complete their depolarization. The spread of depolarization through the left ventricular myocardium begins to dominate the electrical forces, reaching a maximum magnitude at about 0.08 s. These mid and late instantaneous vectors become increasingly oriented more posteriorly and leftward (Fig. 7–3). The final 0.04 s of the prolonged QRS represents completion of the delayed activation of the left ventricle. The electrocardiogram shows a broad, slurred, or splintered monophasic R wave in leads I, V_5, and V_6 with an intrinsicoid deflection beginning at 0.08 s or later. The right precordial leads will display a broad monophasic QS wave or an rS configuration, and the precordial transition zone will be rotated leftward.

An ST-T Vector Opposite the Mean QRS Vector When the sequence of ventricular depolarization is altered, the sequence of repolarization is correspondingly affected. In left bundle branch block the repolarization forces develop in a rightward, anterior direction, approximately 180° from the mean QRS vector. The ST segment will be depressed and the T wave inverted in leads with a predominant R wave; ST-segment elevation and an upright T wave are seen in leads with a predominant negative deflection. The QRS-T angle approaches 180°. The ST-segment deviation may be very impressive in some patients with a left bundle branch block.

Important Considerations

- A left bundle branch block should be easily recognized because of the prolonged QRS interval, decreased or absent anterior forces, and a splintered configuration of the QRS in the left precordial leads.

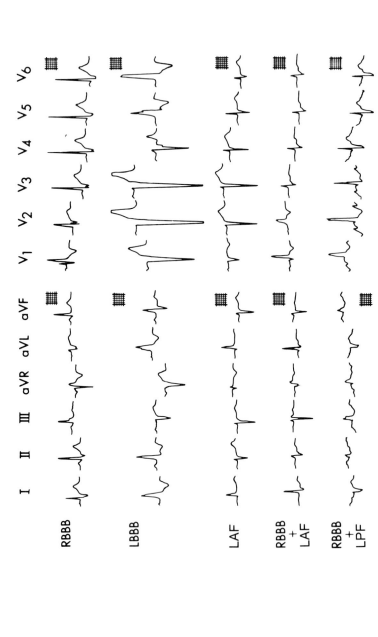

FIG. 7–2. Intraventricular conduction abnormalities. Illustrated are right bundle branch block (RBBB); left bundle branch block (LBBB); left anterior fascicular block (LAF); right bundle branch block with left anterior fascicular block (RBBB + LAF); and right bundle branch block with left posterior fascicular block (RBBB + LPF).

[From R. J. Myerburg in Petersdorf et al. (eds.), *Harrison's Principles of Internal Medicine*, 10th ed., chapter 249, McGraw-Hill, New York, 1982.]

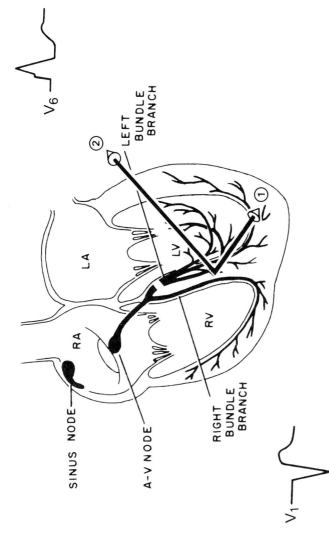

FIG. 7-3. Left bundle branch block. A left bundle branch block is present as illustrated by a separation of the left bundle branch. The initial septal force illustrated in Fig. 7-1 is replaced by a vector directed inferiorly, anteriorly, and leftward due to depolarization of the right side of the septum and the anterior right ventricle. The initial r wave in V_1 is reduced or absent while the q wave in V_6 is no longer present. Vector 2 includes mid and late forces which are directed leftward and posteriorly. This force is responsible for the broad S wave in V_1 and the broad or splintered R wave in V_6. The ST vector is oppositely directed to the QRS vector; therefore, the ST segment is elevated in V_1 and depressed in V_6.

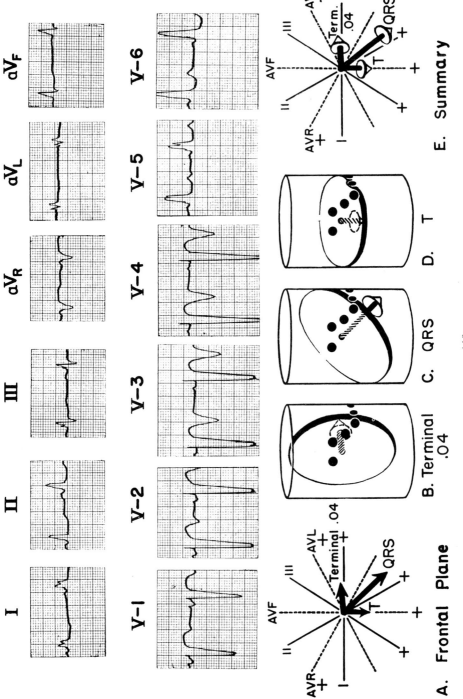

FIG. 7–4. The electrocardiogram of a hypertensive patient showing left bundle branch block and extensive anterior myocardial ischemia.

(A) The frontal plane projection of the mean QRS, T, and terminal 0.04 s vectors.

(B) The terminal 0.04 s vector is directed approximately 60° posteriorly since the terminal portion of the QRS complex is negative in V_1, V_2, V_3, and V_4 and is positive in V_5 and V_6.

(C) The mean QRS vector is rotated approximately 50° posteriorly because the transitional pathway passes between electrode positions V_4 and V_5.

(D) The mean T vector is rotated approximately 50° posteriorly since the T waves are inverted in V_1, V_2, V_3, and V_4 and upright in V_5 and V_6.

(E) Summary. The QRS duration is 0.16 s in V_3 and is approximately 0.12 s in all of the frontal leads, suggesting that a certain portion of the terminal QRS forces is relatively perpendicular to the frontal plane. The terminal 0.04 s vector is directed to the left and posteriorly. The mean T vector is directed abnormally posteriorly away from the anterior surface of the heart and indicates anterior myocardial ischemia. The mean T vector is almost always directed anteriorly in uncomplicated bundle branch block and can be considered abnormal when directed posteriorly. In this case the enclosed QRS-T angle lies posteriorly and therefore the ventricular gradient is directed abnormally posteriorly.

- Because the initial forces are affected, a left bundle branch block produces q waves in the anteroseptal leads and sometimes in the inferior leads which may simulate a myocardial infarction. Similarly, when a left bundle branch block is present, a myocardial infarction cannot usually be detected from inspection of the QRS. There is some evidence that a broad Q wave in lead I or a small q wave in leads I and V_5 to V_6 are evidence for an old anterior or septal infarction, while an inferior Q wave indicates an inferior scar. Serial ST-T wave changes may still point to the diagnosis of an acute injury.

- The marked ST segment deviation due to left bundle branch block may fool the inexperienced interpreter into thinking an acute anteroseptal infarction or ventricular aneurysm is present.

- Patients with an intermittent left bundle branch block may have T-wave inversion in the mid-precordial leads, falsely suggesting ischemia, when normal conduction is present. The reason for this persistent repolarization abnormality when the QRS changes of left bundle branch block are not present is not known.

- A left bundle branch block also obscures the diagnosis of left or right ventricular hypertrophy. Since the right and left ventricles are depolarizing at different times, normal cancellation of simultaneously occurring forces does not occur. Therefore, criteria for right ventricular hypertrophy and left ventricular hypertrophy, which are based on normal conduction, cannot be used.

- When significant left ventricular hypertrophy is present, anterior forces are often small, and the QRS mildly prolonged to 0.10 or 0.11 s. It may be difficult to tell

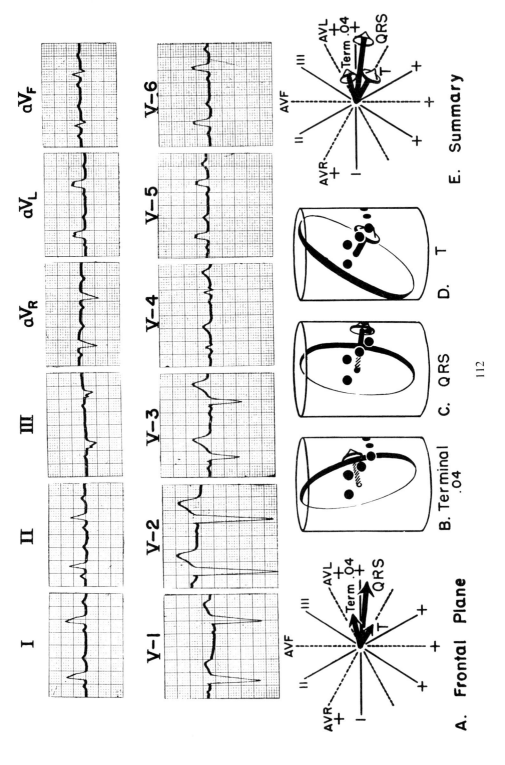

FIG. 7-5. The electrocardiogram of a clinically normal 44-year-old male, showing left bundle branch block.

(A) The frontal plane projection of the mean QRS, T, and terminal 0.04 s vectors. Note that the terminal portion of the QRS complex is positive in lead II and negative in leads III and aV_F. This terminal 0.04 s of the QRS complex can be represented by a mean vector located between the positive limb of leads I and aV_L.

(B) The terminal 0.04 s QRS vector is tilted approximately 40° posteriorly because that portion of the QRS complex is negative in leads V_1, V_2, and V_3 and positive in leads V_5 and V_6.

(C) The mean QRS vector is rotated approximately 30° posteriorly because the transitional pathway passes between electrode positions V_3 and V_4.

(D) The mean T vector is rotated approximately 30° anteriorly because all the precordial T waves are positive and the T wave in V_1 is only slightly larger than the T wave in V_6.

(E) Summary. The QRS duration is 0.13 s, indicating bundle branch block. The terminal 0.04 s vector is directed to the left and posteriorly pointing toward the left ventricle and therefore indicates left bundle branch block.

if the proper diagnosis is left ventricular hypertrophy or a left bundle branch block.

• Rarely, small q waves of less than 0.03 s in duration can be present in leads I, aV_L, V_5, and V_6 in left bundle branch block.

• There is disagreement concerning the authenticity of an "incomplete" left bundle branch block. Some authorities do not accept this diagnosis and use the term left bundle branch block only when the QRS is 0.12 s or greater.

Right Bundle Branch Block *(Figs. 7-2, 7-7 to 7-10)*

Electrocardiographic Criteria for Right Bundle Branch Block (RBBB)

A Late Conduction Delay Producing a Terminal Vector Directed to the Right and Anteriorly When the right bundle branch is blocked, right ventricular depolarization is delayed for at least 0.04 s, during which time the septum, apex, and anterior wall of the left ventricle are stimulated. By 0.04 s the wave of depolarization has spread to the right ventricle. The left ventricular forces continue to dominate the QRS morphology until about 0.06 s. As the right ventricle musters up forces, the left ventricular forces begin to subside as depolarization of the anterolateral and basilar areas of the left ventricle is completed. The delayed, unopposed right ventricular forces now add a terminal vector directed anteriorly and rightward (Fig. 7-7). The electrocardiographic expression of the right bundle branch block is therefore a prolonged QRS interval, a normal-appearing QRS until about 0.06 s, a broad R' wave in V_1 and aV_R, and a broad S wave in I, aV_L, and V_6. Occasionally lead V_1 will show a monophasic rR' pattern.

An ST-T Vector Opposite the Terminal QRS Vector As in left bundle branch block, the ST-T vector shifts 180°

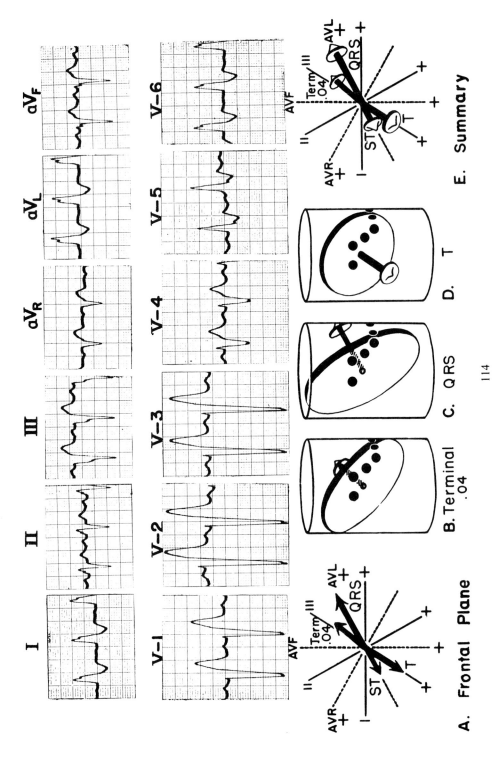

FIG. 7–6. The electrocardiogram of a 50-year-old male who had a classical clinical picture of myocardial infarction illustrating how left bundle branch block can mask the findings of myocardial infarction.

(A) Frontal plane projection of the mean spatial QRS, ST, T, and terminal 0.04 s vectors. Note that the direction of the initial 0.04 s vector is normal, that is, the initial deflection of the QRS complex is positive in lead I and II and V_1 through V_6. The terminal 0.04 s portion of the QRS complex is negative in leads II, III, and aV_F and approaches resultant zero in aV_R. (Note that the PR interval in lead II is 0.16 s and the QRS duration is 0.16 s. The PR interval in lead aV_R is also 0.16 s but the QRS interval is only 0.12 s. This suggests that the terminal portion of lead aV_R is almost isoelectric and can be represented by a vector perpendicular to lead aV_R.) This marked left axis deviation in the presence of left bundle branch block suggests the possibility of coexistent conduction abnormality in the radiation of the anterior fascicle of the left bundle branch.

(B) The terminal 0.04 s vector is rotated approximately 60° posteriorly since the terminal portion of the QRS complex is negative in leads V_1, V_2, V_3, V_4, and V_5, and is positive in V_6.

(C) The mean QRS vector is rotated approximately 50° posteriorly because the transitional pathway passes between electrode positions V_4 and V_5.

(D) The mean T vector is rotated approximately 75° anteriorly.

(E) Summary. The QRS duration of 0.16 s indicates bundle branch block. The terminal 0.04 s vector is directed to the left and posteriorly indicating left bundle branch block. A prominent ST vector is present but because it is relatively parallel with the mean T vector it probably represents early repolarization. The ST segment displacement can become quite marked in bundle branch block and does not necessarily indicate myocardial infarction. The patient had a myocardial infarction several months before the electrocardiogram shown above was made. Left bundle branch block may completely obscure the QRS, ST, and T abnormalities. The abnormal left axis deviation suggests the possibility of abnormal conduction in the anterior fascicle combined with main left bundle branch block.

away from the area of the heart that is depolarized last. The secondary ST-T changes of a right bundle branch block are usually slight compared to a left bundle branch block. The T wave may be inverted in V_1 and V_2, and slight ST-segment depression may be seen in the same leads. The QRS-T angle approaches 180°.

Important Considerations

A right bundle branch block should cause no diagnostic problems. The QRS is prolonged and, in addition to this, a prominent R' wave in V_1 sticks out like a flag.

- Occasionally a right bundle branch block can be confused with other causes of a prominent R wave in V_1, including right ventricular hypertrophy, a posterior myocardial infarction, and the Wolff-Parkinson-White syndrome. A careful appraisal of other leads as well as the configuration of V_1 should usually separate a right bundle branch block from these other problems.
- An rSr' configuration in V_1 is sometimes present in

115

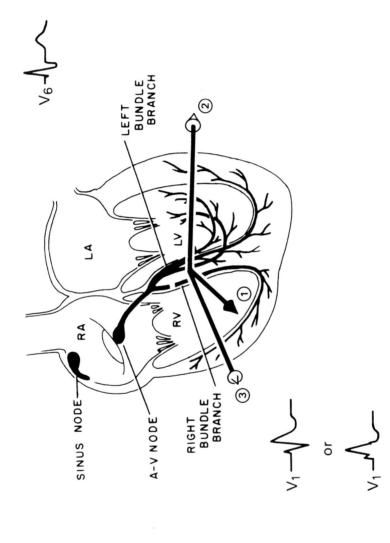

FIG. 7-7. Right bundle branch block. A right bundle branch block is present as demonstrated by a separation of the right bundle branch. Vectors 1 and 2 are unaffected. Vector 3, due to late activation of the right ventricle, is directed anteriorly and rightward producing the broad R' wave in V_1 and slurred S wave in V_6.

normal, often young, people; however, the r' wave is usually lower than the initial r wave and the QRS is not prolonged.

- It is tempting to suggest right ventricular hypertrophy when the r' wave in V_1 is very prominent. For reasons stated in the section on left bundle branch block, ventricular hypertrophy should not be diagnosed when the two ventricles are not stimulated by normal conducting pathways.
- Since a right bundle branch block does not alter initial forces, a myocardial infarction involving the anterior or inferior wall, but not an isolated posterior infarction, can still be detected.

Nonspecific Intraventricular Block

The term *nonspecific intraventricular block* is used to describe a QRS that is widened, usually in the range of 0.10 to 0.12 s, without clearcut evidence of a specific bundle branch block. This may be seen in a small percentage of normal subjects as a toxic effect of potassium or drugs such as procainamide and certain psychotropic agents, and as a result of diffuse heart disease. Minor notching or slurring of the QRS is not necessarily abnormal but is sometimes a sign of an abnormal spread of depolarization.

SI, SII, SIII Pattern *(Fig. 7–11)*

In most normal subjects the basilar portion of the left ventricle is last to undergo depolarization. Therefore, the terminal QRS forces are directed to the left and posteriorly. In an occasional normal subject the right ventricle contributes large terminal forces which are directed to the right and may be anterior or posterior to or flush with the frontal plane. Unlike bundle branch block, the QRS duration is not prolonged. In such cases the QRS loop is not normally elongated but is bean-shaped. This configuration of the QRS loop produces positive and negative deflections on many of the frontal and precordial leads, frequently resulting in S waves in leads I, II, and III and in many of the precordial leads. In some cases the R and S waves are of the same amplitude in nearly all leads. Under such circumstances it is often very difficult and of little value to plot a mean QRS vector. The exact cause of this unusual sequence of depolarization is not known; perhaps there are multiple causes. Some have felt that the crista supraventricularis, the muscular ridge high in the right ventricle, is the source of rightward terminal QRS forces. Others have suggested that a QRS loop of this sort results from a congenital defect of the Purkinje system.

The *SI, SII, SIII pattern* is one electrocardiographic syndrome where a wide spatial QRS-T angle is encountered with a QRS interval that is normal. The

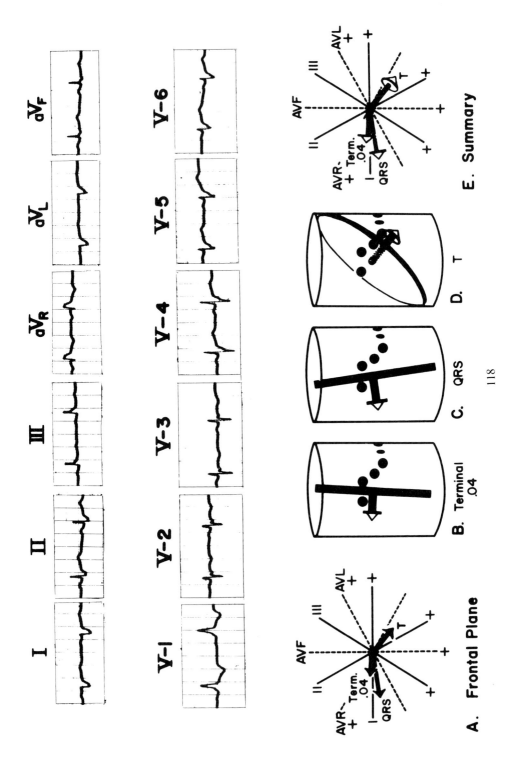

FIG. 7–8. Electrocardiogram showing right bundle branch block and probable left posterior fascicular block. An earlier electrocardiogram in this patient showed right bundle branch block with a normal QRS axis.

(A) The frontal plane projection of the mean spatial QRS, T, and terminal 0.04 s QRS vectors. The QRS complex is slightly positive in lead aV_F and is negative in lead I. Therefore the QRS is almost perpendicular to lead axis aV_L. The T wave is slightly positive in lead III and aV_L. Therefore the mean T vector is located as shown. The mean vector representing the terminal 0.04 s portion of the QRS is directed to the right and is nearly perpendicular to lead axis aV_F because the terminal 0.04 s portion of the QRS is small but negative in aV_F and positive in lead III.

(B) The mean spatial terminal 0.04 s vector oriented in the cylindrical replica of the chest. The mean terminal 0.04 s vector is flush with the frontal plane because the terminal 0.04 s portion of the QRS is positive in lead V_1 and negative in V_2, and the edge of the transitional pathway, which is perpendicular to the vector, must pass between these two electrode positions.

(C) The mean QRS vector oriented in the cylindrical replica of the chest. The mean QRS vector is flush with the frontal plane because the edge of the transitional pathway must pass between electrode position V_1, where the QRS complex is positive and V_2 where it is slightly negative.

(D) The mean T vector oriented in the cylindrical replica of the chest. The edge of the transitional pathway of the mean T vector must pass between electrode positions V_3 and V_4 since the T wave is negative in V_3 and positive in V_4. Since the transitional pathway is perpendicular to the vector, it follows that the mean T vector must be rotated slightly posteriorly to meet the conditions described.

(E) Final summary figure illustrating the mean spatial QRS, T, and terminal 0.04 s vectors. Note that the QRS is 0.12 s in duration and that the mean QRS and terminal 0.04 s vectors are directed far to the right. These characteristics suggest right bundle branch block plus left posterior fascicular block, since earlier tracings had shown right bundle branch block with a normal axis.

ventricular gradient is normal because the mean T vector is frequently increased in magnitude and normal in direction.

The Concept of Fascicular Block

Electrophysiologically, the conducting pathways branching from the His bundle can be conceptualized as consisting of three major fascicles: a right bundle branch to the right ventricle; an anterior division of the left bundle branch to the left ventricle; and a posterior division of the left bundle branch to the left ventricle. There is also some evidence for a third, middle branch of the left bundle. Normally, conduction proceeds at uniform speed through the three agreed-upon fascicles. When disease impairs or blocks conduction through one or more of these fascicles, activation of the muscle innervated by that fascicle is delayed compared with other areas of the ventricle. This is termed a *unifascicular, bifascicular,* or *trifascicular block* depending on the number of fascicles involved. In addition, the conduction over one or more fascicles may

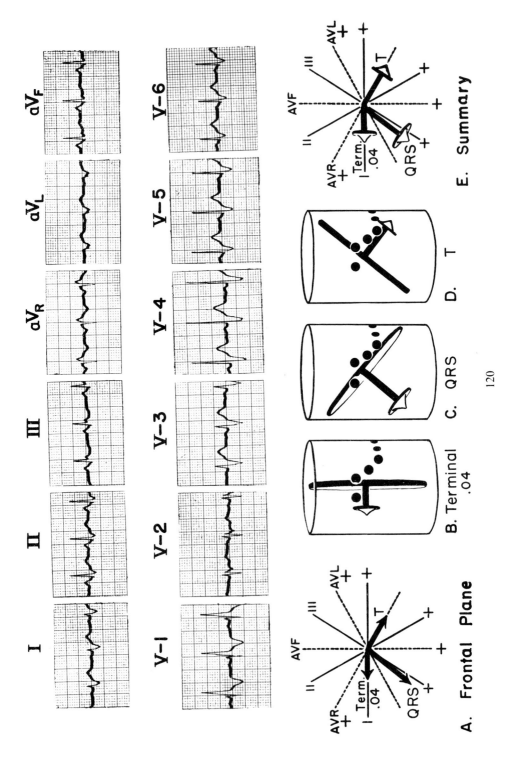

FIG. 7-9. The electrocardiogram of a hypertensive patient, 63 years of age, showing right bundle branch block and probable left posterior fascicular block.

(A) Frontal plane projection of the mean QRS, T, and terminal 0.04 s vectors. In this case there is a deep S wave in lead I, and the terminal 0.04 s of the QRS complex in lead aV_F is resultantly zero. Therefore the terminal 0.04 s vector is directed to the right and is perpendicular to lead aV_F. The mean QRS vector is about $+125°$ with an initial 0.02 s QRS vector pointing leftward and superiorly. Later QRS forces swing rightward. This is compatible with a left posterior fascicular block.

(B) The terminal 0.04 s vector is approximately flush with the frontal plane because the transitional pathway for the terminal 0.04 s vector passes between V_1 and V_2. The terminal 0.04 s portion of the QRS complex is positive in lead V_1 but negative in V_2, V_3, V_4, V_5, and V_6.

(C) The mean QRS vector is approximately flush with the frontal plane since the QRS complex is resultantly positive in V_1 but resultantly negative in the remaining precordial leads.

(D) The mean T vector is flush with the frontal plane since the transitional pathway for the T wave passes through electrode position V_2.

(E) Final summary figure showing the spatial arrangement of the vectors. The QRS duration is 0.12 s, indicating bundle branch block. The terminal 0.04 s vector is directed to the right and indicates right bundle branch block.

posterior-inferior aspect of the ventricle is stimulated before the anterior-superior area.

Electrocardiographic Criteria for Left Anterior Fascicular Block

The Initial 0.02 s QRS Vector Is Oriented Inferiorly and to the Right The early activation of the posterior-inferior wall produces a small r wave in leads II, III, and aV_F and a small q wave in leads I, aV_L, and sometimes V_5 and V_6.

The Initial 0.04 s QRS Vector Is Oriented to the Left and Superiorly A tall R wave follows the q wave in leads I and aV_L, and a deep S wave appears after the r wave in II, III, and aV_F (QI–SIII pattern).

The Mean QRS Axis Is -45° or Greater The most important diagnostic criterion is left axis deviation. A

be partially, intermittently, or completely blocked. The types of possibilities include: right bundle branch block, left bundle branch block, left anterior fascicular block, left posterior fascicular block, or a combination of any of these conduction defects. We have previously discussed the findings of right and left bundle branch block and will now consider the changes produced by anterior and posterior fascicular block and trifascicular block.

Left Anterior Fascicular (Divisional, Hemi-) Block
(Figs. 7-2, 7-12, 7-13)

The anterior fascicle of the left bundle carries the electrical stimulus from the summit of the ventricular septum toward the anterior papillary muscle. When conduction is delayed or disrupted over this fascicle, the

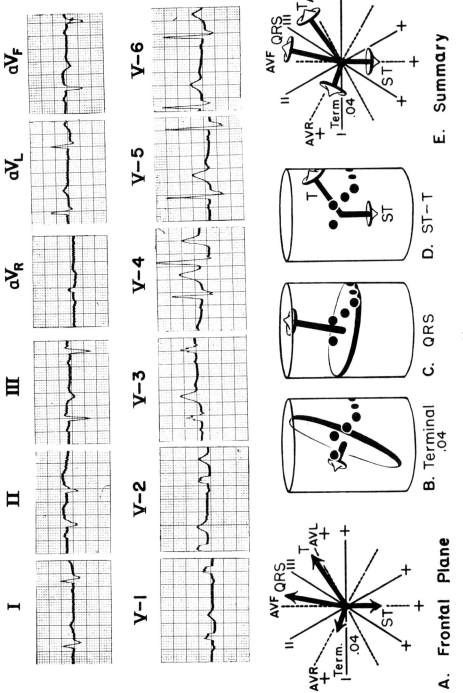

FIG. 7–10. The electrocardiogram of a patient, 60 years of age, showing inferior myocardial infarction and right bundle branch block.

(A) The frontal plane projection of the mean QRS, ST, T, and terminal 0.04 s vectors. Note that the last 0.04 s of the QRS complex is large and negative in leads I and II, slightly positive in lead III, and slightly negative in lead aV_L. This portion of the QRS complexes can be represented by a vector located between the negative limb of lead I and the positive limb of lead aV_R.

(B) The terminal 0.04 s vector is rotated approximately 20° anteriorly because the last portion of the QRS complex is positive in V_1 and V_2 and negative in leads V_3, V_4, V_5, and V_6.

(C) The mean QRS vector is rotated approximately 30° anteriorly, producing resultantly positive QRS deflections in all the precordial leads. Note how leads V_4, V_5, and V_6 are recording near the transitional pathway and that these complexes are resultantly less positive than the complexes recorded from the remaining precordial leads.

(D) The mean ST vector is rotated slightly posteriorly and the mean T vector is rotated slightly anteriorly.

(E) Summary. The QRS duration is 0.13 s, indicating bundle branch block. The terminal 0.04 s QRS vector is directed to the right and anteriorly, indicating right bundle branch block. The QRS-T angle is in an abnormal position because the mean QRS and T vectors are located above the lead I axis. The T vector is directed away from an area of inferior ischemia. There is a prominent ST vector present directed toward the inferior surface of the heart identifying epicardial injury in that region. This electrocardiogram illustrates the simultaneous occurrence of right bundle branch block and inferior myocardial infarction. The superior QRS axis in this example may be due to a loss of inferior forces rather than a left anterior fascicular block.

QRS axis above -45° is generally regarded as evidence for left anterior fascicular block. There is disagreement concerning the significance of a QRS mean axis between -30 and -45° and whether left axis deviation is always due to a conduction defect.

The QRS Interval Is Slightly Lengthened Conduction time between the two papillary muscles is only about 0.025 s. The QRS is therefore only slightly prolonged, in the range of 0.09 to 0.11 s, when a fascicular block is present.

Repolarization Is Not Affected Unless additional disease is present, a fascicular block does not alter the ST or T vector.

Left Posterior Fascicular (Divisional, Hemi-) Block (*Figs. 7–2, 7–8, 7–9*)

The posterior fascicle brings the electrical impulse from the origin of the left bundle to the posterior papillary muscle of the left ventricle. A delay or block in conduction in this fascicle allows the anterior-superior portion of the left ventricle to depolarize before the pos-

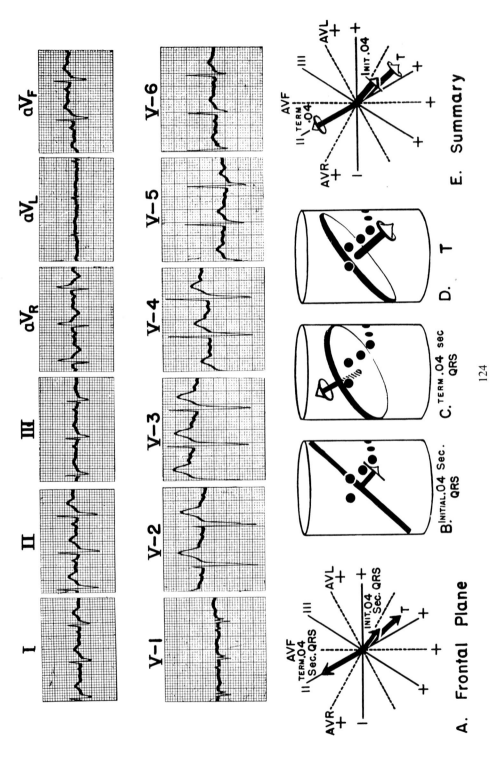

FIG. 7-11. The electrocardiogram of a normal subject, 24 years of age, showing the SI, SII, SIII pattern.

(A) Frontal plane projection of the initial and terminal 0.04 s vectors and the mean T vector. Note that all the QRS complexes are approximately equiphasic in the frontal leads. The initial 0.04 s vector is slightly positive in lead aV_L and the terminal 0.04 s vector is resultantly zero in lead aV_L. The initial 0.04 s vector is directed toward the positive pole of lead II and the terminal 0.04 s vector is directed toward the negative pole of the same lead.

(B) The initial 0.04 s vector is approximately flush with the frontal plane since there is an initial Q wave of 0.04 s duration in lead V_1 and an initial R wave of 0.04 s duration in leads V_3, V_4, V_5, and V_6.

(C) The terminal 0.04 s vector is directed approximately 15° posteriorly because terminal S waves are recorded in all of the precordial leads. Note that the transitional pathway for the terminal 0.04 s vector lies very near electrode position V_1. Sometimes the terminal 0.04 s vector is even more anteriorly directed with an R' at V_1 and even V_2.

(D) The mean T vector is rotated approximately 5° anteriorly since the transitional pathway is located between V_1 and V_2.

(E) Final summary figure. The QRS duration is only 0.08 to 0.09 s. The terminal portion of the QRS is located to the right and is directed slightly posteriorly. This type of tracing illustrates right ventricular conduction delay with normal QRS duration.

terior-inferior aspect. A conduction defect of the posterior fascicle is far less common than its anterior companion.

Electrocardiographic Criteria for Left Posterior Fascicular Block

The Initial 0.02 s QRS Vector Is Directed to the Left and Superiorly The early depolarization of the anterior-superior left ventricular wall produces a small r wave in leads I and aV_L and a small q wave in the inferior leads.

The Initial 0.06 QRS Vector Faces Inferiorly The late activation of the posterior-inferior wall swings the later ventricular forces toward the inferior leads where tall R waves are seen and away from leads I and aV_L, which register S waves.

The Mean QRS Axis Is Rightward of +80° A new posterior fascicular block shifts the mean QRS rightward. The vector may be anywhere from +80 to +140°; +120° is common.

The QRS Interval Is Slightly Lengthened As indicated under anterior fascicular block, conduction is only mildly delayed. The QRS may prolong up to 0.025 s but still remains within or near normal limits.

Repolarization Is Not Affected A posterior fascicular block, by itself, does not cause an abnormal ST or T vector.

Combinations of Fascicular Block *(Fig. 7-2)*

The following possible combinations of fascicular block may occur:

125

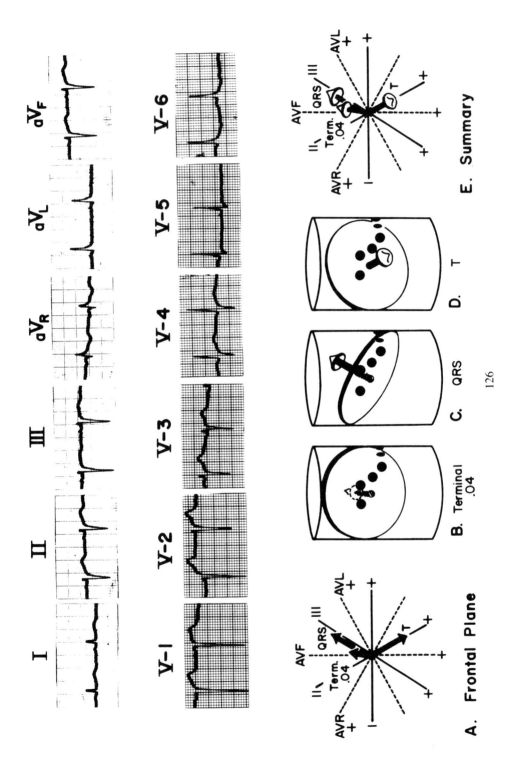

FIG. 7–12. Electrocardiogram showing left anterior fascicular block.
(A) The frontal plane projection of the mean QRS, T, and terminal 0.04 s vectors. The QRS complex is slightly positive in lead III. Accordingly, the mean QRS vector is drawn almost perpendicular to lead axis aV_R. The terminal 0.04 s portion of the QRS complex represented as a mean vector is isoelectric in lead I and is drawn perpendicular to lead I. The mean T vector is isoelectric in lead aV_L and is drawn perpendicular to that lead.
(B) The mean spatial terminal 0.04 s vector oriented in the cylindrical replica of the chest. The mean terminal 0.04 s vector is rotated a marked degree posteriorly since the terminal portion of the QRS complexes is negative in leads V_1, V_2, V_3, V_4, and V_5.
(C) The mean spatial QRS vector is oriented in the cylindrical replica of the chest. The mean QRS vector is rotated slightly posteriorly since the edge of the transitional pathway, which is perpendicular to the vector, lies close to V_4.
(D) The mean T vector is rotated anteriorly to a marked degree since the T waves are positive in leads V_1, V_2, V_3, and V_4, but are negative in lead V_6.
(E) Final summary illustrating the mean spatial QRS, T, and terminal 0.04 s vectors. Note that the left axis deviation of the QRS is greater than $-60°$; that the terminal 0.04 s vector of the QRS is $-90°$; and that the duration of the QRS complexes is normal (0.08 s). The initial 0.04 s vector representing the initial depolarization of the ventricles is directed to the left and inferiorly. These features are characteristic of left anterior fascicular block.

Right Bundle Branch Block and Left Anterior Fascicular Block A right bundle branch block is present and the QRS axis is leftward of -45°. A QI–SIII pattern is present. Leads II and III show small r waves.

Right Bundle Branch Block and Left Posterior Fascicular Block A right bundle branch block is present and the QRS axis is rightward of +80° (usually). An SI–QIII pattern is present. Leads II and III show tall R waves.

A Left Anterior and Posterior Fascicular Block A left bundle branch block will be seen. A left axis may be present.

A Complete Trifascicular Block Complete atrioventricular block with an escape pacemaker below the level of the block is present.

An Incomplete Trifascicular Block All three fascicles show some degree of conduction impairment but at least one fascicle is capable of conducting impulses to the ventricle. An example would be a right bundle branch block, left anterior fascicular block, and a first-degree or second-degree block over the left posterior fascicle. The conduction impairment may vary depending on heart rate and unknown factors. Without a His bundle recording, it is impossible to tell whether the first-degree or second-degree block is located in the fascicle or above the bundle branches.

Important Considerations

- The diagnosis of a fascicular block should be reserved for electrocardiograms that meet carefully de-

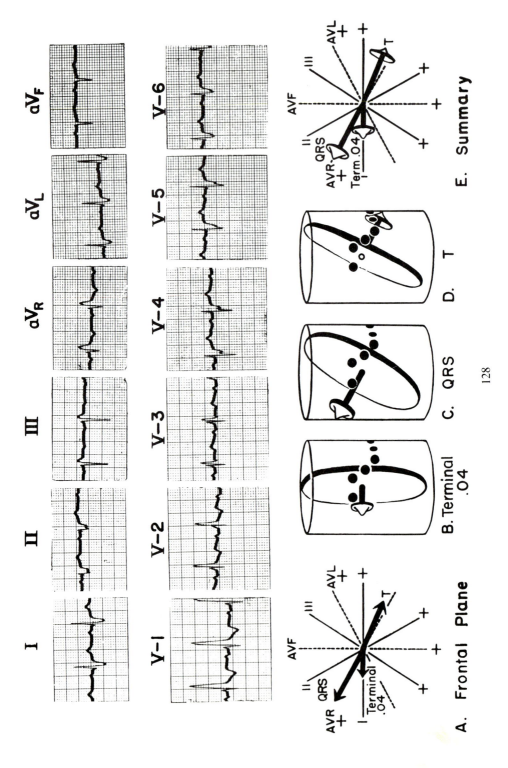

FIG. 7–13. The electrocardiogram of hypertensive patient, 76 years of age, showing right bundle branch block and left anterior fascicular block.

(A) The frontal plane projection of the mean QRS, T, and terminal 0.04 s vectors. The terminal 0.04 s portion of the QRS complex is markedly negative in lead I and isoelectric in lead aV_F. The mean vector representing this portion of the QRS complex would be directed perpendicular to lead aV_F and toward the negative pole of lead I. The initial 0.02 s QRS vector is inferior and rightward while the terminal QRS vector is superiorly directed. This suggests a left anterior fascicular block in addition to the right bundle branch block.

(B) The terminal 0.04 s vector is rotated 30° anteriorly because this portion of the QRS complex is positive in V_1 and V_2 and negative in V_4, V_5, and V_6.

(C) The mean QRS vector is rotated 30° anteriorly because the transitional pathway passes between electrode positions V_3 and V_4. In such a case V_1, V_2, and V_3 will record resultantly positive deflections and V_4, V_5, and V_6 will record resultantly negative deflections.

(D) The mean T vector is rotated 15° posteriorly because the transitional pathway for the T wave is located between electrode positions V_2 and V_3.

(E) Summary. The QRS duration is 0.12 s. The terminal 0.04 s vector is directed to the right and anteriorly, indicating right bundle branch block. The midportion of the QRS is directed markedly superiorly, suggesting block in the anterior fascicle of the left bundle branch.

---

fined criteria. A QRS axis between -30 and -45° should be called left axis deviation because it is not clearly due to a left anterior fascicular block. A vertical or slightly rightward QRS axis may be normal or related to right ventricular hypertrophy or lung disease rather than a posterior fascicular block.

• Fascicular blocks may mimic infarct patterns—an anterior fascicular block may produce the appearance of an anteroseptal or inferior infarction; a posterior fascicular block can suggest an anterior infarction.

• Myocardial infarctions can also be obscured by the development of a fascicular block.

• Ventricular hypertrophy may also be simulated by a fascicular block.

• A trifascicular block pattern does not necessarily indicate that the level of block is within the ventricular conducting system. The delayed conduction may be partially within the atrium or AV node or completely within the His bundle.

Chapter 8
Preexcitation Syndromes

Normally the sinus node impulse is propagated from the sinus node to the ventricular conducting pathways via the AV node and His bundle. The PR interval measures the total duration of this electrical journey and, in the normal adult, is from 0.12 to 0.20 s in duration. Depending on autonomic tone, 0.06 to 0.13 s of the normal PR interval is due to AV nodal conduction delay. Preexcitation is present when a portion or all of the ventricular myocardium is activated sooner than would be expected by conduction over the normal conducting pathways. This occurs when accessory conduction pathways allow conduction to bypass the AV node and reach the ventricular myocardium without the expected delay. A number of potential accessory pathways have been described, including a number of atrioventricular connections (also called Kent bundles) located away from the AV nodal area and several bypass tracts present in or around the AV node. These accessory pathways may or may not participate in the transmission of the electrical impulse to the ventricle; the impulse may reach the ventricle by antegrade conduction over the normal or the accessory conduction system or by simultaneous conduction over both. If the impulse travels exclusively over the normal conducting system, avoiding the accessory pathway, the electrocardiogram will be unchanged. However, if the impulse propagates through an accessory pathway to depolarize part or all of the ventricle, characteristic changes of preexcitation will be seen depending upon the location of the bypass tract and the extent to which

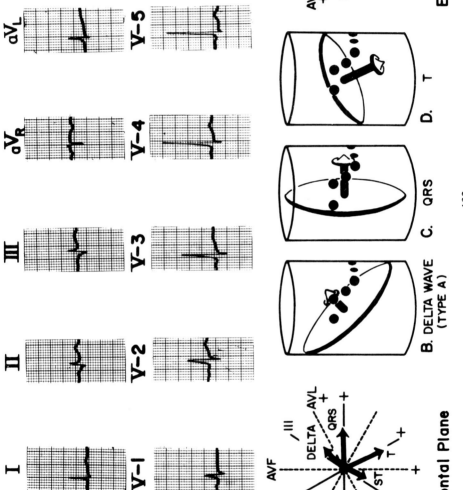
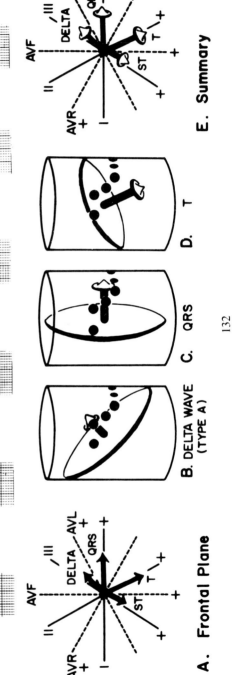

FIG. 8-1. Electrocardiogram showing a Wolff-Parkinson-White conduction abnormality (preexcitation syndrome).

(A) The frontal plane projection of the mean spatial QRS, ST, T, and delta wave vectors. The QRS complex is slightly negative to and delta wave vectors. The QRS complex is slightly negative to lead axis aV$_F$ and is largest and positive in lead I. The mean QRS vector is drawn almost perpendicular to lead aV$_F$. The T wave is largest in lead II and slightly negative in lead aV$_L$. This makes it possible to diagram the mean T vector almost parallel to lead II. The delta wave—represented by the initial 0.04 s portion of the QRS complex—is largest and negative in lead III and is slightly negative in lead II yet is resultantly negative in lead aV$_R$. The mean delta wave vector is illustrated.

(B) The mean spatial delta wave vector oriented in the cylindrical replica of the chest. The mean delta wave vector must be rotated anteriorly since the initial portion of the QRS complex is positive in lead V$_1$. The degree of anterior rotation is not extreme since the delta wave is nearly isoelectric in lead V$_6$. The anterior rotation of the mean spatial delta wave identifies this electrocardiogram as a type A Wolff-Parkinson-White conduction abnormality (preexcitation syndrome).

(C) The mean spatial QRS vector is oriented in the cylindrical replica of the chest. Since the QRS complex is resultantly positive in lead V$_1$, the mean spatial QRS vector is flush with the frontal plane.

(D) The mean spatial T vector is rotated slightly anteriorly since the edge of the zero potential plane, which is perpendicular to the mean spatial vector, must pass through lead V$_1$.

(E) Final summary figure illustrating the mean spatial QRS, ST, T, and delta wave vectors. The delta wave vector identifies this tracing as a Wolff-Parkinson-White conduction abnormality (preexcitation syndrome). Note the typical slurring of the initial portion of the QRS complex in lead V$_4$ along with the short PR interval of 0.1 to 0.13 s and QRS duration of 0.11 s. Warning! This type of electrocardiogram may simulate inferoposterior myocardial infarction.

the impulse may also reach the ventricle via simultaneous AV nodal conduction.

Electrocardiographic Criteria for Preexcitation (Figs. 8–1 to 8–3)

The PR Interval Is Short The PR interval is usually, but not always, less than 0.12 s. A normal or borderline short PR interval can occur, particularly in leads in which the delta wave is not apparent or when AV nodal conduction is also contributing to ventricular depolarization.

A Delta Wave May Be Present The delta wave is a slurred, slanting, initial portion of the QRS complex due to early excitation and slow conduction through ventricular muscle remote from the AV node. This is the major feature of the Wolff-Parkinson-White (W-P-W) syndrome. A delta wave vector can be plotted using the same approach as outlined earlier for the analysis of the initial 0.04 s QRS forces. The spatial orientation of the delta wave vector has been used to infer the location of the bypass tract—an anteriorly oriented delta wave vector (type A) indicating a bypass to the left ventricle (Fig. 8–1) and a posteriorly oriented one

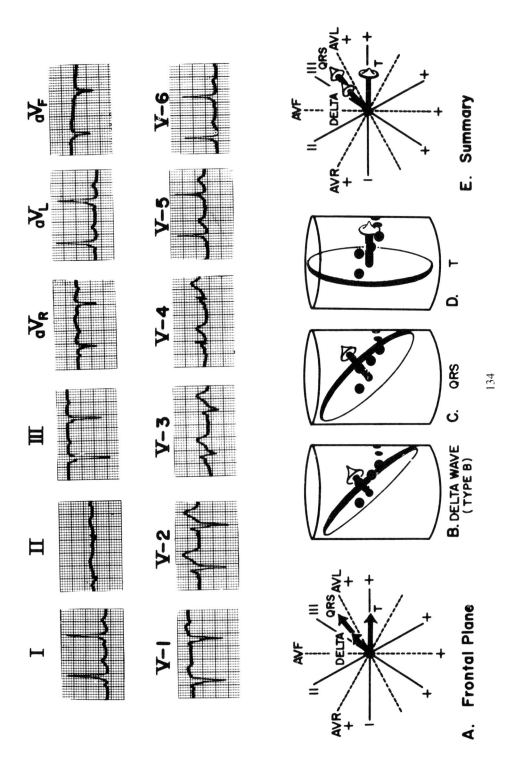

FIG. 8–2. Electrocardiogram showing a Wolff-Parkinson-White conduction abnormality (preexcitation syndrome).

(A) The frontal plane projection of the mean spatial QRS, T, and delta wave vectors. The QRS complex is almost resultantly zero in lead II and the mean QRS vector is illustrated as being almost perpendicular to that lead axis. (It is actually slightly negative in lead II so it is diagrammed to project negative in that lead). The T wave is smallest and slightly positive in lead aV_F. The delta wave—represented by the initial 0.04 s portion of the QRS complex—is largest and positive in lead aV_L and small and negative in lead II. Therefore, the mean delta wave vector is nearly perpendicular to lead II.

(B) The mean spatial delta wave vector oriented in the cylindrical replica of the chest. The mean delta wave vector is directed slightly posteriorly to the frontal plane since the initial 0.04 s portion of the QRS complex is resultantly slightly negative in lead V_1.

(C) The mean spatial QRS vector is oriented in the cylindrical replica of the chest. The QRS complexes are almost resultantly zero in leads V_3 and V_4. Accordingly, the edge of the zero potential plane, which is perpendicular to the mean QRS vector, must pass near them. Therefore, the mean QRS vector is rotated slightly posteriorly.

(D) The mean spatial T vector is rotated slightly anteriorly since the T wave in lead V_1 is resultantly slightly positive.

(E) Final summary figure illustrating the mean spatial QRS, T, and delta wave vectors. Since the mean spatial delta wave vector is slightly posterior to the frontal plane rather than being anterior, the electrocardiogram is identified as being a type B Wolff-Parkinson-White conduction abnormality (preexcitation syndrome). The mean delta wave vector is usually posteriorly directed in such tracings. Note the typical slurring of the initial QRS complex in most leads. The PR interval is 0.08 to 0.09 s and the QRS duration is 0.12 s. Warning! This type of electrocardiogram can be misinterpreted as being due to inferior, or sometimes anterior, myocardial infarction.

related to a right ventricular bypass (Fig. 8–2). This electrocardiographic-anatomic correlation may be inaccurate because of multiple accessory connections and other reasons.

The QRS Interval May Be Prolonged or Normal The QRS interval will be normal if the bypass tract is in or adjacent to the AV node and conduction over the bundle branches is not impaired. When preexcitation occurs outside the AV nodal area, a delta wave is seen and the QRS is correspondingly prolonged.

ST-T Wave Changes May Occur Repolarization abnormalities with an ST-T vector opposite to the delta wave and the mean QRS vectors are seen when conduction spreads abnormally through the myocardium.

Arrhythmias Are Frequent Arrhythmias are common, though not invariable, in patients with preexcitation. The arrhythmias are usually supraventricular, usually involving a circular movement reaching the ventricle via the AV node and reentering the atrium by retrograde conduction over the accessory pathway. Less frequently the arrhythmia conducts antegradely to the ventricle by the anomalous pathway and retrogradely through the AV node to the atrium. Atrial tachycardia is the most common arrhythmia, followed by atrial

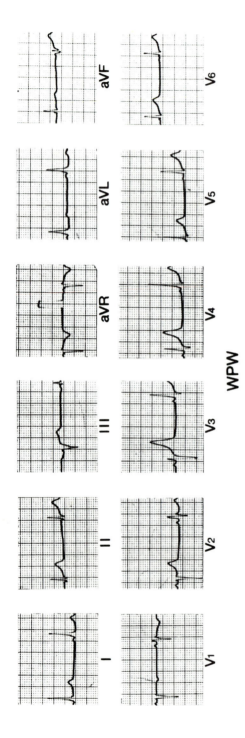

FIG. 8-3. Wolff-Parkinson-White syndrome. Intermittent conduction over the anomalous pathway is present as illustrated by delta waves and a prolonged QRS in the second complex of leads I, aV$_L$, and V$_2$ to V$_4$. Note the appearance of a "pseudo Q wave" in lead aV$_F$ due to a negative delta wave. The delta wave can be represented as a mean vector directed to the left and anteriorly.

fibrillation and then atrial flutter. Ventricular fibrillation may also rarely occur.

Important Considerations

- The Wolff-Parkinson-White syndrome is one type of preexcitation and is diagnosed when a short PR interval is associated with delta waves and a prolonged QRS interval. The abnormal QRS is considered a fusion complex since it is formed by ventricular depolarization due to simultaneous AV nodal conduction and bypass conduction. There is an association of W-P-W with Ebstein's anomaly of the tricuspid valve, mitral valve prolapse, and hypertrophic cardiomyopathy. Patients with W-P-W may also have unrelated heart disease of any type.
- The Lown-Ganong-Levine (L-G-L) syndrome is a form of preexcitation manifested by a short PR interval

and a narrow QRS complex. The bypass is in or around the AV node. This is also known as the short PR interval syndrome when associated with arrhythmias.

• The electrocardiogram may be constantly normal, intermittently abnormal, or always abnormal in patients with an accessory pathway (Fig. 8–3). The reasons that favor conduction over an accessory pathway at one time but not another are uncertain. The propensity for arrhythmias of some patients with preexcitation, but not others with a similar electrocardiogram, is also puzzling.

• Preexcitation may falsely suggest other electrocardiographic entities. Type A W-P-W, in which the delta wave is directed anteriorly, may mimic right bundle branch block, posterior myocardial infarction, and right ventricular hypertrophy. A posterior delta wave, as seen in type B W-P-W, may suggest left bundle branch block, anterior myocardial infarction, and left ventricular hypertrophy. When the bypass connection is on the inferior surface, the delta wave is oriented superiorly and an inferior infarction may be wrongly suggested. Repolarization abnormalities due to preexcitation may produce a false-positive exercise test. Atrial fibrillation is often mistaken for ventricular tachycardia when the anomalously conducted fibrillatory impulses result in bizarre QRS complexes with a rapid ventricular rate. The irregularity of the rhythm, the presence of interspersed complexes that are more normally conducted, and extremely short RR intervals should provide the correct diagnosis.

Section B
Acquired Diseases that Affect the Electrocardiogram

Chapter 9
Coronary Artery Disease

The electrocardiogram is often asked to reveal the presence and severity of acute or chronic coronary artery disease. Although it may offer very valuable information in this regard, nonspecific ST-T abnormalities or nondiagnostic Q waves may also mislead the interpreter to an erroneous diagnosis of coronary disease. Conversely, the electrocardiogram may be normal despite severe double- or triple-vessel coronary disease or even an acute myocardial infarction. In the following discussion the accepted diagnostic criteria for the diagnosis of coronary artery disease will be mentioned and important considerations about the fallibility of these criteria indicated.

Myocardial Infarction

The electrocardiogram of a patient with an acute myocardial infarction may be normal or unchanged from a prior recording. This important fact, which is sometimes ignored, is particularly true in the early stages of infarction; with infarctions that are small or located in certain "silent" areas of the heart; or when the electrocardiogram is distorted by preexisting abnormalities. In the majority of patients, however, the electrocardiogram is abnormal, though not necessarily specific for an acute infarction.

Electrocardiographic Criteria for the Diagnosis of Myocardial Infarction *(Figs. 9–1 to 9–25)*

The diagnosis of infarction depends upon one or more of the three following observations.

A Mean T-Wave Vector Initially Directed Toward and Later Away from the Site of Infarction (*Figs. 9–10, 9–25*)

At the onset of myocardial injury a broad tall T wave, due to subendocardial ischemia, is often seen in leads facing the injured area. This *hyperacute T wave*, as it is sometimes called, may merge with an elevated, upward-slanting ST segment or antecede the ST elevation. As the injury develops, the initial T-wave vector quickly begins to rotate away from the affected area and may not be present or discernible at the time the patient is initially evaluated. Later in the course, as the ST-segment elevation begins to regress, the T-wave vector is directed away from the site of infarction. T-wave inversion, which ranges from shallow to deep, is pointed, and often has symmetrically down-slanting sides, then develops in the same and sometimes nearby leads. This T-wave inversion tends to persist for prolonged periods after an infarction and does not necessarily indicate continuing ischemia. When the infarction is small or does not extend to the epicardial surface, T-wave inversion may be the only electrocardiographic expression of injury.

A Mean Spatial ST Vector Directed Toward a Transmural or Epicardial Injury or Away from a Subendocardial Infarction

This is known as a current of injury (Figs. 9–6 to 9–11, 9–20, 9–21, 9–25).

ST-segment elevation is produced by an epicardial or transmural infarction; ST-segment depression is seen with a subendocardial or posterior infarction. The extent of ST-segment displacement may be slight, only a millimeter or so, or it may reach as high or higher than the R wave. As it takes off from the descending limb of the R wave, the ST-segment elevation usually assumes a convex upward or upward-slanting configuration. ST-segment depression may also vary from a

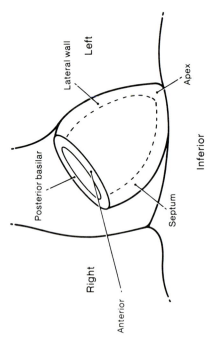

FIG. 9–1. Diagram illustrating a frontal view of the left ventricle as seen within the cardiac silhouette. The dashed lines indicate the endocardial surface. Various regions of the left ventricle are identified.

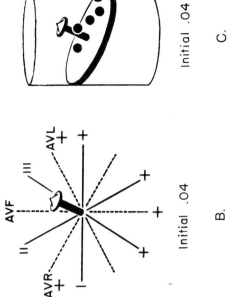
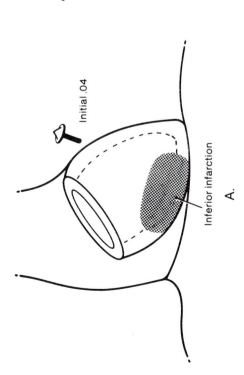
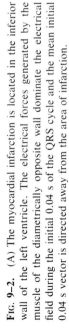

Fig. 9–2. (A) The myocardial infarction is located in the inferior wall of the left ventricle. The electrical forces generated by the muscle of the diametrically opposite wall dominate the electrical field during the initial 0.04 s of the QRS cycle and the mean initial 0.04 s vector is directed away from the area of infarction.

(B) The mean initial 0.04 s vector is treated as though it originates in the center of the chest, and the hexaxial reference system has been superimposed. This enables one to study the projection of the mean initial 0.04 s vector on the frontal lead axes. In this case a Q wave will be written in leads II, III, and aV$_F$, and an R wave will be written in leads I, aV$_R$, and aV$_L$. This type of myocardial infarction is usually called an inferior infarction.

(C) This figure illustrates how the mean initial 0.04 s vector shown in (A) will influence the precordial leads. In this case there will be initial R waves in all the precordial leads.

slight degree of shallow scooping displacement to a deep, excavated appearance that is horizontal or downward-sloping compared to the isoelectric line. Since ST-segment elevation or depression can also occur transiently with acute ischemia and can be caused by factors other than coronary disease, the ST-segment deviation should be new and persistent before infarction is suggested.

A Mean Initial 0.04 s QRS Vector Pointing Away from the Site of Infarction (Figs. 9–2 to 9–9, 9–11 to 9–16, 9–18 to 9–24) The normal initial 0.01 to 0.02 s QRS vector

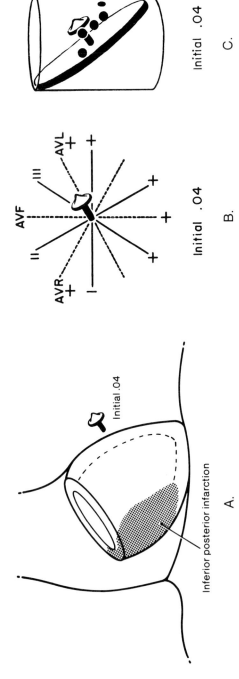

FIG. 9–3. (A) The myocardial infarction is located on the inferior and posterior surface of the left ventricle. The electrical forces generated by the diametrically opposite part of the heart dominate the electrical field during the initial 0.04 s of the QRS cycle and the mean initial 0.04 s vector is directed away from the area of infarction.

(B) The mean initial 0.04 s vector is treated as though it originates in the center of the chest, and the hexaxial reference system has been superimposed. This enables one to study the projection of the mean initial 0.04 s vector on the frontal lead axes. In this case a Q wave will be recorded in leads II, III, aV$_F$, and aV$_R$, and an R wave will be recorded in leads I and aV$_L$.

(C) This figure illustrates how the mean initial 0.04 s vector shown in (A) will influence the precordial leads. In this case initial R waves will be recorded in all the precordial leads.

is always anterior but may be superior or inferior, rightward or leftward. Leads on the opposite side of this vector will record a normal narrow q wave. Therefore the QRS complex in leads I, II, III, aV$_L$, aV$_F$, and V$_3$ to V$_6$ may begin with a small q wave, depending upon the exact spatial position of this initial vector. By 0.04 s, however, the QRS vector should always be between 0° and +90°, nearly parallel to the mean QRS vector in the frontal plane, and anterior to the mean QRS vector in the precordial plane. A myocardial infarction causes a partial or total loss of these early electrical forces, allowing unopposed forces from the opposite

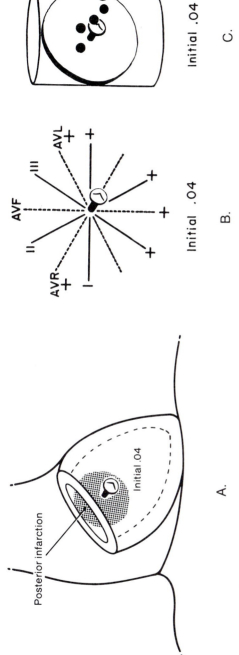

FIG. 9–4. (A) The myocardial infarction is located on the posterior wall of the left ventricle. This figure illustrates a "true" posterior infarct. The electrical forces generated by the anterior surface of the heart dominate the electrical field during the initial 0.04 of the QRS cycle.

(B) The mean initial 0.04 s vector is treated as though it originates in the center of the chest, and the hexaxial reference system has been superimposed. This enables one to study the projection of the mean spatial 0.04 s vector on the frontal lead axes. In this case the frontal plane projection of the vector is quite small, producing an R wave in leads I, II, aV_F, and aV_L, and a Q wave in lead a V_R. The mean 0.04 s vector is perpendicular to lead III, and therefore the initial 0.04 of the QRS complex in lead III will be resultantly zero.

(C) This figure illustrates how the mean initial 0.04 s vector shown in (A) will influence the precordial leads. In this case initial R waves will be recorded in all the precordial leads and the R wave in the right precordial leads will be quite large.

region of the heart to dominate during this time period. As a consequence, the 0.04 s initial mean QRS vector points away from the site of infarction; abnormally wide and deep Q waves are recorded in leads providing direct information about the infarcted area.

Definition of an Abnormal Q Wave

By the usual definition, an abnormal Q wave spans 0.04 s or more in duration and reaches a certain depth, often stated as greater than 25 percent of the following

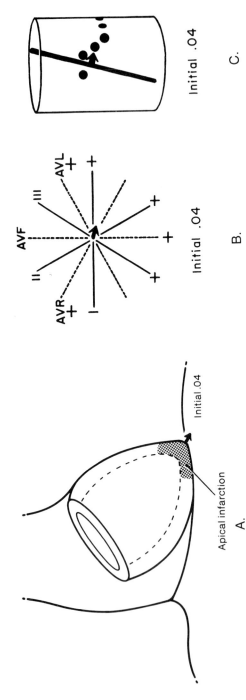

FIG. 9–5. (A) The myocardial infarction is located in the apical portion of the left ventricle. If the infarcted area is relatively small there may be little change in the QRS contour other than reduced magnitude. This is because a large number of normal initial QRS forces can still be generated by the intact muscle. In addition there may be little ventricular muscle opposite to the area of infarction located at the apex and therefore few opposing forces are generated.

(B) The mean initial 0.04 s vector is treated as though it originates in the center of the chest, and the hexaxial reference system is superimposed. This enables one to study the projection of the mean initial 0.04 s vector on the frontal lead axes. In this case the initial 0.04 s vector will be quite small and is directed in a normal manner. A small Q wave will be recorded in lead III, but leads I, II, aV_L, and aV_F will record a resultant positive deflection for the first 0.04 of the QRS cycle.

(C) This figure illustrates how the mean 0.04 s vector shown in (A) will influence the precordial leads. In this case an initial Q wave will be recorded in lead I and positive R waves will be recorded in leads V_2, V_3, V_4, V_5, and V_6.

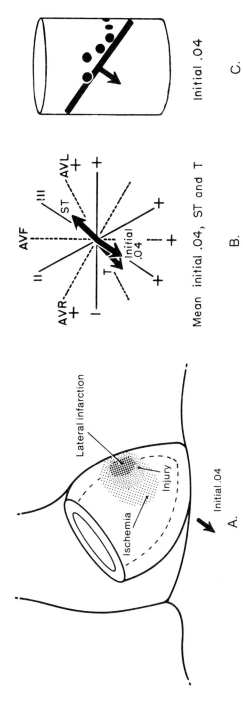

FIG. 9–6. (A) The myocardial infarction is located in the lateral portion of the left ventricle. The electrical forces generated in the opposite portion of the heart dominate the electrical field during the initial 0.04 s of the QRS cycle, and the mean initial 0.04 s vector is directed away from the infarction. The area of infarcted tissue is surrounded by an area of myocardial injury which is located predominantly in the epicardial region of the left ventricle. The mean ST vector will be directed toward the area of epicardial injury. The area of dead and injured tissue is surrounded by an area of epicardial ischemia. The mean T vector will be directed away from the area of epicardial ischemia.

(B) The mean initial 0.04, ST, and T vectors are treated as though they originate in the center of the chest, and the hexaxial reference system has been superimposed. This enables one to study the projection of the vectors on the lead axes. In this case a Q wave will be recorded in leads I and aV_L, and an R wave will be recorded in leads II, III, and aV_F. The mean initial 0.04 s vector is perpendicular to lead aV_R, and therefore the initial 0.04 of the QRS complex in lead aV_R will be resultantly zero. The ST segment will be elevated in leads I and aV_L and depressed in leads II, III, aV_F, and aV_R. The T wave will be inverted in leads I and a V_L and upright in leads II, III, aV_F, and aV_R.

(C) This figure illustrates how the mean initial 0.04 s vector shown in (A) will influence the precordial leads. In this case a Q wave will be recorded in leads V_2, V_3, V_4, V_5, and V_6. Although it is not illustrated, the ST segment would be elevated in leads V_2, V_3, V_4, V_5, and V_6 and depressed in lead V_1. The T wave would be inverted in V_2, V_3, V_4, V_5, V_6, and upright in lead V_1.

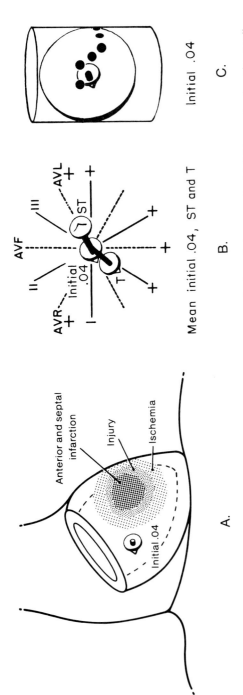

FIG. 9–7. (A) The myocardial infarction is located in the anterior and septal region of the left ventricle. The electrical forces generated in the opposite portion of the ventricular muscle dominate the electrical field during the initial 0.04 s of the QRS cycle, and the mean initial 0.04 s vector is directed away from the infarcted area. The area of infarction is surrounded by an area of epicardial myocardial injury. The mean ST vector will be directed toward the area of injury. The area of dead and injured tissue is surrounded by a zone of epicardial ischemia. The mean T vector will be directed away from the area of epicardial ischemia.

(B) The mean initial 0.04 s, ST, and T vectors are treated as though they originate in the center of the chest, and the hexaxial reference system has been superimposed. This enables one to study the projection of the vectors on the frontal lead axes. In this case the frontal plane projection of the mean initial 0.04 s vector is quite small, producing a Q wave in leads I and a V_L and an R wave in leads III, aV_F, and aV_R. The mean 0.04 s vector is perpendicular to lead II, and therefore the initial 0.04 s of the QRS complex in lead II will be resultantly zero. The ST segment will be elevated in leads I and aV_L and will be depressed in leads III, aV_F, and aV_R. There will be no ST-segment displacement in lead II. The T wave will be inverted in leads I and aV_L and will be upright in leads II, III, aV_F, and aV_R.

(C) This figure illustrates how the mean initial 0.04 s vector shown in (A) will influence the precordial leads. In this case the Q wave will be recorded in all the precordial leads. Although it is not illustrated, the ST segment would be elevated and the T waves would be inverted in all the precordial leads.

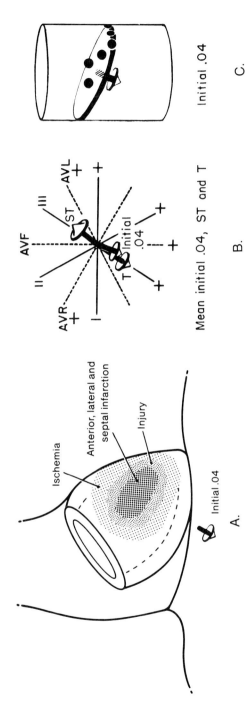

FIG. 9–8. (A) The myocardial infarction is located in the anterior, lateral, and septal portion of the left ventricle. The electrical forces generated in the opposite portion of the heart dominate the electrical field during the initial 0.04 s of the QRS cycle, and the mean initial 0.04 s vector is directed away from the infarcted area. The area of dead tissue is surrounded by an area of epicardial myocardial injury, and the ST vector will be directed toward the area of epicardial injury. Surrounding the latter area is an area of epicardial myocardial ischemia. The mean T vector will be directed away from the area of epicardial ischemia.

(B) The mean initial 0.04 s, ST, and T vectors are treated as though they originate in the center of the chest, and the hexaxial reference system has been superimposed. This enables one to study the projection of the vectors on the frontal lead axes. In this case a Q wave will be recorded in leads I, aV_L, and aV_R and an R wave will be recorded in leads II, III, and aV_F. The ST segment will be elevated in leads I and aV_L and depressed in leads II, III, aV_F, and aV_R. The T wave will be inverted in leads I and aV_L, resultantly zero in lead aV_R, and upright in leads II, III, and aV_F.

(C) This figure illustrates how the mean initial 0.04 s vector shown in (A) will influence the precordial leads. In this case a Q wave will be recorded in leads V_1, V_2, and V_3, and the initial 0.04 s of the QRS cycle will be resultantly zero in leads V_4, V_5, and V_6. Although it is not illustrated, the ST segment would be elevated in leads V_1, V_2, and V_3, and isoelectric in leads V_4, V_5, and V_6. The T waves would be inverted in leads V_1, V_2, and V_3 and flat in Leads V_4, V_5, and V_6.

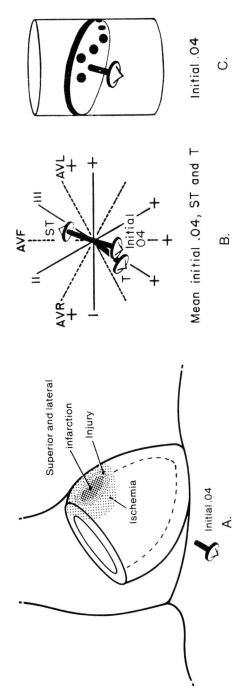

FIG. 9-9. (A) The myocardial infarction is located in the superior-lateral wall of the left ventricle. The electrical forces generated in the opposite portion of the ventricular muscle dominate the electrical field during the initial 0.04 s of the QRS cycle and the mean initial 0.04 s vector is directed away from the infarcted area. The area is surrounded by a zone of epicardial injury, and the mean ST vector will be directed toward the area of epicardial injury. The zone of injury is surrounded by a zone of epicardial ischemia and the mean T vector will be directed away from such an area.

(B) The mean initial 0.04 s, ST, and T vectors are treated as though they originate in the center of the chest, and the hexaxial reference system has been superimposed. This enables one to study the projection of the vectors on the frontal lead axes. In this case a Q wave will be recorded in leads I, aV_L, and aV_R and an R wave will be recorded in leads II, III, and aV_F. The ST segment will be elevated in leads I, aV_L, and aV_R and depressed in leads II, III, and aV_F. The T wave will be inverted in leads I and aV_L and upright in leads II, III, aV_F, and aV_R.

(C) This figure illustrates how the mean initial 0.04 s vector would influence the precordial leads in this particular case. Initial R waves will be recorded in all the precordial leads. Although it is not illustrated, the ST segment would be slightly depressed in all of the precordial leads. The T waves would be upright in all the precordial leads.

R wave (if present) in leads I, III, aV$_F$, and V$_2$ to V$_6$ and greater than 50 percent in aV$_L$. Actually, an abnormal Q wave may be less than 0.04 s in duration and may not be 25 percent of the R wave. Accordingly, in practice it may be difficult to tell a normal from an abnormal Q wave, particularly if the deflection in question meets only part of the criteria. Additional evidence that the Q wave is abnormal includes a notching or slurring of the downstroke of the Q wave, chronic ST- or T-wave changes in the same leads, and a prior recording that did not show Q waves. An abnormal Q wave can rarely occur acutely with transmural ischemia but most often appears hours to several days after a myocardial infarction. It is, therefore, not an initial finding of an acute myocardial infarction. Since the posterior surface of the heart is not directly sampled by the anterior chest leads, the diagnosis of a posterior infarction is deduced by analyzing V$_1$ and V$_2$ for reciprocal changes—an increase in the amplitude and width of the R wave is the reciprocal of an abnormal Q wave.

Important Considerations

- A broad Q or QS configuration may occasionally be found in lead III or aV$_L$ alone. Although this may be the only remnant of a myocardial infarction, it can also be a finding in normal individuals and should be interpreted with caution unless other evidence for a myocardial infarction is present.

- An even more perplexing problem occurs when there is a new reduction in R-wave amplitude without the development of a Q wave. This may be caused by myocardial infarction, a shift in the mean QRS axis, constitutional or technical factors, or a normal day-to-day variation in R-wave amplitude. Serial tracings, clinical correlations, and close attention to the ST-T vector may be useful.

- The presence of ventricular hypertrophy, right and left bundle branch block, valvular disease, and cardiomyopathy greatly reduces the accuracy of diagnosing an infarction from the initial QRS vector.

- The presence of an old infarction hinders the diagnosis of a new infarction in the same area. Serial ST-T changes may still be reliable witnesses.

- A small infarction or a new infarction in an area opposite from an old infarction may not result in a Q wave.

- There are many causes of ST-segment displacement other than myocardial infarction (Fig. 9–25). An ST vector pointing inferiorly, anteriorly, and laterally occurs with pericarditis; however, no QRS abnormalities occur. The ST vector associated with digitalis is oppositely directed to the mean QRS vector and may resemble subendocardial injury; the mean T vector as-

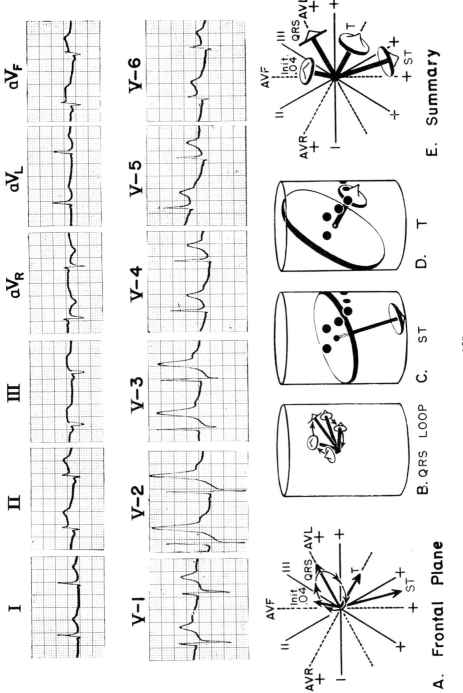

FIG. 9–10. The electrocardiogram of a patient, 55 years of age, showing an acute inferior-posterior myocardial infarction with lateral involvement.

(A) The frontal plane projection of the mean QRS, ST, T, and initial 0.04 s vectors are shown. The frontal plane projection of the spatial QRS loop is also shown. Note that the QRS complex is equiphasic in lead II and can be represented by a mean vector directed perpendicular to lead II. The T wave is smallest in lead III and can be represented by a mean vector directed perpendicular to lead III. The ST segment is markedly elevated in lead II, and slightly depressed in lead aV_L. This ST-segment displacement can be represented by a mean vector directed just to the right of the positive limb of lead II. The initial 0.04 s of the QRS loop is resultantly negative in lead III and aV_F and is positive in lead aV_R. A mean vector representing the forces generated during the initial 0.04 s of the QRS cycle will be directed just to the right of the negative limb of lead III. The QRS loop travels in a clockwise manner.

(B) The spatial QRS loop is shown. The initial portion of the loop, represented by the first vector, is directed slightly to the right and anteriorly; the second portion of the loop, represented by the second vector, is directed slightly to the left and anteriorly; and the third portion of the loop, represented by the third vector, is directed to the left and is flush with the frontal plane. The subsequent portions of the loop are directed to the left and posteriorly.

(C) The mean ST vector is rotated approximately 30° posteriorly because the transitional ST pathway passes between electrode positions V_3 and V_4.

(D) The mean T vector is rotated approximately 30° anteriorly because all of the precordial leads record tall, upright T waves.

(E) Final summary figure showing the spatial arrangement of the vectors. The mean spatial initial 0.04 s vector is located abnormally to the left of the horizontally directed mean QRS vector and indicates an inferior infarction. The mean ST vector is directed downward, to the left, and slightly posteriorly toward the area of inferior and lateral epicardial injury. The mean T vector is in a normal position but has tremendous magnitude. This "hyperacute" T wave indicates generalized subendocardial ischemia. This finding occurs transiently at the onset of myocardial infarction; later the mean T vector will be directed away from the area of epicardial ischemia surrounding the infarct.

sociated with digitalis is usually small and normally directed and the QT interval is short. The ST vector, occasionally seen in the normal person, in patients with left ventricular hypertrophy, and in patients with left bundle branch block, is usually relatively parallel with the mean T vector. This is quite different from the ST-T vector relationship of myocardial infarction. A mean QRS vector directed opposite to the mean QRS vector can be seen with angina pectoris or tachycardia, after exercise or arrhythmia, following a pulmonary embolus, or with hyperventilation or standing. An interpretation of the etiology should be made with extreme caution unless the clinical details are known.

Extent of the Infarction

At autopsy a myocardial infarction may be considered to be subendocardial, epicardial, or transmural de-

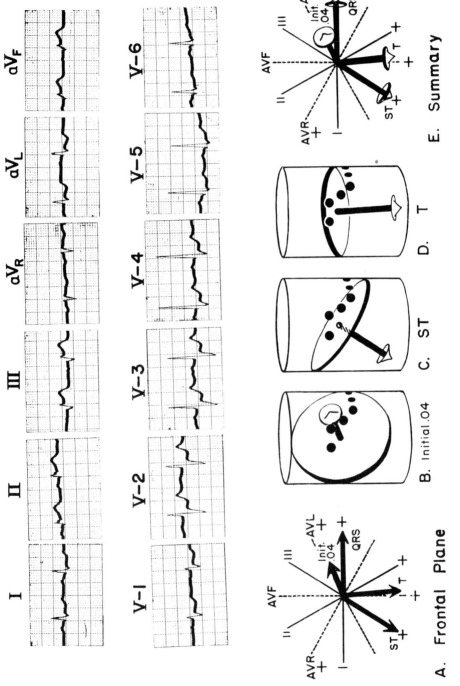

FIG. 9–11. The electrocardiogram of a patient, 62 years of age, showing an acute inferior-posterior myocardial infarction.

(A) The frontal plane projection of the mean QRS, ST, T, and initial 0.04 s vectors. The mean QRS vector is directed perpendicular to lead aV_F because the QRS complex is resultantly zero in lead aV_F. The ST-segment displacement is greatest in lead III and least in lead aV_R and can be represented by a mean vector directed parallel with the positive limb of lead III. The mean T vector is directed just to the left of the positive limb of lead aV_F because the T wave is slightly positive in lead I and large and positive in lead aV_F. The initial 0.04 s of the QRS complex is negative in lead III and aV_F and is resultantly slightly positive in lead II. The initial 0.04 s of the QRS cycle can be represented by a mean vector directed relatively perpendicular to lead II, but located so that a small positive quantity will be projected on lead II.

(B). (C). (D). The mean spatial initial 0.04 s vector is rotated approximately 80° anteriorly because the initial 0.04 s of the QRS complex is resultantly positive in V_1, V_2, V_3, and V_4. (The Q wave in V_5 is 0.02 s in duration and the transitional pathway for the initial 0.04 s vector lies near V_6.) The mean spatial ST vector is rotated posteriorly since the ST segment is depressed in all the precordial leads. The mean spatial T vector is tilted at least 15° anteriorly since all the precordial leads record upright T waves.

(E) The mean spatial initial 0.04s vector is abnormal in position because it is located too far to the left of the horizontally directed mean spatial QRS vector. The mean spatial ST vector is directed toward the area of inferior and posterior epicardial injury, and the mean spatial initial 0.04 s vector is directed away from the area of posterior myocardial necrosis. The infarction is clinically only 3 h old and the mean T vector has not yet rotated away from the ischemia surrounding an area of necrosis.

pending on its location and extent within the thickness of the myocardial wall. The electrocardiogram is often used to predict the underlying pathology—a new Q wave implies transmural involvement while serial ST-T changes alone indicate a nontransmural (epicardial or subendocardial) infarction. Although the presence of an abnormal Q wave does correlate, in general, with a loss of myocardium exceeding 50 percent of the ventricular thickness, there are flaws to this concept. Permanent Q waves may form when the infarction is only subendocardial; Q waves may be absent with a proven transmural infarction. Finally, Q waves may also appear transiently with intense myocardial ischemia.

Site of the Infarction

The electrocardiogram furnishes a fairly accurate anatomic localization of a myocardial infarction, though the extent of the damage is often more widespread than the electrocardiogram might predict. The apical, posterior, and lateral areas of the left ventricle, both atria, and the right ventricle are poorly represented by the electrocardiogram. Infarctions in these areas are often electrocardiographically "silent." The anterior, septal, and inferior walls are more adequately sampled, and infarctions in these areas are more easily recognized. The various directions of the mean spatial initial

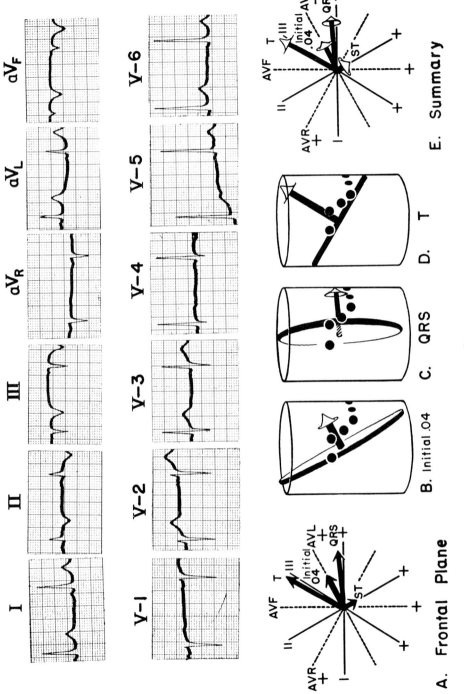

FIG. 9–12. The electrocardiogram of a patient, 50 years of age, showing an old inferior myocardial infarction.

(A) The mean initial 0.04 s vector is resultantly zero in lead II and is therefore perpendicular to lead II. It is drawn in the direction indicated because deep Q waves are present in leads III and aV_F. The QRS complex is largest and positive in lead I and slightly negative in lead aV_F and can be represented by a mean vector located just to the left of the positive limb of lead aV_F. The T wave is just barely positive in lead aV_R and is largest and negative in lead III. Accordingly, the T waves can be represented by a mean vector directed just to the right of the negative limb of lead III.

(B), (C), (D) The mean spatial initial 0.04 s vector is tilted 10° anteriorly because initial R waves of 0.04 s duration are found in leads V_2, V_3, V_4, V_5, and V_6. The mean QRS vector is tilted 20° posteriorly because the transitional pathway passes between V_2 and V_3. The mean T vector is flush with the frontal plane. Note how the T waves are low and upright in leads V_1 and V_4 but large and upright in leads V_2, V_3, V_5, and V_6. When the mean T vector is located as indicated, it is possible for the electrodes located in the V_1 and V_4 positions to record near the transitional pathway produced by the T wave.

(E) The mean spatial initial 0.04 s and T vectors are abnormally directed to the left of the horizontally directed mean QRS vector. These vectors are directed away from the inferior surface of the left ventricle. Since the infarction in this case is 4 months old, the ST vector is quite small.

0.04 s vector caused by an infarction in different locations of the left ventricle are illustrated by Figs. 9–2 to 9–24. Part A of each figure indicates the location of the myocardial infarction. A mean initial 0.04 s vector is drawn opposite to the infarcted area to indicate the direction of unopposed ventricular forces. A myocardial infarction is bordered by an injured area as well as an ischemic zone, as illustrated in the last four figures. Part B of each figure shows the mean spatial initial 0.04 s vector transposed to the center of the hexaxial reference system. From this diagram the projection of the vector on the frontal leads can be visualized. Part C of each diagram illustrates the position of the spatial 0.04 s vector in a cylindrical replica of the chest. The projection of this vector on the precordial leads can be seen. The following correlations have been made between the electrocardiographic leads and the underlying cardiac anatomy:

Anterior Infarction (*Figs. 9–1, 9–7, 9–8, 9–16, 9–18 to 9–23*)

The mean initial 0.04 s vector will be directed abnormally posteriorly. A decrease in the initial r wave or a Q wave is seen in the precordial leads. Frontal plane leads are usually unchanged. Since there are many causes of decreased or absent anterior forces—age, sex, left ventricular hypertrophy, lung disease, obesity, incorrect precordial lead placement—the diagnosis of an old anterior myocardial infarction should be made with caution. A particular problem is a QS

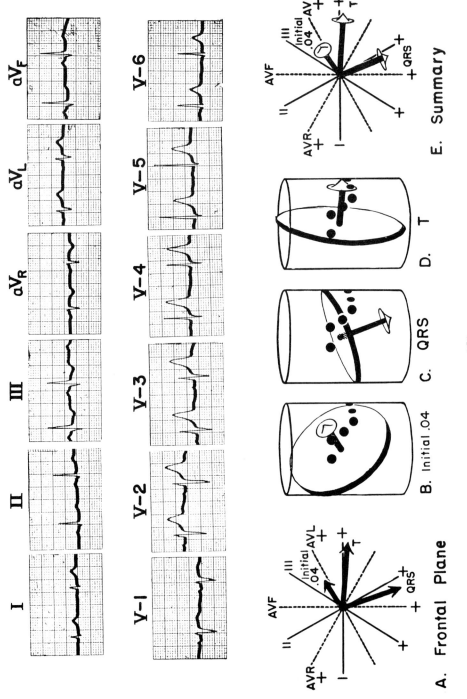

FIG. 9–13. The electrocardiogram of a patient, 49 years of age, showing an old inferior myocardial infarction with only QRS changes.

(A) The first 0.04 s of the QRS complexes is positive in lead I and negative in lead II and largest and negative in lead III. This QRS abnormality can be represented by a mean vector directed relatively perpendicular to lead II. The mean QRS vector is slightly negative in lead aV_L and slightly positive in lead I and can be represented by a vector located slightly to the right of the positive limb of lead II. The T wave is largest in lead I and slightly positive in lead aV_F and can be represented by a mean vector directed relatively parallel with lead I but directed so that a small positive quantity will be projected on lead aV_F.

(B), (C), (D) The initial 0.04 s of the QRS complexes is large and positive in leads V_1, V_2, V_3, V_4, and V_5 and approaches resultant zero at V_6. The mean initial 0.04 s vector must be rotated approximately 75° anteriorly to produce such findings in the precordial leads. The mean spatial QRS vector is rotated 20° posteriorly because the transitional pathway passes through electrode position V_3. The mean spatial T vector is rotated 15° anteriorly because all the precordial T waves are upright, V_1 being the smallest.

(E) The mean spatial initial 0.04 s vector is directed to the left of a vertically directed mean QRS vector. The spatial QRS-T angle is approximately 65°. The only definite abnormality is that of the position of the mean initial 0.04 s vector. This patient had a clinical history and electrocardiographic evidence of an inferior myocardial infarction 15 years prior to the above tracing. At times it is extremely difficult to determine when an old inferior infarction is present. If the 0.04 s vector is located far enough to the left to produce a Q wave in leads II, III, and aV_F—the latter of 0.04 s duration—and the mean QRS vector is in a vertical position, then inferior myocardial infarction is likely. (See QRS loop in Fig. 9-24A.)

Inferior (Diaphragmatic) Infarction (Figs. 9–1 to 9–3, 9–10 to 9–15)

The mean initial 0.04 s QRS vector is directed superiorly and leftward toward the shoulder and away from the inferior wall. Abnormal Q waves will be recorded in leads II, III, and aV_F while an R wave will be present in leads I and aV_L. At times an abnormal Q wave will be present in only one or two of the three inferior leads. Lead aV_F then provides the most specific evidence of inferior infarction. Because normal q waves 0.02 s in duration can be recorded in these inferior leads, particularly in normal young people with a vertical mean configuration in V_1 to V_2, which may be within normal limits, or an apparent decrease or absent r wave in V_1 to V_3 which is miraculously present on the next tracing. Acutely, ST-segment elevation and hyperacute T waves may be seen in the precordial leads. Serial evolutionary changes confirm the diagnosis. The close proximity of leads V_1 to V_4 makes precise electrocardiographic-anatomic correlations fairly inaccurate; however, anterior wall infarctions are often partitioned into septal (V_1, V_2), anteroseptal (V_1 to V_4), anterior (V_3, V_4), anterolateral (I, aV_L, V_3 to V_6), and extensive anterior (I, V_1 to V_6) locations.

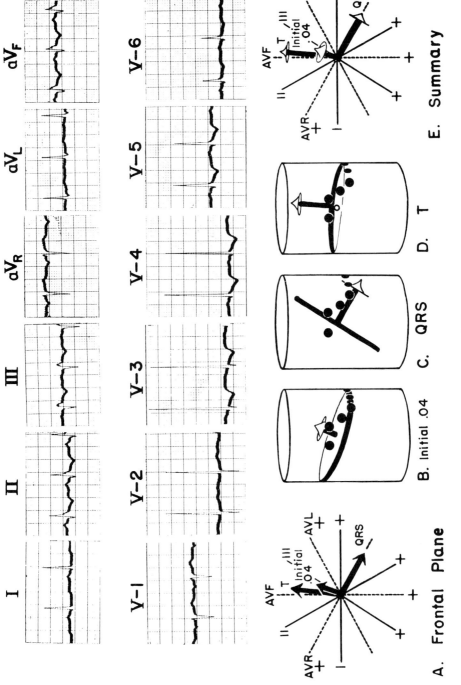

FIG. 9-14. The electrocardiogram of a patient, 34 years of age, showing an old inferior myocardial infarction.

(A) The frontal plane projection of the mean QRS, T, and initial 0.04 s vectors. The initial 0.04 s of the QRS complex is resultantly negative in leads III and aV_F and resultantly slightly negative in lead II and resultantly slightly positive in lead aV_R. These initial forces can be represented by a mean vector directed relatively parallel with lead III but located so that a small positive quantity will be projected on lead aV_R. The QRS complex is resultantly zero in lead III and can be represented by a vector perpendicular to lead III. The T waves are large and negative in leads II and III and slightly positive in lead I. Such T waves can be represented by a mean vector directed relatively parallel with the negative limb of lead aV_F but located so that a small positive quantity will be projected on lead I.

(B), (C), (D) The mean spatial initial 0.04 s vector is directed approximately 15° anteriorly because V_1, V_2, and V_3 are resultantly positive during the first 0.04 s of the QRS cycle and leads V_4, V_5, and V_6 record from the transitional pathway for they are negative during the first 0.02 s and positive during the next 0.02 s. The mean QRS vector is flush with the frontal plane since V_1 records a resultantly negative deflection and V_2 records a resultantly positive deflection. The mean spatial T vector is rotated 5° posteriorly since the T waves are upright in V_1 and V_2 and negative in V_3, V_4, V_5, and V_6.

(E) The mean spatial initial 0.04 s and T vectors are directed abnormally to the left of the mean spatial QRS vector. The QRS-T angle is approximately 115°. The 0.04 s and T vectors are directed away from the inferior and posterior surface of the left ventricle. The magnitude of the QRS complex in V_3 is suggestive but not diagnostic of left ventricular hypertrophy.

QRS vector as well as patients with lung disease and left ventricular hypertrophy, the diagnosis of an old inferior infarction can be difficult to make. Acutely, the ST vector of inferior infarction points inferiorly and rightward toward lead III, which usually shows the greatest degree of ST-segment elevation. Simultaneous ST-segment depression may be present in the mid-precordial leads. This anterior ST-segment depression has previously been considered to be due to reciprocal changes from an inferior-posterior orientation of the ST vector. There is some evidence that this ST-segment depression may also indicate a compromised blood flow to the anterior subendocardial or posterolateral wall. If the evidence of infarction involves leads II, III, aV_F, aV_L, V_5, and V_6, the infarction is said to involve the inferolateral area of the heart. Pathologically, inferior infarctions often involve the lateral and posterior wall and the right ventricle, even when this is not apparent on the electrocardiogram.

Posterior (True Posterior) Infarction (*Figs. 9-1, 9-3, 9-4, 9-10, 9-11*)

The mean initial 0.04 s vector is directed anteriorly toward V_1. An RV_1 to V_2 duration $\geq$ 0.04 s or an R/S ratio in $V_1 \geq 1$, in the absence of right ventricular hypertrophy, Wolff-Parkinson-White syndrome, or right bundle branch block, is suggestive of a posterior infarction. Acutely, the ST vector will point away from V_1 and V_2, causing ST-segment depression in those leads. Infarction of the posterobasilar wall is often as-

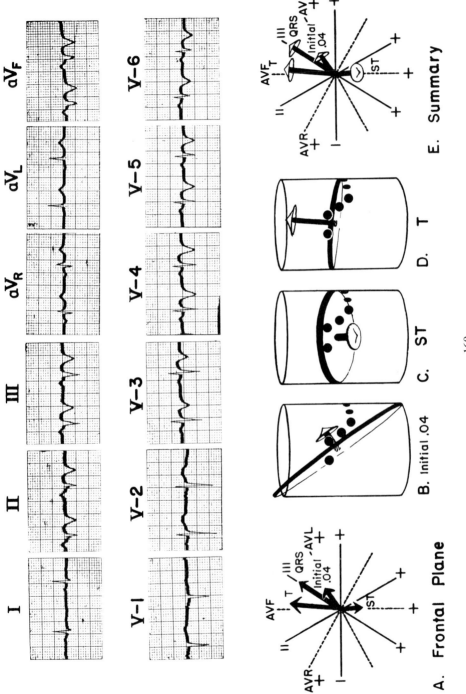

FIG. 9–15. The electrocardiogram of a patient, 53 years of age, recorded 11 days after an acute inferior infarction.

(A) The QRS complex is largest and negative in lead III and resultantly zero in lead aV$_R$. QRS complexes with these characteristics can be represented by a mean vector parallel to the negative limb of lead III. The first 0.04 s of the QRS complex is deeply negative in lead III and slightly negative in lead II and can be represented by a mean vector directed relatively parallel with the positive limb of lead aV$_L$, but directed so that a small negative quantity will be projected on lead II. The T waves are deeply inverted in leads II, III, and aV$_F$ and slightly positive in lead I. Such T waves can be represented by a mean vector directed relatively parallel with the negative limb of lead aV$_F$ but directed so that a small positive quantity will be projected on leads II and III and isoelectric in lead I and can be represented by a mean vector directed perpendicular to lead I.

(B), (C), (D) The mean initial 0.04 s spatial vector is approximately flush with the frontal plane because the initial forces are negative in lead V$_1$ and positive in leads V$_2$, V$_3$, V$_4$, V$_5$, and V$_6$. The mean spatial ST vector is rotated at least 15° anteriorly because the ST segment is slightly elevated in all the precordial leads. The mean T vector is rotated about 5° posteriorly because the T waves are positive in leads V$_1$ and V$_2$ and negative in leads V$_3$, V$_4$, V$_5$, V$_6$.

(E) Final summary figure illustrating the spatial arrangements of the vectors. The mean initial 0.04 s vector has a normal relationship with the mean QRS vector, but the irregularity of the initial portion of the QRS loop is suggestive of infarction. (Note notching of initial 0.04 s portion of QRS in lead II.) In this case many of the inferior QRS forces have been destroyed, thereby altering the mean QRS so that marked left axis deviation results. The mean T vector is located abnormally to the left of the mean QRS vector and is directed away from the inferior, anterior, and apical surfaces of the left ventricle. The mean QRS-T angle is only 25°. The inverted T waves in leads V$_4$, V$_5$, and V$_6$ are interesting, and it should be pointed out that a large zone of anterolateral ischemia surrounding a single infarction can produce such a finding and that one need not postulate two infarctions. The mean spatial ST vector is directed toward an area of inferior and anterior injury.

sociated with an inferior infarction since these areas share a right coronary blood supply in most hearts. Therefore, signs of inferior infarction will often accompany posterior infarction. The presence of an old inferior infarction will often help decide if a broad RV$_1$ is due to an old posterior infarction. Because the terms "inferior" and "posterior" have sometimes been used interchangeably, an infarction of the posterobasilar wall is often called a *true posterior infarction* to prevent confusion. A combination of an abnormally wide R wave in V$_1$ and an abnormal Q wave in lateral leads I, aV$_L$, or V$_6$ may properly be called a posterolateral infarction.

Apical Infarction (*Figs. 9–1, 9–5, 9–23*)

An apical infarction may occur with either an inferior or anterior infarction. Its presence cannot usually be detected from the electrocardiogram because infarction in this area does not cause a loss of the myocardium that generates initial forces. In addition, there is relatively little ventricular muscle diametrically opposite to the cardiac apex to create an abnormal vector.

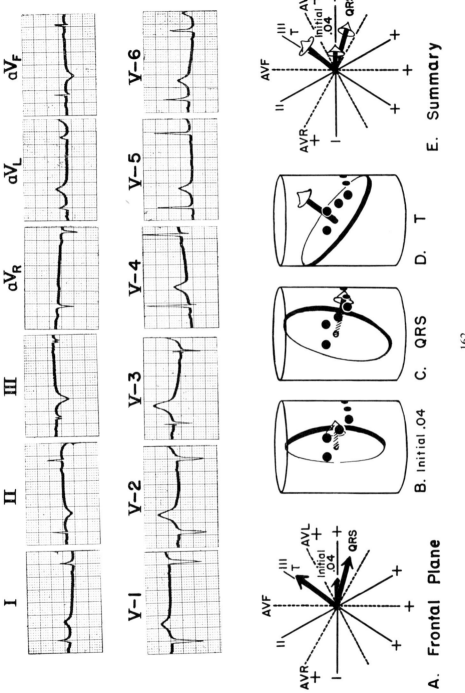

FIG. 9–16. The electrocardiogram of a patient, 74 years old, showing an anteroseptal infarction and inferior ischemia.

(A) The first 0.04 s of the QRS cycle is negative in lead III and isoelectric in lead aV_F. The forces generated during the initial 0.04 s of the QRS cycle can be represented by a mean vector directed perpendicular to lead aV_F and directed toward the positive pole of lead I. The QRS complex is largest in lead I and slightly negative in lead III and positive in lead aV_F. Such complexes can be represented by a mean vector located between a perpendicular to lead III and a perpendicular to lead aV_F. The T wave is large and negative in lead III and slightly negative in lead aV_R. Such T waves can be represented by a mean vector directed relatively parallel with the negative limb of lead III but directed so that a small negative quantity will be projected on lead aV_R.

(B), (C), (D) The mean initial 0.04 s vector is rotated posteriorly approximately 30° because the transitional pathway passes through electrode position V_3. It should be noted that the R wave is absent in V_1 and V_2. There is a Q wave of 0.02 s duration in V_3 and an R wave for the second 0.02 s in lead V_3. This indicates that the first 0.02 s forces are directed more posteriorly than the next 0.02 s forces. This finding is characteristic of anteroseptal infarction. The mean QRS vector must be rotated 40° posteriorly because the transitional pathway passes between V_3 and V_4. The mean T vector is rotated an unknown number of degrees anteriorly since all precordial T deflections are upright.

(E) The mean spatial initial 0.04 s vector is directed in a normal manner when viewed in the frontal plane. The initial forces are abnormal when viewed in space because the initial 0.02 s forces are directed more posteriorly than the next 0.02 s forces, indicating anteroseptal infarction. The mean T vector is rotated abnormally to the left and anteriorly and is directed away from an area of posterior and inferior myocardial ischemia. (See QRS loop in Fig. 9–24B.)

The finding of an inferoanterior ST vector producing ST-segment elevation in leads II, III, aV_F, V_3, and V_4, or the simultaneous development of abnormal Q waves in the same leads can be used to suggest the diagnosis.

Subendocardial Infarction *(Fig. 9–17)*

The ST vector points away from the injured subendocardial area. New ST-segment depression lasting more than 24 h is seen in leads representing the infarcted area. T-wave inversion may occur. Q waves do not usually develop unless the infarction extends to the epicardium.

Subepicardial Infarction

The ST vector points toward the injured area. New ST-segment elevation is present in leads corresponding to the area and Q waves do not occur.

Right Ventricular Infarction

An infarction of the right ventricle usually, if not always, occurs in association with inferior or posterior infarction. It can be suggested only when ST-segment elevation is seen in leads V_4R, V_1, or V_1 to V_2, usually in conjunction with typical findings of an inferior or posterior infarction.

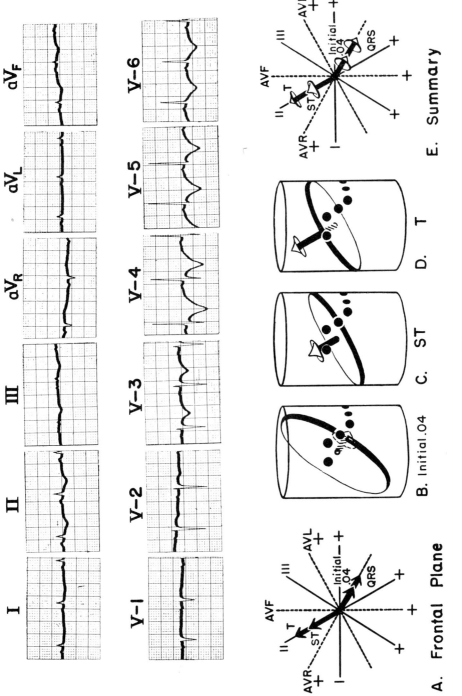

FIG. 9-17. The electrocardiogram of a patient, 71 years of age, with a myocardial infarction showing ST-T wave changes.

(A) The frontal plane projection of the mean QRS, ST, T, and initial 0.04 s vectors. The QRS complex is resultantly zero in lead III and positive in leads I and II. Accordingly, the mean QRS vector is directed perpendicular to lead III. The T wave is isoelectric in lead aV_L and negative in leads II and III and can be represented by a mean vector directed parallel with the negative limb of lead II. The ST-segment displacement is slight but is greatest and negative in lead II and least in lead aV_L and can be represented by a mean vector directed parallel with the negative limb of lead II. The initial 0.04 s of the QRS cycle is positive in leads I, II, aV_L, and aV_F and negative in lead aV_R. This portion of the QRS complex is isoelectric in lead III and can be represented by a mean vector directed perpendicular to lead III. (When the mean initial 0.04 s vector is difficult to plot, one is often obliged simply to identify the fact that the initial forces of the QRS cycle are normally directed.)

(B), (C), (D) The mean spatial initial 0.04 s vector is rotated posteriorly approximately 20° because the transitional pathway passes through V_3. There is a small initial R wave in leads V_1 and V_2 of 0.01 to 0.02 s duration, but the resultant of the forces during the first 0.04 s is negative in leads V_1 and V_2. The mean ST vector is rotated approximately 20° anteriorly since the ST segment is slightly elevated in V_1 and V_2 and depressed in V_4, V_5, and V_6. The mean T vector is rotated approximately 10° posteriorly because the T wave is flat in V_1 and negative in V_2, V_3, V_4, V_5, and V_6.

(E) Final summary figure illustrating the spatial arrangement of the vectors. The principal abnormality is that of the direction of the T vector. The QRS-T angle is 150° and the T vector is quite large. The T vector is directed away from the apical region of the left ventricle and probably represents severe ischemia of that region. Although this is the only definite abnormality, one can usually be sure that a certain amount of cell death has occurred when T waves with this magnitude are seen in a patient with a clinical history compatible with a myocardial infarction.

Atrial Infarction

Because the forces of atrial repolarization are very small, atrial infarction is rarely diagnosed. The diagnosis can be suggested when the PR segment (ST_a) is deviated producing PR-segment elevation or depression depending on the lead and the location of the infarction. This is usually, but not always, associated with evidence of acute ventricular infarction. Similar PR-segment shift can also be observed in pericarditis, early repolarization, and some normal tracings, and its significance will depend on clinical correlations and supportive evidence of acute ventricular infarction. The P wave may become notched or widened. Atrial arrhythmias frequently occur.

Estimating the Age of the Infarction

The age of an acute myocardial infarction is roughly estimated by analyzing the stage of the ST-T evolution. Hyperacute T waves are often the first sign of an epicardial or transmural infarction, but may not be seen at the time of presentation. A new, persistent ST vector is the major evidence for an acute infarction; the greater the displacement above or below the isoelectric line,

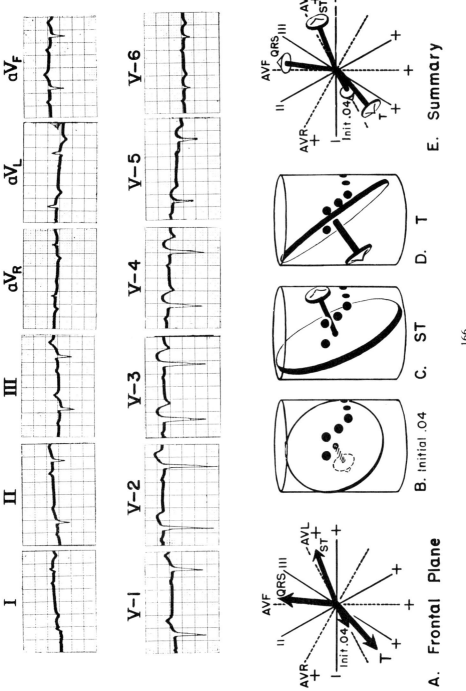

FIG. 9–18. The electrocardiogram of a patient, 48 years of age, showing an extensive anterior myocardial infarction with septal and lateral involvement.

(A) The QRS complexes are resultantly negative in leads II and III and slightly positive in lead I and can be represented by a mean vector directed relatively parallel with the negative limb of lead aV_F but directed so that a small positive quantity will be projected on lead I. The initial 0.04 s portion of the QRS cycle is negative in leads I and aV_L and positive in lead III and can be represented by a small mean vector directed perpendicular to lead II. The T wave is large and positive in lead III and slightly positive in lead aV_R and can be represented by a mean vector directed just to the right of the positive limb of lead III. The ST segment is elevated in leads I, II, and aV_L and slightly depressed in leads III, aV_R, and aV_F. Accordingly, the mean ST vector is directed relatively parallel with the positive limb of aV_L but directed so that a small positive quantity will be projected on lead II.

(B), (C), (D) The mean initial 0.04 s vector is rotated markedly posteriorly and deviated from the frontal plane approximately 80° because the initial 0.04 s is negative in all the precordial leads. The mean ST vector is rotated at least 45° anteriorly because the ST segment is elevated in all the precordial leads but is less elevated in V_1 and V_6. The mean T vector is approximately flush with the frontal plane because the T wave is upright in lead V_1 and inverted in leads V_2, V_3, V_4, V_5, and V_6.

(E) Final summary figure illustrating the spatial arrangement of the vectors. The mean spatial initial 0.04 s vector is located abnormally to the right and is posteriorly directed. This vector is directed away from a large area of anterior infarction. The mean ST vector is directed toward an area of epicardial injury located in the anterior and lateral portion of the left ventricle. The mean T vector is rotated away from an area of anterior and lateral epicardial ischemia. It is interesting to note that the tracing was made three months after the acute infarction and that the abnormal ST vector is still present, suggesting the likelihood of a ventricular aneurysm at the site of infarction.

the more likely the injury is very recent. Unless reinfarction or pericarditis intervenes, the ST-segment deviation often decreases during the first 24 to 48 h, though usually it remains abnormal for several days to several weeks. A ventricular aneurysm should be suspected when the ST segment remains elevated for more than 2 weeks, particularly when abnormal Q waves reside in the same leads as the ST-segment elevation. As the ST-segment elevation regresses, the T-wave vector rotates away from the infarcted area. T-wave inversion appears within one to several days following the infarction and may last indefinitely or gradually return to normal over a period of days to months. Q waves may develop during the same time frame but can appear in the first few hours. Although a fresh myocardial infarction is relatively simple to diagnose, it may be quite difficult to tell whether the infarction is recent or old after several days. Obviously the age of the infarction is best determined by correlating the clinical history with the electrocardiographic changes.

The diagnostic changes of an infarction may gradually revert to a normal tracing in a small percentage of patients with abnormal Q waves and about a third of patients with only ST-T changes. The return to nor-

| I | II | III | aV$_R$ | aV$_L$ | aV$_F$ |

| V-1 | V-2 | V-3 | V-4 | V-5 | V-6 |

A. Frontal Plane

B. Initial .04

C. ST

D. T

E. Summary

FIG. 9–19. The electrocardiogram of a patient, 56 years of age, showing a large anteroseptal and lateral myocardial infarction.

(A) The QRS complex is large and negative in lead II and resultantly slightly positive in lead aV_R. QRS complexes with these characteristics can be represented by a mean QRS vector directed relatively parallel with the negative limb of lead III but directed so that a small positive quantity will be projected on lead aV_R. The first 0.04 s of the QRS loop is resultantly zero in lead aV_R, positive in lead III, and negative in lead aV_L and can be represented by a mean vector directed perpendicular to lead aV_R. The ST segment is depressed in leads I and II and elevated in lead aV_R and can be represented by a mean vector directed just to the right of the negative limb of lead aV_F. The mean T vector is directed perpendicular to lead II because the T wave is resultantly zero in lead II.

(B), (C), (D) The mean spatial initial 0.04 s vector is rotated 80° posteriorly because the initial 0.04 s of the QRS complex is negative in V_1, V_2, V_3, V_4, and V_5 and is resultantly zero in V_6. The mean ST vector is rotated approximately 20° anteriorly because the ST segment is elevated in V_1, V_2, and V_3, and is depressed in V_4, V_5, and V_6. The mean T vector is flush with the frontal plane because the transitional pathway passes between V_1 and V_2.

(E) Final summary figure illustrating the spatial arrangement of the vectors. The mean initial 0.04 s vector is directed abnormally posteriorly. It is directed away from the anterior surface of the left ventricle. The mean T vector is located abnormally to the right and is directed away from an extensive area of anterolateral ischemia.

mal is completed by 18 to 24 months in the majority of these patients. Other patients are left with residual, nondiagnostic q waves, reduced R-wave amplitude, or ST-T changes that may raise the possibility of an old infarction.

Myocardial Ischemia (Fig. 9–25)

Myocardial ischemia may induce no apparent alteration of the electrocardiogram, or it may alter the direction or magnitude of the ST and T vector depending on the site and the severity of the ischemia. Intense transmural ischemia may produce ST-segment elevation in leads overlying the ischemic area. This is usually due to coronary artery spasm, which may occur with or without fixed atherosclerotic obstruction, and resolves quickly as the blood flow is restored. With subendocardial ischemia, the ST vector points away from the ischemic region and transient ST-segment depression results. In general, the mean T-wave vector tends to be directed away from epicardial ischemia and to be inverted in leads overlying the area. When the T vector is directed away from an area of ischemia located in the left ventricle, the QRS-T angle may be more than 90°. If there is ischemia of the inferior surface, the T vector will tend to rotate leftward and superiorly so that the T wave will be inverted in leads II, III, and aV_F. Under these circumstances, the mean T vector is almost always located to the left of the mean QRS vector and the QRS-T angle may be abnormally wide. When the ischemia is anterolateral in

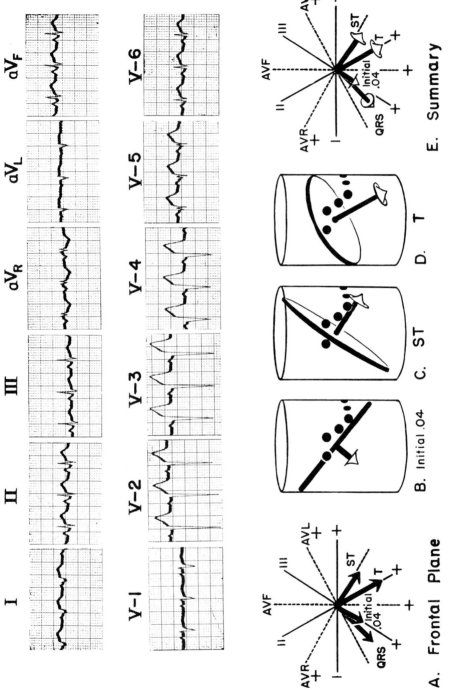

FIG. 9–20. The electrocardiogram of a patient, 59 years of age, showing a recent anterior and lateral myocardial infarction.

(A) The QRS complex is negative in lead I and is resultantly slightly positive in leads II and aV$_R$. QRS complexes with these characteristics can be represented by a mean vector directed slightly to the right of the positive limb of lead III. The 0.04 s of the QRS loop is resultantly zero in lead aV$_R$ and can be represented by a mean vector directed perpendicular to that lead. The ST segment is greatly elevated in leads I and II and is isoelectric in lead III and can be represented by a mean vector directed perpendicular to lead III. The T wave is large and positive in lead II and is resultantly zero in lead aV$_L$, and can be represented by a mean vector directed parallel to the positive limb of lead II.

(B), (C), (D) The mean initial 0.04 s vector is flush with the frontal plane since the initial 0.04 s of the QRS complex is resultantly zero in lead V$_1$. Abnormal Q waves are recorded in Leads V$_2$, V$_3$, V$_4$, V$_5$, and V$_6$. The mean ST vector is rotated approximately 10° anteriorly because the transitional pathway passes near electrode position V$_1$. ST-segment elevations of the magnitude illustrated almost always indicate epicardial injury or severe transmural ischemia due to coronary artery spasm. The mean T vector is rotated 15° or more anteriorly because the T waves are upright in all the precordial leads.

(E) Final summary figure illustrating the spatial arrangement of the vectors. The mean initial 0.04 s vector is directed abnormally to the right as is the entire QRS loop. The 0.04 s vector is directed away from an area of anterolateral myocardial necrosis. The ST vector is directed toward an area of anterolateral epicardial injury. It is not uncommon for the mean T vector to be quite large and normally directed during the early hours of myocardial infarction. In subsequent electrocardiograms in this patient the T vector became nearly parallel to the 0.04 s vector. The ST vector and the 0.04 s vector are not diametrically opposite in direction because the areas of necrosis and injury are not concentric.

location, the T vector is rotated to the right causing T-wave inversion in leads I and aV$_L$. Under these circumstances, the mean T vector is located to the right of the mean QRS vector, and the QRS-T angle may be abnormally wide. If the ischemia is located at the apex or involves the epicardial surface of the entire left ventricle, the T vector will point toward the right shoulder, causing T-wave inversion in leads I, II, III, aV$_L$, and aV$_F$ and producing a markedly abnormal QRS-T angle. If the ischemia involves the anterior portion of the left ventricle, the mean T vector may be directed abnormally posteriorly, and the T wave in V$_1$ to V$_3$ will become inverted. Although the T-wave inversion seen with ischemia or injury is often in the nonspecific category, a deep, symmetrical T-wave inversion or serial T-wave changes can be used to suggest an ischemic etiology. With subendocardial ischemia the T-wave vector may become larger but retain a fairly normal position.

An inverted U wave, seen best in the mid and left precordial leads on the resting or exercise electrocardiogram, is an occasional finding of myocardial ischemia or infarction, especially with left anterior descending coronary artery disease (Fig. 9–26). An inverted U wave can also occur with hypertension, aortic and mitral regurgitation, and left ventricular hypertrophy;

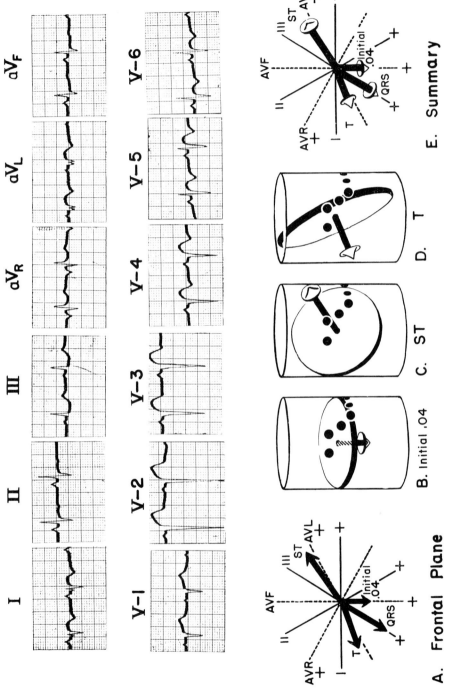

FIG. 9–21. The electrocardiogram of a patient, 58 years of age, showing an extensive anterolateral and septal myocardial infarction.

(A) The QRS complex is positive in lead III, resultantly slightly positive in lead II, and resultantly zero in lead aV_R and can be represented by a vector directed parallel with lead III. The initial 0.04 s of the QRS cycle is positive in leads II, III, and aV_F and negative in leads aV_R and aV_L, and resultantly zero in lead I. Accordingly, the mean initial 0.04 s vector is directed perpendicular to lead I. The ST-segment displacement is positive in leads I and aV_L, negative in leads III and aV_F, and slightly negative in lead II and can be represented by a mean vector located between the positive limb of lead aV_L and the negative limb of lead III. The T wave is large and negative in lead I, slightly negative in lead II, and slightly positive in lead aV_F and can be represented by a mean vector located just to the right of the negative limb of aV_L.

(B), (C), (D) The mean initial 0.04 s vector is rotated approximately 35° posteriorly because the transitional pathway passes through V_4. (Note that the QRS duration appears to be shorter in the deflection at V_4 than it is at V_3 and V_5, suggesting that the initial portion of V_4 deflection is almost isoelectric, which means that the vectors are perpendicular to the axis of this lead during this interval.) The mean ST vector is rotated approximately 80° anteriorly since all the precordial deflections have elevated ST segments. The mean T vector is rotated approximately 10° anteriorly since the T wave is upright in V_1 and V_2 and isoelectric in V_3 and inverted in V_4, V_5, and V_6.

(E) Final summary figure illustrating the spatial arrangement of the vectors. The mean initial 0.04 s vector is directed abnormally posteriorly and points away from the anteroseptal region of the left ventricle. The ST vector is directed toward the anterior region of epicardial injury. The mean T vector is directed away from an area of anterolateral ischemia. It is interesting to note that myocardial infarction can superficially resemble right ventricular hypertrophy. In this case there is right axis deviation and there is a deep S wave in V_5 and V_6. The mean initial 0.04 s and mean QRS vectors are directed posteriorly in this case rather than anteriorly as in right ventricular hypertrophy. A large abnormal ST vector having the direction shown above is not seen in right ventricular hypertrophy. (See QRS loop in Fig. 9–24C.)

in some elderly people with peripheral vascular disease; and, rarely, in the absence of apparent heart disease.

Electrocardiographic Mimics of Myocardial Infarction or Ischemia

- The presence of an abnormal Q wave, ST-segment deviation, or T-wave inversion does not certify that coronary artery disease is the cause. Abnormal Q waves may be seen when normal myocardium is replaced with fibrosis or a disease process, with alteration of forces due to ventricular hypertrophy, and with various conduction defects. Various causes of pseudoinfarct wave patterns are listed in Table 9–1.

- ST-segment elevation can be present normally in V_1 to V_3, with early repolarization in the mid-precordial and sometimes inferior leads, or be found in pericarditis, hyperkalemia, hypothermia, left bundle branch block, and left ventricular hypertrophy. Examples of various ST abnormalities are illustrated in Fig. 9–25.

- ST-segment depression is a frequent nonspecific find-

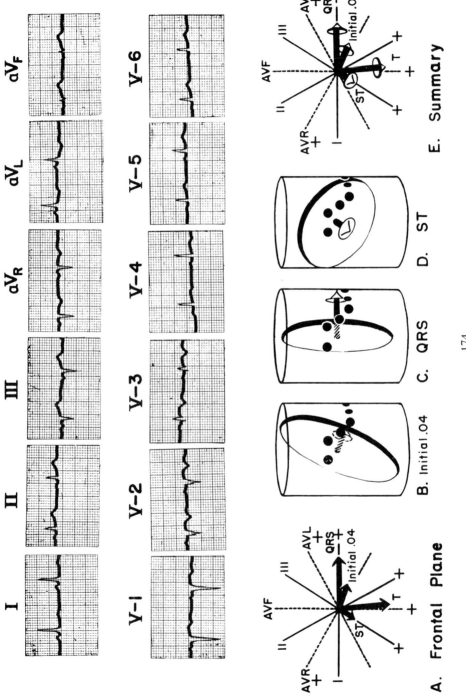

174

FIG. 9–22. The electrocardiogram of a patient, 62 years of age, showing an old anteroseptal infarction.

(A) The mean QRS vector is directed perpendicular to lead a V_F because the QRS is resultantly zero in lead aV_F. The initial 0.04 s of the QRS complex cycle is positive in leads I, II, aV_L, and aV_F and negative in lead III and can be represented by a mean vector directed between the negative limb of aV_R and the positive limb of lead I. There is very little ST-segment displacement but this interval appears elevated in lead III and slightly elevated in lead II. The ST-segment displacement can be represented by a mean vector directed parallel with the positive limb of lead III. (Actually, in such a case the ST segment should be depressed in lead I. When such small forces are studied the range of error is greater and one must be content with an approximate plot. The most accurate plot is accomplished by studying all the leads. For instance, in this tracing the ST segment appears isoelectric in lead I, but in such a case leads II and III would record equally positive displacements and the ST segment would be depressed in lead aV_R. In reality, however, the ST segment is not depressed in lead aV_R. Accordingly, the mean ST vector must be directed to the right of the positive limb of lead aV_F.) The mean T vector is directed just to the left of the positive limb of aV_F because the T wave is upright in leads II, III, and aV_F but is only slightly positive in lead I.

(B), (C), (D) The mean spatial initial 0.04 s vector is rotated 30° posteriorly because there is an initial negative deflection in V_1, V_2, and V_3 and an initial positive deflection of the QRS in V_4, V_5, and V_6. The mean QRS vector is rotated 20° posteriorly because the transitional pathway passes between V_2 and V_3. The mean ST vector is small and is rotated about 80° anteriorly because the ST segment is slightly elevated in V_1, V_2, V_3, V_4, and V_5.

(E) Final summary figure illustrating the spatial arrangement of the vectors. Note that the initial 0.04 s vector is directed posteriorly to the mean QRS vector and points away from the anteroseptal region of the left ventricle. Whenever the initial portion of the QRS loop is directed more posteriorly than the subsequent portion of the QRS loop, an area of infarction on the anterior surface of the heart is probably present. The ST vector is directed toward the anterior surface of the heart while the T vector is directed away from the anterior surface. (See QRS loop in Fig. 9–24D.)

ing. Left ventricular hypertrophy, right ventricular hypertrophy, digitalis, hyperkalemia, hypokalemia, hyperventilation, mitral valve prolapse, left bundle branch block, right bundle branch block, and preexcitation are some of the causes of ST-segment depression similar to that found in coronary disease.

• Numerous cardiac and systemic disorders, as well as physiologic states such as hyperventilation, emotion, exercise, and food ingestion, may lower the T-wave amplitude or cause a nonspecific T-wave inversion (Fig. 9–25). Since the T-wave abnormality of many different conditions, some serious and some benign, may be similar, other electrocardiographic and clinical data must be applied to try to explain the finding. For example, a T vector that produces an inverted T wave in V_1 to V_3, may be due to anterior ischemia from coronary artery disease, right ventricular strain from a pulmonary embolus, or a normal juvenile pattern.

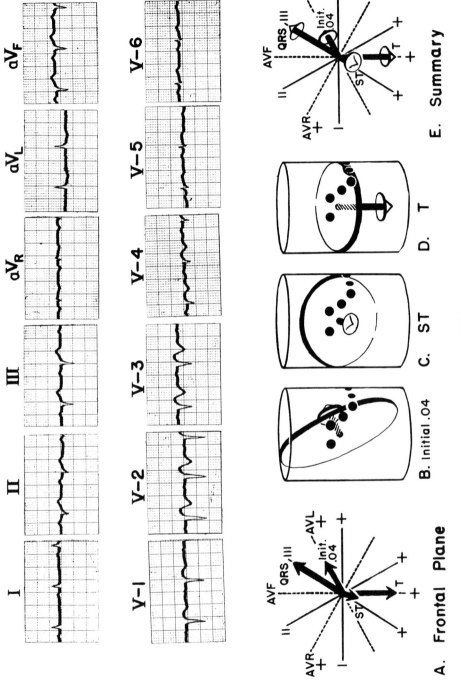

FIG. 9–23. The electrocardiogram of a patient, 70 years of age, showing an anteroseptal and inferior myocardial infarction.

(A) The mean QRS vector is directed parallel with the negative limb of lead III because the QRS complex is large and negative in lead III and resultantly zero in lead aV_R. The initial 0.04 s of the QRS complex is negative in leads III and aV_F and appears isoelectric in lead II and negative in lead aV_R. Accordingly, the mean initial 0.04 s vector is directed perpendicular to lead II. The mean ST vector is almost perpendicular to lead I and is extremely small when viewed in the frontal plane. The mean T vector is perpendicular to lead I because the T wave is isoelectric in that lead.

(B), (C). (D) The mean spatial initial 0.04 s vector is rotated approximately 40° posteriorly because there is an initial negative deflection of 0.04 s duration in leads V_1, V_2, and V_3 and an initial positive deflection in leads V_5 and V_6. (The initial 0.04 s appears resultantly zero in V_4.) The mean ST vector is rotated approximately 80° anteriorly since the ST segment is elevated in leads V_1, V_2, V_3, V_4, V_5. The mean T vector is rotated 45° posteriorly because the transitional pathway for the T wave passes between electrode positions V_4 and V_5.

(E) Final summary figure illustrating the spatial arrangement of the vectors. The mean initial 0.04 s vector is rotated to the left and abnormally posteriorly, pointing away from the anterior and inferior region of the left ventricle. The QS deflections in lead III and aV_F suggest an inferior myocardial infarction and the absent initial R waves in V_1, V_2, and V_3 suggest an anteroseptal infarction. One infarction involving the anterior wall and apex can produce such an electrocardiogram and one need not postulate two myocardial infarctions. The mean spatial ST vector is directed toward an area of anterior-inferior epicardial injury.

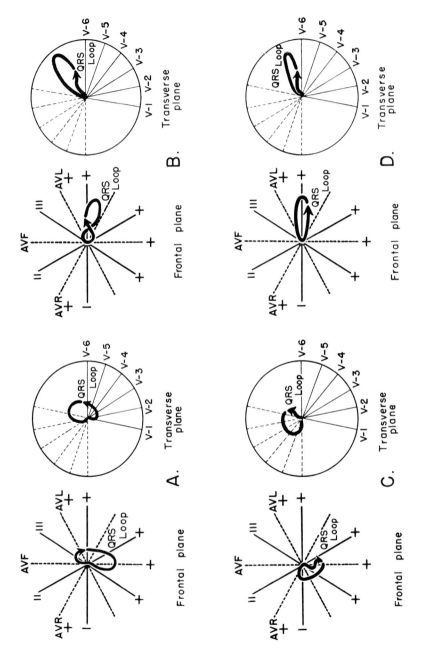

FIG. 9–24. The frontal and transverse plane QRS loops of several myocardial infarcts. One should recall that the QRS loop in the normal subject is narrow and elongate (Fig. 2–23). Normally the initial forces are anterior to and relatively parallel with the mean QRS vector. In the normal subject a line drawn through the termini of the instantaneous vectors passes in a smooth and orderly manner to encompass the mean spatial QRS vector, although one or another view of the loop may reveal a crisscrossed figure.

(A) The QRS loop of the electrocardiogram shown in Fig. 9–74. The frontal plane QRS loop is abnormal because the initial forces are directed too far to the left of the mean QRS, indicating an inferior myocardial dead zone. The transverse plane QRS loop is normal.

(B) The QRS loop of the electrocardiogram shown in Fig. 9–77. The QRS loop crosses itself when viewed in the frontal plane but such is frequently seen normally. The initial portion of the QRS loop is deformed as seen in the transverse plane and indicates an anteroseptal myocardial infarction.

(C) The QRS loop of the electrocardiogram shown in Fig. 9–82. The entire QRS loop is located abnormally to the right and markedly posteriorly and the initial portion of the loop is deformed. This type of loop indicates an extensive anterior myocardial infarction.

(D) The QRS loop of the electrocardiogram shown in Fig. 9–83. The frontal plane QRS loop is entirely normal. The initial portion of the QRS loop is deformed as seen in the transverse plane. This type of deformity is seen in anteroseptal infarction.

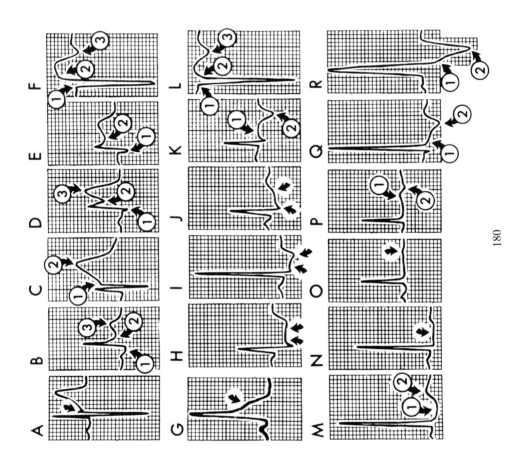

FIG. 9–25. ST-segment and T-wave changes. Arrows in each panel indicate the major features of each complex.

(A) Early repolarization (J-point elevation), normal variant.
(B) Acute pericarditis: (1) depressed T_a; (2) elevated ST; (3) normal T.
(C) Early acute myocardial infarction (AMI): (1) elevated ST; (2) tall, peaked T wave; steep angle between 1 and 2.
(D) AMI: (1) small Q wave; (2) elevated ST segment; (3) tall, peaked T wave with steep 2→3 angle.
(E) AMI: (1) pathologic Q wave; (2) elevated ST segment.
(F) AMI: (1) Q wave; (2) elevated ST segment; (3) terminal T-wave inversion.
(G) Angina pectoris (Prinzmetal variant) with ST elevation during pain.
(H), (I) Angina pectoris (usual form) with horizontal or downward sloping ST segment during pain or exercise.
(J) J-point depression with upsloping ST segment during exercise, normal response.
(K) Primary T-wave inversion (2) in ischemia or primary muscle disease.
(L) Myocardial infarction (healed): (1) pathologic Q; (2) ST returning to base line; (3) symmetrically inverted T wave.
(M) Digitalis effect: (1) downward coving of ST segment, merging into (2) an upright T wave.
(N–P) Nonspecific ST-segment and T-wave changes often seen in chronic ischemic heart disease.
(Q) Left ventricular hypertrophy ST-T pattern with (1) downsloping ST segment and (2) asymmetrically inverted (secondary) T wave.
(R) Downsloping ST segment merging into a deeply inverted T wave in ventricular conduction abnormality.

From R. J. Myerburg in Petersdorf et al. (eds.), Harrison's Principles of Internal Medicine, 10th ed., chapter 249, McGraw-Hill, New York, 1982.

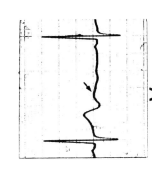

FIG. 9–26. Abnormal U waves. Tracings are from different patients. On the left is shown an inverted U wave (arrow) due to myocardial ischemia. An abnormally prominent U wave (arrow) from a patient with a stroke is shown on the right.

Table 9–1

Conditions That May Produce a Pseudoinfarction Pattern

Amyloidosis
Athletic heart
Chronic lung disease
Congestive cardiomyopathy
Dextrocardia
Friedreich's ataxia
Hyperkalemia
Hypertrophic nonobstructive cardiomyopathy
Hypertrophic obstructive cardiomyopathy
Intracranial hemorrhage
Left anterior fascicular block
Left bundle branch block
Left ventricular hypertrophy
Muscular dystrophy
Myocarditis
Pneumothorax
Primary and metastatic tumors to the heart
Pulmonary embolus
Right ventricular hypertrophy
Traumatic heart disease
Wolff-Parkinson-White syndrome

Chapter 10
Lung Disease

Chronic Obstructive Lung Disease *(Fig. 10–1)*

The electrocardiogram remains normal or is only minimally affected by mild to moderate lung disease. As the lung disease worsens, electrocardiographic changes may occur that reflect the more vertical position of the heart, the effect of the low diaphragm, the presence of hyperinflated lungs, and the development of cor pulmonale.

Electrocardiographic Criteria for Chronic Obstructive Lung Disease

An Enlarged P Vector Which Is Shifted Rightward, Inferiorly, and Anteriorly The normal frontal plane P vector lies near $+60°$, parallel to lead II. With chronic lung disease the P vector is $\geq +80°$, though rarely exceeding $+90°$ (Fig. 10–1). Though not always present, this rightward shift of the P-wave vector is the most sensitive finding for lung disease. In lead II and/or aV_F, the P wave may become tall and peaked, equaling or exceeding 2.5 mm; lead I shows an isoelectric or barely positive P wave. The P-wave deflection in V_1 may also be tall and pointed. At times the P wave in lead II may be broad and notched, suggesting a left atrial abnormality.

A Mean QRS Vector That Is Shifted Rightward in the Frontal Plane and Posteriorly in the Horizontal Plane Depending on the severity of the lung disease, the degree of right ventricular hypertrophy, and the

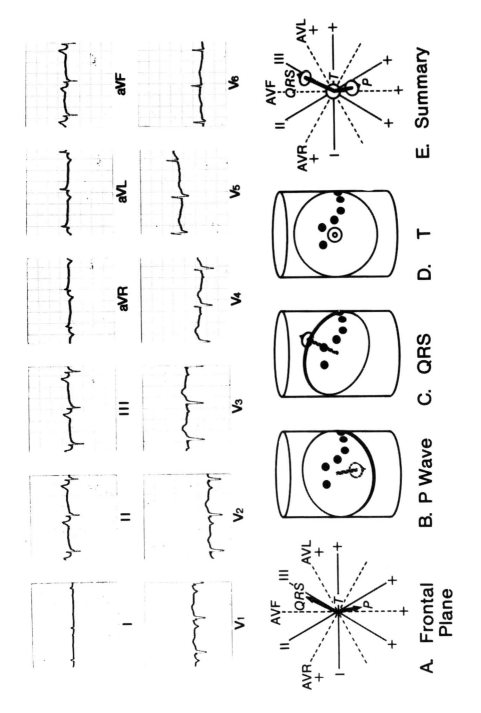

FIG. 10-1. Chronic obstructive lung disease. The tracing is from a 60-year-old man.

(A) Frontal plane projection of the mean P, QRS, and T vectors.

(B) The mean P wave vector is slightly positive in lead 1 and strongly positive in the inferior leads. The vector is therefore located just to the left of lead aV_F.

(C) The mean QRS vector is almost perpendicular to leads 1 and aV_R and is posteriorly directed with the transitional plane at approximately lead V_5. (Note that one QRS complex in lead V_5 is equiphasic while the other is upright.)

(D) The mean T vector must be perpendicular to the frontal plane since the voltage is virtually zero in all leads.

(E) Final summary figure showing the spatial arrangement of the vectors. Typical findings of lung disease include an apparent left axis deviation, a vertical P vector, peaked and broad P waves, low-voltage QRS complexes, and decreased amplitude of lead V_6.

position of the heart relative to the precordial leads, the mean QRS vector shifts rightward toward or beyond +90°, and a posterior rotation occurs so that the QRS axis may become almost perpendicular to the frontal plane. The effect is a "clockwise" rotation shifting the precordial transition zone leftward of V_4. Anterior forces appear decreased and QS or rS complexes may be seen in most or all of the precordial leads. When the r wave in V_1 to $V_3 \leq 3$ mm, the proper terminology is *decreased anterior forces*. In some patients the frontal plane mean QRS axis is indeterminate or there is an illusory left axis deviation, possibly caused by a slight superior angulation to the posterior QRS vector or to an extreme right axis deviation. An SI, SII, SIII pattern is another consequence of the posterior QRS vector.

Decreased Magnitude of Ventricular Forces Because of the hyperinflated, diseased lungs, less electrical forces are transmitted through the chest. Low voltage, particularly in the frontal leads, is therefore a common finding. Precordial plane forces are also reduced because of the posterior QRS vector and the lower, more vertical position of the heart relative to the precordial leads. Leads V_5 and V_6 may show lower total amplitude than lead V_4.

Increased Right Ventricular Forces (Fig. 10-2) Advanced lung disease may eventually lead to right ventricular hypertrophy and an increase in anterior-rightward forces. These findings, which include further right axis deviation, a prominent R or R' wave in V_1, and a deeper S wave in V_6, are often obscured, in patients with advanced lung disease, by the masking electrocardiographic effects of lung disease and left ventricular hypertrophy. The diagnosis of right ventricular hypertrophy is made ante mortem in less than 30 percent of patients who have this finding at autopsy.

Important Considerations

- The diagnosis of lung disease is greatly strengthened when two or more criteria are present. In particular,

A. Frontal Plane

B. P Wave

C. QRS

D. T

E. Summary

FIG. 10-2. Cor pulmonale. The electrocardiogram is from a 73-year-old female with lung disease and cor pulmonale.

(A) Frontal plane projection of the mean P, QRS, and T vectors.

(B) The mean P wave vector is slightly positive in lead aV_L and greatest in magnitude in lead II. The vector is therefore slightly leftward of lead II (note that leads II and aV_L are perpendicular to each other). Leads V_1 and V_2 show biphasic P waves due to prominent initial right atrial forces, which are anteriorly directed, and late posterior forces due to the left atrium.

(C) The mean QRS vector is directed rightward towards lead III, which is strongly positive and near the perpendicular to lead aV_R.

(D) The T-wave vector is resultantly zero in lead aV_F and strongly positive in lead I. The vector is therefore parallel to lead I.

(E) Final summary figure showing the spatial arrangement of the vectors. Lung disease is suggested by the decreased frontal plane voltage, biatrial abnormality, and decreased initial forces. Right ventricular hypertrophy is indicated by the reversal of the normal R/S ratio in leads V_1 and V_6.

the combination of an abnormal P vector with right axis deviation, low QRS voltage, or an SI, II, III pattern enhances the specificity of the diagnosis.

- A reduced or absent r wave in V_1 to V_3 may be found in lung disease, anteroseptal myocardial infarction, left ventricular hypertrophy, right ventricular hypertrophy, and in some normal people. If recordings of V_1 to V_4 taken one intercostal space lower show an R wave that exceeds 3 mm, lung disease is the probable reason for the apparent reduction in anterior forces.

Pulmonary Embolus *(Fig. 10-3)*

Pulmonary emboli seldom cause electrocardiographic changes, other than sinus tachycardia, unless the acute stress is severe. This usually occurs when 50 percent or more of the pulmonary vasculature is obstructed and the mean pulmonary artery pressure is above 30 mmHg. The electrocardiographic signs are attributed to acute dilatation of the right side of the heart and to the secondary effects produced by hypoxemia, hemodynamic changes, and altered coronary blood flow.

Electrocardiographic Criteria for Acute Pulmonary Embolus

The Mean QRS Vector May Be Shifted to the Right or Sometimes to the Left Either right or left axis deviation may be produced by an acute pulmonary embolus. The right axis deviation is attributed to acute right heart strain. The reason for the left axis deviation is unknown.

The Initial QRS Forces Are Shifted Superiorly, Posteriorly, and Leftward While Terminal Forces Are Directed Superiorly, Posteriorly, and Rightward An SI, QIII, TIII pattern, produced by the shifts mentioned above, is one of the more classic findings for pulmonary embolization. When the terminal forces are delayed, a

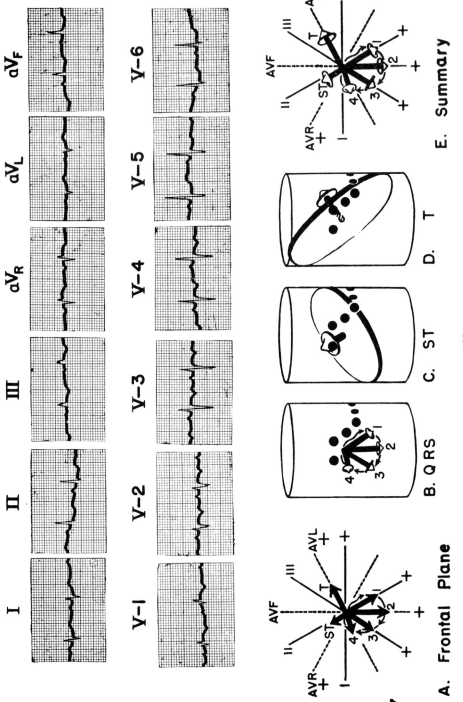

FIG. 10–3. The electrocardiogram of a patient, 54 years of age, made shortly after pulmonary embolism.

(A) The frontal plane projection of the mean spatial QRS loop and ST and T vectors.

(B) The QRS loop is broken down into four successive spatial instantaneous vectors. Each of these instantaneous vectors is oriented in space producing a rough outline of the mean spatial QRS loop.

(C) The mean ST vector is rotated 40° anteriorly because the ST segment is elevated in V_1, V_2, and V_3 and depressed in V_5 and V_6.

(D) The mean T vector is rotated approximately 20° posteriorly because the T wave is inverted in V_1, V_2, V_3, and V_4 and upright in V_5 and V_6. Note that when the mean T vector, or any vector, is in this position, only a small amount of posterior rotation is necessary to produce inverted T waves in several of the precordial leads.

(E) Final summary figure illustrating the spatial arrangement of the vectors. The QRS loop is rotund and is inscribed in a clockwise manner. The initial forces are to the left and are rotated anteriorly, producing an initial R wave in lead V_1. Vector four, illustrating the terminal QRS vectors, is directed to the right and anteriorly, producing an S wave in leads I, V_2, V_3, V_4, V_5, and V_6 and an R wave in V_1. The mean ST vector is directed toward the right shoulder and indicates subendocardial injury, while the mean T vector is directed to the left and posteriorly indicating right ventricular ischemia. These findings are typical of acute cor pulmonale secondary to pulmonary embolism. At times only right ventricular ischemia may be present.

right ventricular conduction delay or right bundle branch block may be noted. Prior to the development of a right bundle branch block, the S wave in V_1 may become slurred.

The QRS Vector Is Shifted Posteriorly in the Horizontal Plane This posterior rotation moves the precordial transition zone leftward of V_3.

The ST Vector Points Anteriorly or Posteriorly ST-segment elevation or depression may develop in V_1 to V_3.

A T Vector Is Directed Superiorly and Posteriorly T-wave inversion in V_1 to V_3 and in the inferior leads is often the only evidence for acute right heart strain.

A Right Atrial Abnormality May Be Seen A transient right atrial abnormality, as previously defined, may occur.

Important Considerations

- The electrocardiogram is often normal or shows nonspecific changes with acute pulmonary embolization, particularly when the embolus is not severe.
- When the electrocardiographic changes listed previously are transient in appearance, the diagnosis should be suspected.
- An inferior myocardial infarction can be mimicked by a pulmonary embolus; however, the Q wave is usually less than 0.04 s.

fused with coronary artery disease or severe lung disease.

Electrocardiographic Criteria for Left Pneumothorax

Shift of the Mean QRS Axis to the Right

Decrease in Anterior Forces Resulting in a Smaller R Wave V_1 to V_6

Decrease in QRS Voltage

Shift in the T Vector Producing T-Wave Inversion in the Precordial Leads

- A pulmonary embolus may also suggest an anterior myocardial infarction by producing an elevated ST segment and T-wave inversion in the right precordial leads. Simultaneous inferior T-wave inversion should point to the correct diagnosis of the pulmonary embolus.

Left Pneumothorax

A left pneumothorax, either spontaneous or iatrogenic, is an occasional cause of chest pain, dyspnea, and electrocardiographic changes that may be con-

Chapter 11
Pericarditis

The electrocardiogram of a patient with pericarditis will vary depending upon the acuteness, severity, and extent of the inflammation, the presence and size of a pericardial effusion, the cause of the pericarditis, and preexisting changes on the electrocardiogram.

Acute Pericarditis *(Figs. 11–1, 11–2)*

When acute pericarditis is accompanied by a pericardial friction rub, the electrocardiogram will be abnormal 80 to 90 percent of the time. The incidence of an abnormal tracing in a patient who is asymptomatic or does not have a rub is unknown. A normal electrocardiogram does not exclude acute pericarditis and cannot be used as evidence against this diagnosis.

Electrocardiographic Criteria for Acute Pericarditis

An ST Vector Directed Anteriorly, Inferiorly, and Leftward The ST vector of pericarditis points in the general direction of the cardiac apex. Therefore, ST-segment elevation is most commonly seen in leads I, II, and V_4 to V_6. Depending on the exact direction of this vector, leads III, aV_L, aV_F, V_2, and V_3 may also display ST-segment elevation. Contrary to a popular belief, reciprocal ST-segment depression can occur and may be noted in leads aV_R, V_1, and rarely III. The configuration of the ST-segment elevation is usually

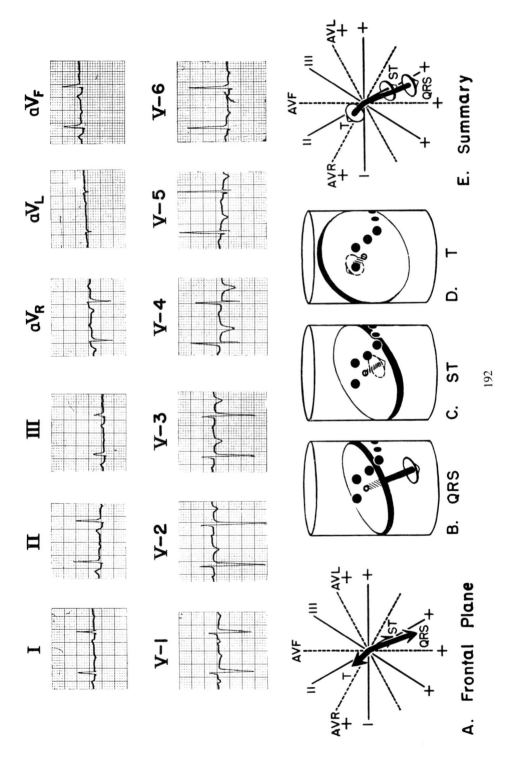

FIG. 11-1. The electrocardiogram of a patient, 37 years of age, with the clinical findings of benign idiopathic pericarditis.

(A) The frontal plane projection of the mean spatial QRS, ST, and T vectors.

(B) The mean QRS vector is tilted 30° posteriorly because the transitional pathway passes between electrode positions V_3 and V_4.

(C) The mean ST vector is tilted 50° posteriorly because the transitional pathway passes between electrode positions V_4 and V_5.

(D) The mean T vector is rotated almost 80° away from the frontal plane, producing inverted T waves in all the precordial leads.

(E) Final summary figure illustrating the spatial arrangement of the vectors. The mean spatial ST vector is directed toward the centroid of diffuse epicardial injury and is nearly parallel with the mean spatial QRS vector. The mean spatial T vector is directed away from an area of diffuse epicardial injury. These findings are typical of pericarditis.

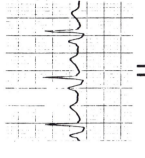

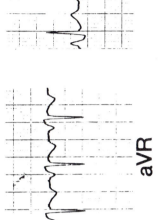

Atrial Injury

FIG. 11-2. Atrial injury. Deviation of the PR segment—upward in lead aV_R and downward in lead II—in a patient with pericarditis.

193

slightly concave, with a magnitude seldom exceeding 5 mm. The onset of the ST segment may originate from an S wave that appears pulled up from the isoelectric line. The ST-segment elevation may last from a few days to several weeks, ultimately returning to the isoelectric line as the acute inflammation subsides.

A PR-Segment Vector Directed Superiorly and Rightward (Fig. 11-2) Deviation of the PR segment, probably due to atrial epicardial injury, is a subtle, helpful clue to the presence of pericarditis. The PR segment in aV_R is stretched up, while depression of the PR segment may be seen in leads II, aV_F, and V_2 to V_6 in 80 percent of patients with unequivocal pericarditis.

A T Vector Pointing Superiorly and Rightward During the later stages of acute pericarditis, usually after the ST-segment elevation has resolved, the T-wave vector rotates rightward and superiorly away from the mean QRS vector. Widespread T-wave inversion is seen in leads with an upright QRS complex. The T wave may have a notched or biphasic contour.

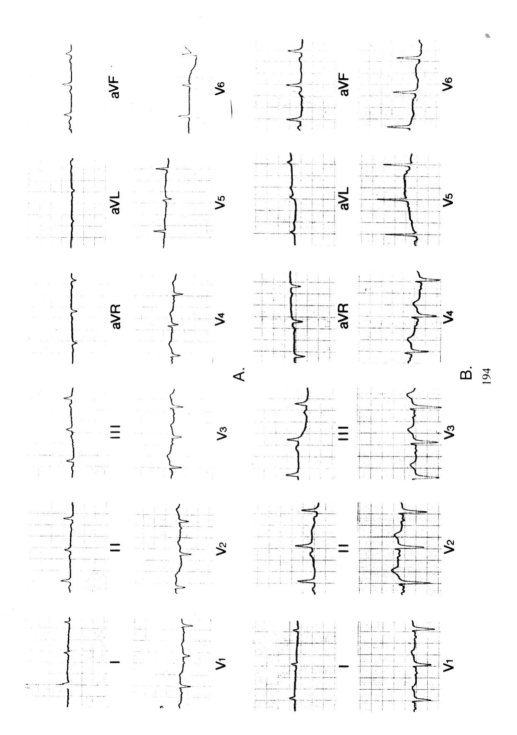

Fig. 11–3. (A) Pericardial effusion. A generalized low-voltage and electrical alternans (seen best in leads V_4 to V_5) in a 53-year-old male with a malignant pericardial effusion due to metastatic cancer of the lung. (B) Same patient after effusion has been removed. Note increase in voltage and disappearance of electrical alternans.

Important Considerations

- The ST-segment changes of pericarditis may be difficult to separate from an acute inferolateral infarction. The following points may be helpful:
- The ST-segment elevation of pericarditis is usually widespread; reciprocal ST-segment depression is seen only in aV_R and V_1 in pericarditis but is usually present with acute infarction.
- ST-segment elevation greater than 5 mm is unlikely to be due to pericarditis. The ST-segment elevation is often concave in pericarditis and convex in infarction.
- In pericarditis the T-wave inversion does not usually occur until after the ST segment returns to the baseline. Deeply inverted T waves are not seen in pericarditis but may occur with infarction.
- Q waves do not develop in pericarditis.
- The ST changes of the early repolarization pattern are often similar to pericarditis. The early repolarization pattern and pericarditis share the following common features: an ST vector directed anteriorly, inferiorly, and leftward; ST-segment elevation that does not exceed 4 mm; and absence of reciprocal ST-segment depression (except in aV_R). An early repolarization pattern is suggested when the J point is notched or slurred; the T wave is very tall; the ST-T findings do not evolve; and the clinical findings are negative for pericardial disease.
- PR segment deviation similar to pericarditis can occur with an early repolarization pattern.

Chronic Pericarditis

Virtually all patients with chronic constrictive pericarditis have an abnormal tracing; however the findings are nonspecific.

Electrocardiographic Findings for Chronic Pericarditis

Wide Notched P Waves

Decreased QRS and T-Wave Voltage

Low-Voltage, Flat, or Inverted T Waves

Atrial Arrhythmias, Particularly Atrial Fibrillation

A combination of right axis deviation, a left atrial abnormality, and inferolateral T-wave inversion is more specific and may be due to constrictive pericarditis involving the left ventricle and left atrioventricular groove.

Pericardial Effusion *(Fig. 11–3)*

Electrocardiographic Criteria for Pericardial Effusion

Decreased QRS and T Voltage Low voltage is diagnosed when the summed amplitude of the positive and negative deflection of leads I, II, and III are each less than 5 mm. Precordial plane low voltage implies that the total amplitude of all leads is below 8 mm. Although low voltage is often seen with pericardial effusion, it is not a very sensitive or specific finding. Low voltage can also occur when the mean QRS axis is perpendicular to the frontal or precordial plane; with increased distance, air, or fluid between the heart and electrodes as seen with lung disease, pleural effusion, and obesity; with diseases that replace or infiltrate the myocardium; and with myxedema.

Electrical Alternans of the QRS or QRS-T Amplitudes (Fig. 11–3A) With very large pericardial effusions, an untethered heart may swing rhythmically within the pericardial sac so that the QRS and sometimes the T wave display alternating peaks of amplitude. This may be seen in all leads or only in certain leads. A malignant pericardial effusion is usually present.

Chapter 12
Cardiomyopathy

Since cardiomyopathies usually involve widespread areas of atrial and ventricular myocardium, electrocardiographic abnormalities are often present. Although these abnormalities are rarely specific, consisting for the most part of P-wave changes, ventricular hypertrophy, conduction defects, and secondary ST-T changes, the electrocardiogram may alert the clinician to the presence of myocardial disease or suggest a possible cause. The following discussion will highlight commonly reported findings. Criteria developed in Part III, Section A should be applied.

Idiopathic, Dilated (Congestive) Cardiomyopathy *(Fig. 12–1)*

The diagnosis cannot be made from the electrocardiogram. Common findings include left atrial abnormality, left axis deviation, left bundle branch block, left ventricular hypertrophy (often masked by a conduction defect), absent q waves in leads I, V_5, and V_6, and nonspecific or secondary ST-T changes. The ventricular voltage may be low, a finding associated with a poorer prognosis. A right bundle branch block is un-

I II III aVR aVL aVF

V1 V2 V3 V4 V5 V6

A. Frontal Plane   B. Terminal .04   C. QRS   D. T   E. Summary

FIG. 12–1. Cardiomyopathy. This electrocardiogram is from a 54-year-old man with idiopathic dilated cardiomyopathy.

(A) Frontal plane projection of the mean QRS, terminal 0.04 s, and T vectors.

(B) The terminal 0.04 s vector is superiorly and leftward because the terminal force is positive in leads I and aV_L and the transitional plane is between leads V_5 and V_6. The prominent anterior ST vector makes it difficult to determine where the QRS ends.

(C) The mean QRS vector is resultantly zero in aV_R and strongly positive in aV_L. The vector must be placed at $-60°$ with a transition plane between V_5 and V_6.

(D) The mean T vector is perpendicular to aV_R and anteriorly directed since all precordial leads are upright.

(E) Final summary figure showing the spatial arrangement of the vectors. The prolonged QRS, decreased anterior forces, and terminal leftward forces indicate a left bundle branch block. The oppositely directed ST vector is typical for a left bundle branch block. The left atrial abnormality, superior QRS axis, and very wide QRS are typical, though not diagnostic, of a cardiomyopathy.

common. Coronary artery disease is sometimes falsely suggested by abnormal Q waves, due to fibrosis or conduction defects, and by widespread T-wave inversion. A prolonged PR interval, atrial fibrillation and flutter, premature ventricular complexes, and ventricular tachycardia are frequent arrhythmias.

Hypertrophic Cardiomyopathy

The electrocardiogram is almost always abnormal in patients with obstructive and nonobstructive hypertrophic cardiomyopathy. Although the features are not diagnostic, the electrocardiogram may bring this possibility to the attention of the physician. Common findings include left or right atrial abnormality, left ventricular hypertrophy, abnormal, deep Q waves in inferior and lateral leads, left axis deviation, and secondary ST-T wave changes. Less common changes include right ventricular hypertrophy, Wolff-Parkinson-White pattern, and PR interval prolongation. Particularly helpful clues are the combination of a right atrial abnormality with left ventricular hypertrophy or deep inferolateral Q waves and a tall RV_1 from the increased septal forces. Supraventricular and ventricular arrhythmias are often found with ambulatory monitoring.

Myocarditis

Mild myocarditis may affect the T wave by reducing the amplitude or inverting the T wave. With more severe inflammation, widespread ST-T changes, bundle branch block, sinus tachycardia, and ventricular ectopy may appear. Deep T-wave inversion may be mistaken for ischemia. ST-segment elevation can also occur and may be due to associated pericarditis or, rarely, extensive myocardial injury.

Atrial fibrillation is common in long-standing hypertension.

Infiltrative Cardiomyopathy

Various diseases, including sarcoidosis, amyloidosis, and hemochromatosis, may infiltrate the heart and alter the electrocardiogram. The changes may include conduction defects, diminished QRS voltage, abnormal Q waves suggesting infarction, nonspecific ST-T abnormalities, and arrhythmias. Although the electrocardiogram is never diagnostic, it may provide evidence that the heart is involved by the systemic disease.

Hypertension

A left atrial abnormality and minor changes in T-wave amplitude or direction may be early findings of hypertension. Other findings include left ventricular hypertrophy, ST-T wave changes secondary to the ventricular hypertrophy, and left axis deviation. Widening of the QRS interval or a left bundle branch block may be consequences of long-standing hypertension.

Chapter 13
Aortic and Mitral Valvular Heart Disease

Valvular heart disease may impose a resistance load, a volume load, or both upon one or more of the cardiac chambers. Stenosis of a valve leads to a hypertrophic response of the chamber behind the lesion. Accordingly, aortic stenosis may produce ventricular hypertrophy; mitral stenosis may cause atrial hypertrophy. Valvular regurgitation dilates the receiving chamber. Therefore, ventricular dilatation results from aortic regurgitation while atrial dilatation occurs with mitral regurgitation. Long-standing severe stenosis ultimately leads to chamber dilatation as well as hypertrophy; both stenosis and regurgitation can also cause fibrosis and conduction defects of the atrium and the ventricle.

In the following discussion, various electrocardiographic changes that may occur with isolated, advanced aortic and mitral valvular disease will be presented. Criteria developed in Part III, Section A on altered anatomic or electrophysiologic disturbances should be applied.

Aortic Stenosis *(Fig. 6–1)*

With severe acquired or severe long-standing congenital aortic stenosis, a left atrial abnormality and left ventricular hypertrophy are usually present, although the electrocardiogram may remain normal despite severe aortic stenosis. The increased left ventricular forces produce deep right precordial S waves and tall left

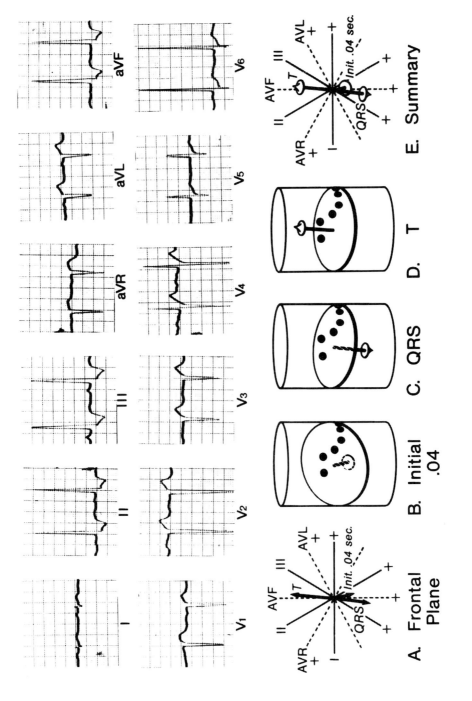

FIG. 13–1. Aortic regurgitation. The electrocardiogram is from a 16-year-old girl with Marfan's syndrome and severe aortic regurgitation.

(A) Frontal plane projection of the mean QRS, initial 0.04 s, and T vectors.

(B) The initial 0.04 s vector is slightly positive in lead I and negative in aV_R and aV_L. Therefore it is just to the left of aV_F.

(C) The mean QRS is resultantly negative in lead I and slightly more positive in lead III compared to lead II. The vector must be just to the right of aV_F.

(D) The mean T vector is opposite the mean QRS vector, and since it is positive in lead I, it is drawn slightly to the left of the perpendicular to lead I.

(E) Final summary figure showing the spatial arrangement of the vectors. The striking ventricular forces and vertical mean QRS axis is common in young people with left ventricular hypertrophy. Decreased anterior forces and ST-segment elevation in V_1 to V_2 are common findings with severe left ventricular hypertrophy.

precordial R waves. When this is accompanied by an ST-T vector opposite the mean QRS vector, the electrocardiogram is sometimes referred to as a *systolic overload pattern*. In children and young adults the QRS voltage often does not reflect the severity of the aortic stenosis; however, a flat, biphasic, or inverted T wave in V_6 is evidence for an aortic valve gradient of 80 mm Hg or greater. Associated left ventricular fibrosis may lead to a left bundle branch block in the adult. Atrial fibrillation rarely occurs until late in the course of the disease or with associated mitral valve disease.

Aortic Regurgitation (Fig. 13–1)

Early findings in aortic regurgitation may include prominent left ventricular and septal forces. The increased QRS amplitude, together with tall left precordial T waves, constitutes a *diastolic overload pattern* which is occasionally present. A left atrial abnormality, decreased anterior forces, enormous left ventricular forces, an ST-T vector opposite the mean QRS vector, and a horizontal or leftward mean QRS axis are later changes. A borderline or prolonged PR interval is common with moderate or severe aortic regurgitation.

Mitral Stenosis (Figs. 6–4, 13–2)

The major, and often the sole, electrocardiographic finding of mitral stenosis is a left atrial abnormality. The P wave is often very broad and notched in lead II and has a prominent negative terminal deflection in V_1. With increasing severity of mitral stenosis and the development of pulmonary hypertension, the mean QRS vector may progressively rotate rightward, and evidence for right ventricular hypertrophy may be seen.

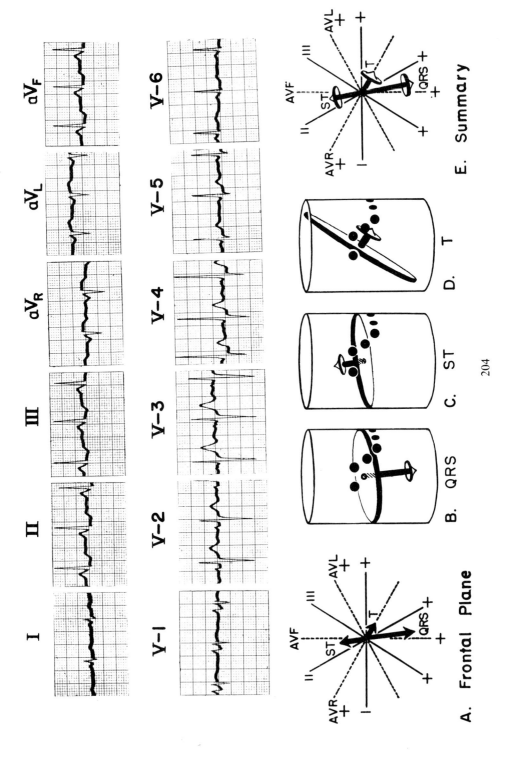

FIG. 13-2. The electrocardiogram of a patient, 35 years of age, with mitral stenosis.

(A) The QRS complex is approximately equal and positive in leads II and III and approximately equal and negative in leads aV_R and aV_L. The QRS complex is resultantly slightly positive in lead I. The mean QRS vector is directed downward and located so that a small positive quantity will be projected on lead I. The ST segment displacement is greatest and negative in lead II and slightly negative in lead I. The mean ST vector is directed cephalad and located so that a small negative quantity will be projected on lead I. The T waves (the last portion of the ST-T segment) are small in the frontal plane and appear to be isoelectric in lead III. Accordingly, the mean T vector is directed perpendicular to lead III.

(B), (C), (D) The spatial orientation of the mean QRS, ST, and T vectors. The mean QRS vector is rotated roughly 30° posteriorly because the transitional pathway passes between V_3 and V_4. The mean ST pathway passes through V_2. Note that the ST segment is elevated in V_1 and depressed in V_3, V_4, V_5, and V_6. The mean T vector is rotated 5° anteriorly because the transitional pathway passes between V_1 and V_2 and is almost resultantly zero in V_1.

(E) Final summary figure. The mean spatial QRS vector is directed vertically and slightly posteriorly. The characteristic electrocardiographic evidence of right ventricular hypertrophy, namely, that the mean QRS vector is directed to the right and anteriorly, is not present here. The mean QRS vector shown above can be perfectly normal or may be present in right ventricular hypertrophy. This is especially true in cases of chronic cor pulmonale and in minor degrees of right ventricular hypertrophy resulting from mitral stenosis. The prominent P waves in the above tracing suggest mitral stenosis or cor pulmonale. The ST and T vectors are the result of digitalis medication. The mean ST vector is fairly large and is directed opposite to the mean QRS vector, while the mean T vector is normally directed but shortened in the frontal plane. The QT interval is 0.32.

The combination of a vertical QRS axis and a left atrial abnormality is highly suggestive of mitral stenosis, although lung disease may produce a similar tracing. Atrial fibrillation is common in long-standing mitral stenosis.

Mitral Regurgitation

A left atrial abnormality may also be seen with chronic, but not usually acute, mitral regurgitation. The QRS amplitude and vectors are often normal; however, left ventricular or biventricular hypertrophy with related ST-T changes may occur. Left ventricular hypertrophy is not as severe as seen in aortic valve disease, since mitral regurgitation allows the left ventricle to eject against a lower resistance. Unlike other causes of left ventricular hypertrophy, the frontal mean QRS axis tends to be inferiorly directed with mitral regurgitation. Atrial fibrillation is common with chronic, severe mitral regurgitation.

The electrocardiogram is often normal with acute mitral regurgitation unless coronary artery disease is the cause. When mitral valve prolapse is the cause of mitral regurgitation, a superior rightward T vector, producing inferolateral T-wave inversion, is sometimes present. Occasionally ST segment depression is seen in the same leads. Atrial and ventricular arrhythmias occur.

Important Considerations

- The findings listed under specific valvular lesions apply to relatively pure, significant valvular disease but may not pertain to patients with mixed (stenosis and regurgitation) or multiple valvular problems, or with early or mild-to-moderate valvular disease.
- Most of the electrocardiographic-valvular correlations have been made with far advanced or fatal rheumatic or syphilitic valvular disease. These studies are not necessarily comparable to the current population of patients with valvular disease because of differences in etiology and advances in medical and surgical treatment.
- In middle-aged and older patients, coexisting problems, such as hypertension, coronary artery disease, lung disease, and aging changes will influence the electrocardiogram.

- In general, the electrocardiogram is relatively insensitive in the detection of chamber dilatation and therefore is not very useful in the evaluation of the severity of valvular regurgitation. There is an improved, though still imperfect, correlation with the severity of valvular stenosis and the electrocardiogram.
- The diastolic overload pattern is relatively infrequent, not very sensitive, and, if present, often evolves into a systolic overload pattern. Some studies doubt the existence of a diastolic overload pattern.
- A systolic overload pattern occurs fairly late in the course of aortic stenosis and can be mimicked by ischemia or digitalis effect.
- Because criteria for left and right ventricular hypertrophy are not very sensitive, many patients will not show abnormalities of ventricular depolarization even when ventricular hypertrophy is present. A left atrial abnormality or ST-T changes may provide earlier evidence of significant valvular disease.
- A left atrial abnormality is best detected in lead V_1 and is a nonspecific finding occurring with any disease affecting the left heart.

Chapter 14
Congenital Heart Disease

The electrocardiogram offers useful information about the type and severity of congenital heart disease, although few specific patterns occur. The changes usually reflect the hemodynamic effects of a volume overload from a left-to-right shunt, a resistance load from a stenotic valve or pulmonary hypertension, or both a volume and resistance load. In the following discussion selected types of congenital heart disease and the most common electrocardiographic changes, particularly in the postadolescent period, will be mentioned.

Atrial Septal Defects *(Fig. 14–1)*

Atrial septal defects are anatomically classified as ostium primum, ostium secundum, and sinus venosum defects. They have the following electrocardiographic manifestations:

- The mean P-wave vector is normal with ostium primum and secundum defects and leftward with a sinus venosum defect. The P-wave configuration is usually normal unless pulmonary hypertension is present. The PR interval may be at the upper limits of normal or prolonged.
- A terminal anterior and rightward QRS vector due to a right ventricular conduction delay is usual; an rSr′, or rSR′ is seen in V_1 to V_2 and aV_R; and a prominent, slurred S wave is present in leads I, II, aV_L, and V_5 to V_6. The QRS interval may be at the upper limits of normal or prolonged up to 0.12 s.

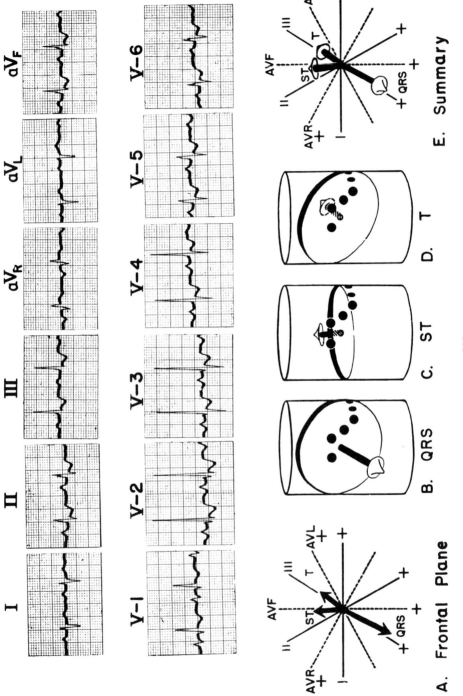

FIG. 14-1. The electrocardiogram of a patient, 38 years of age, with interatrial septal defect, illustrating right ventricular hypertrophy.

(A) The QRS complex is largest in lead III and resultantly slightly negative in lead aV$_R$. When QRS complexes with such characteristics are represented as a mean vector it will be directed just to the left of the positive limb of lead III. It is difficult to identify where the ST segment ends and where the T wave begins, and the ST-T waves could best be illustrated together as a loop. Considering this difficulty, the ST segment, studied in all frontal leads, appears negative in leads II and III and just slightly negative in lead I. A mean vector responsible for the ST-segment displacement will be directed parallel with the negative limb of lead aV$_F$ and slightly to the right of that line since it projects a small negative quantity on lead I. The T wave is positive in lead I and most negative in lead III and slightly negative in lead aV$_R$. These T-wave findings can be represented by a mean vector directed relatively parallel with the negative limb of lead III.

(B), (C), (D) The spatial orientation of the mean QRS, ST, and T vectors. The mean QRS vector is rotated 85° anteriorly because the transitional pathway passes very near electrode V$_6$. A QRS vector so located will cause almost all anterior chest leads to be resultantly positive. The mean ST vector is tilted 10° posteriorly because the ST segment in V$_1$ is isoelectric and the remaining ST segments are negative. (The ST segment in V$_2$ is negative and must have recorded from the negative half of the electrical field. Slight electrode misplacement near electrode position V$_2$ would alter the ST segment a great deal.) The T wave appears negative in all leads, suggesting that the T vector is tilted 85° posteriorly.

(E) Final summary figure showing the spatial arrangement of the vectors. The mean QRS vector is directed downward and to the right and is rotated markedly anteriorly, while the T vector is rotated 170° away from the mean QRS vector. Frequently a mean ST vector will be seen to be relatively parallel with the mean T vector as in this case. Under such circumstances the T vector is large and the ST vector relatively small, while in this case the ST vector is large and the T vector is somewhat smaller than is usually expected. This finding plus a short QT interval (0.28 s) and a slightly prolonged PR interval (0.21 s) indicates digitalis effect in addition to the ST-T change of right ventricular hypertrophy.

- An inferiorly or rightward oriented mean QRS vector is typical for a sinus venosum or secundum defect, while a superior-leftward mean QRS vector is an important clue to an ostium primum defect.
- In an uncomplicated atrial septal defect, the ST and T vectors are usually normal.
- With pulmonary hypertension or a large left-to-right shunt, a right atrial abnormality, taller R′ wave in V$_1$, right axis deviation, and right precordial T-wave inversion may be seen.
- Atrial fibrillation often occurs in middle-aged or older adults with long-standing, large atrial septal defects.

Important Considerations

- The rSr′ configuration of V$_1$ is the most typical feature of an atrial septal defect but is similar to the pattern found in a small percentage of normal, usually young, individuals.

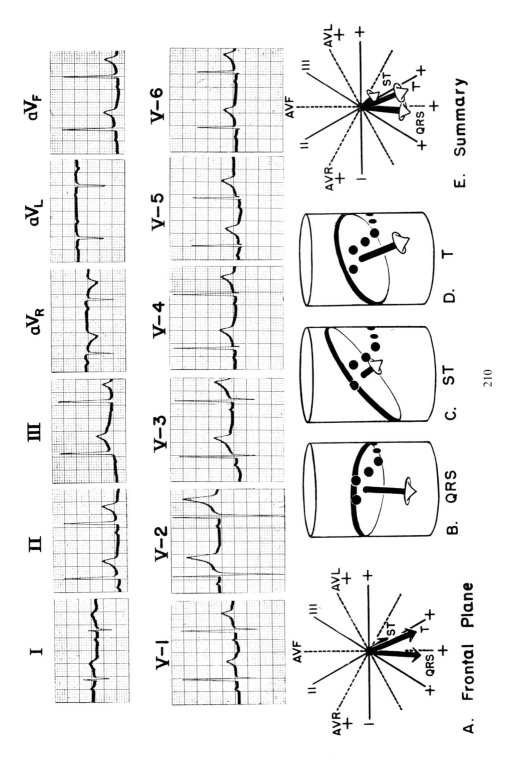

FIG. 14–2. The electrocardiogram of a patient, 8 years of age, with pulmonic stenosis, illustrating right ventricular hypertrophy.

(A) The QRS complex is approximately equal and positive in leads II and III, and equal and negative in leads aV_R and aV_L. The QRS deflection is resultantly slightly negative in lead I. When the QRS force is represented as a vector, it will be drawn parallel to the positive limb of lead aV_F but must project a small negative quantity on lead I. The T wave is largest and positive in lead II and smallest but negative in lead aV_L. Accordingly, the mean T vector will be drawn just to the right of the positive limb of lead II. The ST-segment elevation seen in the first complex in lead III is an artifact due to a wandering baseline. This is known by studying the ST segment in all the other frontal leads and recalling that leads I + III = II, and $aV_R + aV_L + aV_F = 0$. The ST-segment elevation is greatest in lead II, and therefore the ST vector responsible for the ST-segment displacement will be drawn parallel with the positive limb of lead II. Note that the mean ST vector is relatively parallel with the mean T vector.

(B), (C), (D) The spatial orientation of the QRS, ST, and T vectors. The mean QRS vector is rotated 10° anteriorly because the transitional pathway passes between V_1 and V_2. Actually, the QRS complex at V_2 is the only resultantly negative precordial QRS deflection. The mean ST vector is rotated at least 10° anteriorly because the transitional pathway for ST passes through V_1. Since all precordial T waves are positive, the mean T vector is rotated at least 20° anteriorly.

(E) Final summary figure. The mean spatial QRS vector is directed vertically, slightly to the right, and anteriorly. Normal persons may have a mean spatial QRS vector directed just as vertically as in the above case. The differential point lies in the fact that the normal mean spatial QRS vector is directed posteriorly, whereas the mean spatial QRS vector shown above is directed anteriorly, indicating right ventricular hypertrophy.

Ventricular Septal Defect

Depending on its size, a ventricular septal defect imposes a volume load on both ventricles and the left atrium and, if pulmonary hypertension ensues, a resistance load on the right ventricle. The electrocardiographic findings that may occur include the following:

- The mean P vector is normally directed. The P-wave configuration may be normal or, with a
- The electrocardiogram may be normal in an uncomplicated, usually small, atrial septal defect.
- The electrocardiogram of an ostium primum defect—a left axis deviation and right ventricular conduction delay—is a tip-off to this diagnosis in a patient with a left-to-right shunt.
- A left atrial abnormality, in association with a right ventricular conduction delay and a superior-leftward mean QRS axis, suggests an ostium primum defect with mitral regurgitation due to a cleft mitral valve.

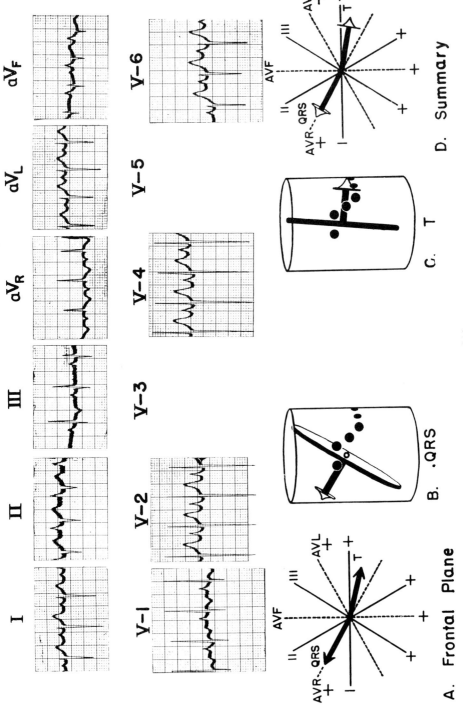

FIG. 14-3. The electrocardiogram of a patient, 3 years of age, with tetralogy of Fallot.

(A) The QRS complexes vary greatly with respiration, but when long strips are studied, it becomes apparent that the QRS complex is smallest and slightly negative in lead aV_F, resultantly zero in lead III, and negative in leads I and II. Such QRS complexes can be illustrated by a mean vector directed parallel to lead aV_R. The T wave also varies with respiration and when studied in a long strip is slightly negative in lead III and slightly positive in lead aV_F. Such a T wave can be illustrated by a vector drawn between a perpendicular to lead III and a perpendicular to lead aV_F.

(B), (C) The spatial orientation of the mean QRS and T vectors. The mean QRS vector is rotated 5° posteriorly because the transitional pathway passes between V_1 and V_2. The T vector is flush with the frontal plane because the transitional pathway passes between the V_1 and V_2 position.

(D) Final summary figure showing the spatial arrangement of the vectors. The mean QRS vector is rotated slightly posteriorly. When the mean QRS vector is rotated *markedly* to the right, slightly posteriorly directed QRS vectors may be encountered, but it is rare for the displacement to be more than 5°. The peaked, narrow P wave in leads II and V_1 indicate a right atrial abnormality. The marked right axis deviation (+210°), tall R wave in V_1, and reversal of expected R/S ratio in V_6 are due to right ventricular hypertrophy.

large left-to-right shunt, suggest a left atrial abnormality. The PR interval is normal.

- A left ventricular diastolic overload pattern—narrow deep Q waves and tall R and T waves in V_5 to V_6—is an early finding after infancy. Since the mean QRS axis is usually inferiorly directed, tall R and T waves in the inferior leads may be evidence for left ventricular hypertrophy, particularly in infants and young children.
- A right ventricular systolic volume overload pattern, consisting of a tall RV_1 and an inverted or upright T wave, may be seen.
- The mean QRS axis may vary widely but is usually between +30° and +150°.
- Terminal QRS forces are usually rightward in the frontal plane producing S waves in leads I, II, and sometimes III.

Important Considerations

- A normal electrocardiogram is seen with a small ventricular septal defect and pulmonary artery pressures below 40 mmHg.
- There is no correlation between the location of the ventricular septal defect and the electrocardiogram.

Patent Ductus Arteriosus

A large patent ductus arteriosus produces a volume load on the left atrium and left ventricle and, as pulmonary pressure increases, a resistance load on the right heart. The findings may include

- A left atrial abnormality with a normally directed mean P vector. The PR interval may be prolonged.
- The mean QRS axis is normal.

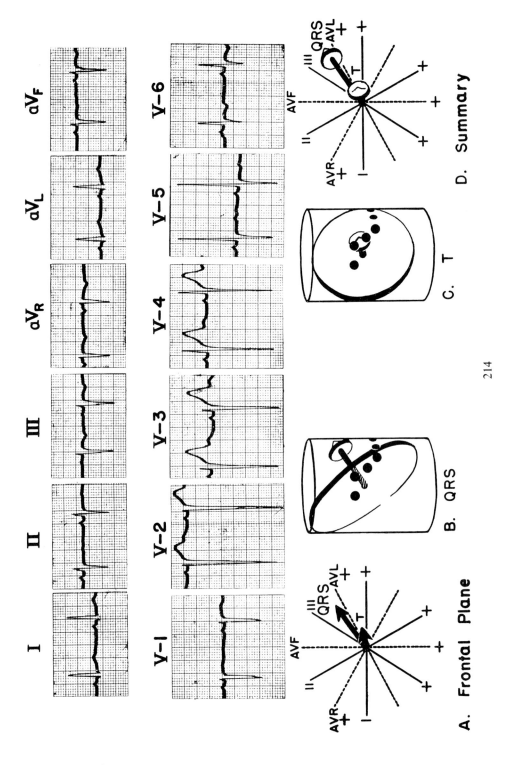

FIG. 14–4. The electrocardiogram of a patient, 15 years of age, with coarctation of the aorta, illustrating left ventricular hypertrophy.

(A) The QRS complex is largest and negative in lead III and slightly negative in lead II. QRS complexes of this nature can be represented by a mean vector directed just cephalad to a perpendicular to lead II and pointing toward the positive pole of aV_L. The T wave is smallest and slightly positive in lead II and slightly negative in lead aV_F. Accordingly, the mean T vector is located between the positive limb of lead I and the positive limb of lead aV_L.

(B), (C) The spatial orientation of the mean QRS and T vectors. The mean QRS vector is rotated 50° posteriorly because the transitional pathway passes between V_4 and V_5. The mean T vector is rotated 85° anteriorly because the transitional pathway lies very near V_6. A mean T vector in this position will be foreshortened in the frontal plane and large in the mid-precordial leads.

(D) Final summary figure showing the spatial arrangement of the vectors. The mean QRS vector is directed markedly leftward and posteriorly. Note that the frontal plane projection of the QRS-T angle is entirely normal but that the spatial QRS-T angle is roughly 135°. Left ventricular hypertrophy is suggested because of the left axis deviation, deep S wave in leads V_2 to V_4, and T abnormality in leads V_5 and V_6.

- A left ventricular volume overload pattern (as described under ventricular septal defect).
- The T-wave vector is parallel to the mean QRS vector. Tall, peaked T waves may be seen.
- In the case of pulmonary hypertension, a biatrial or a right atrial abnormality, rightward deviation of the mean QRS vector, and increasing right ventricular or biventricular hypertrophy may be seen.

Pulmonic Stenosis

Pulmonic stenosis results in a resistance load to the right heart. The following electrocardiographic changes may occur (Fig. 14–2):

- A right atrial abnormality with the occasional development of a giant P wave.
- Signs of right ventricular hypertrophy. With mild or moderate pulmonic stenosis the electrocardiogram may be normal or display only an rSr′ in lead V_1. A reversal of the R/S ratio in V_1 and V_6 and the development of a tall, monophasic, or notched R wave in V_1 indicates severe right ventricular hypertrophy.
- A rightward, anterior shift of the mean QRS axis with a normal QRS interval.
- A leftward, posterior, and superior shift of the T-wave vector in severe pulmonic stenosis (although the T-wave vector may be normal in young children). Inverted T waves in the right precordial and inferior leads are the result.
- Possible shift of the ST vector in the same general direction as the T vector.

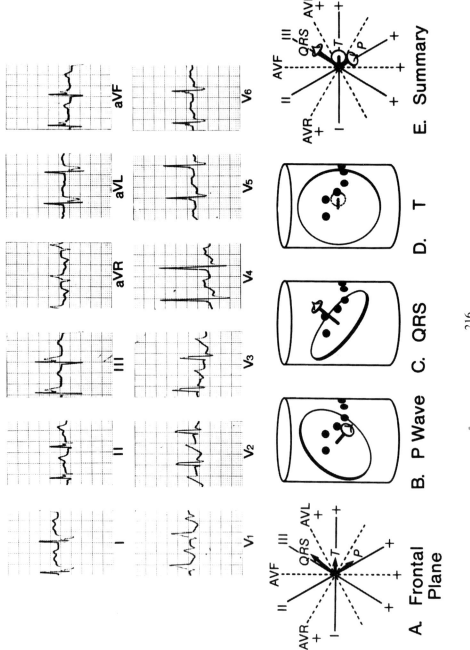

FIG. 14–5. Ebstein's anomaly. The electrocardiogram is from a 20-year-old male.

(A) Frontal plane projection of the mean P, QRS, and T vectors.

(B) The mean P-wave vector is slightly positive in lead aV_L and of greatest magnitude in leads II, V_1, and V_2. The vector is therefore drawn just to the left of lead II and anteriorly.

(C) The mean QRS vector is difficult to plot because the initial and terminal forces are opposite to each other.

(D) The mean T vector is positive in leads I and aV_L and resultantly almost zero in aV_F. The vector is drawn perpendicular to aV_F. The transition plane is between V_4 and V_5.

(E) Final summary figure showing the spatial arrangement of the vectors. The very large P wave, a q wave in V_1, a bizarre right bundle branch block with marked splintering, and a mean QRS vector to the left of lead II are typical findings in Ebstein's anomaly.

Important Considerations

- A mean QRS axis of +90° to +120° may be seen with mild, moderate, or severe pulmonic stenosis; a QRS axis above +120° is most often seen with a pulmonic valve gradient ≥ 50 mmHg.
- A q wave in V_1 correlates with a gradient ≥ 80 mmHg.
- An R wave ≥ 20 mm in V_1 and an S wave of 10 mm in lead I correlates with a gradient ≥ 50 mmHg.

Tetralogy of Fallot *(Fig. 14–3)*

The electrocardiographic findings of tetralogy of Fallot depend on the severity of the right ventricular outflow obstruction and the magnitude and direction of shunting through the ventricular septal defect. The electrocardiogram is usually abnormal and may be indistinguishable from mild-to-moderate valvular pulmonic stenosis with an intact ventricular septum. The following changes may occur:

- The P wave is either normal or mildly peaked without an increase in amplitude.
- The mean QRS vector is usually anterior and rightward but does not lie superior to +170°. On occasion the mean QRS axis is normal or even leftward.
- Right ventricular hypertrophy is present if the outflow obstruction is significant; the most common pattern is an Rs in V_1 and rS in V_5 to V_6.
- The ST and T vectors will rotate leftward and inferiorly with increasing right ventricular hypertrophy.

Important Considerations

- With mild right ventricular outflow obstruction and a large ventricular septal defect, the electrocardiogram may be similar to a ventricular septal defect alone or show mixed features of both abnormalities.
- After total surgical repair, a right bundle branch block and occasionally left axis deviation are present.

A. Frontal Plane   B. P Wave   C. QRS   D. T   E. Summary

FIG. 14-6. Dextrocardia. The electrocardiogram is from a 23-year-old female.

(A) Frontal plane projection of the mean P, QRS, and T vectors.

(B) The mean P-wave vector is resultantly zero in lead II and most strongly positive in lead III. The vector is drawn at +150° and anteriorly.

(C) and (D) The mean QRS and T vectors are similar to the orientation of the mean P-wave vector.

(E) Final summary figure showing the spatial arrangement of the vectors. Typical findings of dextrocardia include a P vector oriented to the right, anteriorly, and inferiorly, absent q waves in V_5 to V_6, a mean QRS vector which is inferior and rightward, and decreasing QRS voltage from V_1 to V_6. The condition can be separated from reversed arm lead placement by noting that the QRS voltage decreases going from leads V_1 to V_6.

bundle branch block is an infrequent finding in the adult.

- With left ventricular hypertrophy, the T-wave vector may rotate away from the QRS vector. Inverted or low-amplitude T waves are noted in leads I, aV_L, and V_5 to V_6.

Ebstein's Anomaly *(Fig. 14–5)*

In Ebstein's anomaly the tricuspid valve is abnormally positioned because malformed posterior and septal leaflets are displaced into the right ventricular cavity. This results in a small right ventricle, an enlarged right atrium, tricuspid regurgitation, and a right-to-left shunt through an atrial septal defect. The electrocardiogram is usually abnormal and may suggest the diagnosis because of the following findings:

- A large or giant P wave which may be peaked or broad is found in most patients. The PR interval is frequently prolonged unless preexcitation is present.

Coarctation of the Aorta *(Fig. 14-4)*

Coarctation of the aorta produces a resistance load on the left heart. Associated problems, including hypertension, aortic stenosis, ventricular septal defect, patent ductus arteriosus, mitral stenosis, and mitral regurgitation are common. The possible findings include:

- The P wave may be normal or show a left atrial abnormality. The PR interval is usually normal.
- The mean QRS vector is usually normal; however, left axis deviation may develop in older patients while right axis deviation is seen under age 3 months.
- Depending on the severity of the coarctation and the presence of other defects, the ventricular forces may be normal or show mild-to-moderate left ventricular hypertrophy. In the infant under age 3 months, right ventricular hypertrophy may occur.
- An rSr' pattern in V_1, due to an unexplained late posterior-rightward vector, may occur. A left

219

the cardiac apex is to the right. The following electrocardiographic findings are seen:

- The P-wave vector is oriented to the right, anteriorly, and inferiorly, about +135° in the frontal plane. The P wave is negative in leads I and aV_L and upright in aV_F and aV_R.
- The initial QRS vector will be oriented leftward, instead of rightward, since the conduction system is inverted. Q waves will be present in right chest leads V_5R to V_6R and absent in V_5 to V_6.
- The mean QRS vector is directed inferiorly and rightward in the frontal plane; lead I will be resultantly negative.
- Left precordial leads show a decreasing QRS voltage between V_1 and V_6 while the QRS voltage increases across the right precordial leads from V_1 to V_6R.

Important Considerations

- Inadvertent switching of the arm leads, a common error, will simulate dextrocardia except that the left precordial leads will show a normal progression of voltage.
- The electrocardiogram can be interpreted using the usual criteria by deliberately reversing the arm leads and recording the precordial leads from the left to right.

- The mean QRS axis is usually inferiorly directed but may be rightward or leftward. It is often difficult to calculate the vector because of the conduction defect.
- A right ventricular conduction delay or complete right bundle branch block, often with a bizarre splintering or slurring in the right precordial leads, and a low-amplitude QRS complex in the frontal leads are typical features.
- A q wave is frequently present in V_1, probably due to right atrial dilatation.
- A preexcitation pattern with a negative delta wave in leads V_1, II, III, and aV_F is present in some patients.
- The T vector may be directed superiorly and leftward producing T-wave inversion in the inferior and right precordial leads.
- Supraventricular arrhythmias are common.

Dextrocardia with Situs Inversus (Fig. 14–6)

In dextrocardia with situs inversus, also known as mirror image dextrocardia, the relative positions of the cardiac chambers and the liver and stomach are reversed. The anatomic right heart and the sinus node are positioned to the left of the left heart chambers and

Chapter 15

Miscellaneous Electrocardiographic Abnormalities

Electrolyte Abnormalities (Fig. 15–1)

High or low serum levels of potassium and calcium may alter the electrocardiogram. The changes are greatly influenced by the rapidity with which the electrolyte abnormality develops, the type and severity of heart disease, if present, and the effects of drugs such as digitalis. In addition, the electrolyte abnormality is rarely, if ever, a pure effect since mixed electrolyte and/or acid-base disturbances and changing hemodynamics are usually present. With the exception of severe hyper- and hypokalemia, the electrocardiographic changes are not very specific and the possibility of an electrolyte disturbance can only be suggested. The clinician, however, can use the electrocardiogram to very good advantage by correlating the changes with the clinical information and using the electrocardiogram to assess the serial progress of the condition.

Hyperkalemia

The possible electrocardiographic changes due to hyperkalemia include (Figs. 15–1 and 15–2)

- Tent-shaped T waves of normal amplitude
- Peaked, narrow-based T waves of increased amplitude

- ST-segment elevation simulating an injury pattern; rarely, ST segment depression
- Prolongation of the QT_c interval as a result of the increased QRS interval
- Arrhythmias, including asystole, ventricular fibrillation, aberrant junctional rhythms, escape rhythms, and atrioventricular block

Important Considerations

- The electrocardiogram is relatively insensitive to the effects of mild hyperkalemia, although tenting or increased T-wave amplitude may be seen when the serum potassium is above 5.5 meq/L. The T-wave changes of mild hyperkalemia may be similar to the prominent T wave seen in some normal individuals, with cerebrovascular events, and with left ventricular volume overload.
- A widened QRS indicates more severe hyperkalemia, usually greater than 6.5 meq/L. The QRS appears pulled apart rather than resembling a bundle branch block. Comparison with previous electrocardiograms is helpful in detecting early changes.
- With severe hyperkalemia exceeding 7.5 meq/L, the electrocardiogram is fairly characteristic with alterations of the P wave, PR interval, QRS duration, and sometimes the ST segment. At this level of potassium the T wave is not peaked. QRS axis deviation may be present.
- Hyperkalemia may simulate myocardial infarction

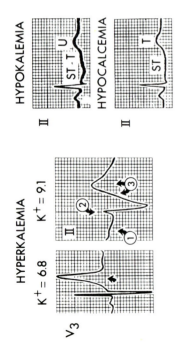

FIG. 15-1. Electrolyte disturbances. Hyperkalemia ($K^+ = 6.8$) with tall, peaked T waves. Severe hyperkalemia ($K^+ = 9.1$) with (1) flattening of the P wave, and ↑ PR interval (1→2), (2) marked widening of the QRS complex (2→3), and (3) merging of the S wave into the T wave. Hypokalemia produces flat or inverted T waves with prominent U waves, causing prolonged "QU" interval, while hypocalcemia produces true prolongation of the ST segment with marked QT prolongation.
[From R. J. Myerburg in Petersdorf et al. (eds.), *Harrison's Principles of Internal Medicine*, 10th ed., chapter 249, McGraw-Hill, New York, 1982.]

- Low-amplitude, widened P waves with eventual disappearance of the P wave
- Prolongation of the PR interval
- Widening of the QRS involving both the initial and terminal forces
- Deviation of the mean QRS axis to the left and superiorly or, rarely, to the right and inferiorly

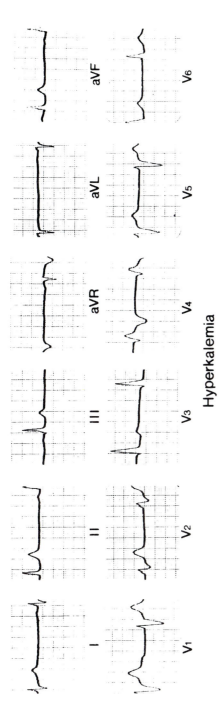

Hyperkalemia

FIG. 15–2. Hyperkalemia. The electrocardiogram is from a patient with chronic renal disease and a K^+ of 8.1 meq/L. Typical findings include a low-amplitude P wave and a diffuse conduction defect resulting in a "pulled-apart" QRS complex.

because the ST segment may be elevated or the initial forces altered.

- Sinusoidal-appearing complexes are a sign of very severe, life-threatening hyperkalemia.

Hypokalemia

The possible electrocardiographic changes attributed to hypokalemia include (Figs. 15–1, 15–3)

- Depression of the ST segment
- Lowering of the T-wave amplitude
- Increase in the U-wave amplitude
- Apparent, but not true, QT_c interval prolongation due to fusion of the T and U waves
- Increase in the amplitude and duration of the P wave
- Slight to moderate PR interval prolongation
- Slight increase in QRS duration and amplitude
- Arrhythmias, including AV block, ectopic supraventricular and ventricular arrhythmias, and ventricular fibrillation

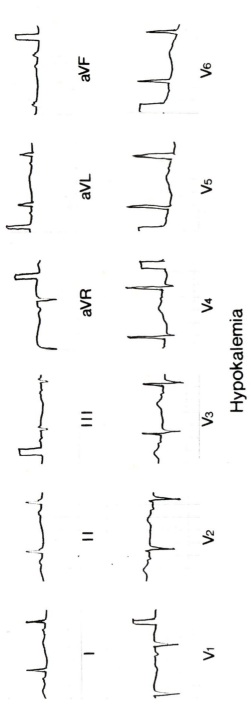

Hypokalemia

FIG. 15–3. Hypokalemia. The electrocardiogram is from a 45-year-old woman with K⁺ of 1.8 meq/L. Findings include ST-segment depression, a prolonged QT interval, low-amplitude T waves, and a prominent U wave.

Important Considerations

- Depression of the ST segment, low-amplitude T waves, and U waves greater than 1 mm are the usual basis for suggesting hypokalemia. Although each of these findings is nonspecific, the triad is very useful.
- The electrocardiogram is insensitive to the effects of hypokalemia until the serum potassium is below 3.2 meq/L. With severe hypokalemia of 2.5 meq/L or less, the correlation is improved though still not highly specific. This is not surprising since serum potassium levels may not be an accurate reflection of total body potassium.
- A U-wave amplitude that exceeds 1 mm or is greater than the T-wave amplitude in the same lead is consid-

ered significant. Other causes of prominent U waves include bradycardia, left ventricular hypertrophy, quinidine, procainamide, phenothiazines, and acute central nervous system disorders. In these situations the T-wave amplitude is often increased rather than decreased as seen with hypokalemia. At rapid heart rates and in certain leads the U wave may merge with the end of the T wave and give the appearance of a bizarre or notched T wave and a prolonged QT_c interval.

Hypercalcemia

The electrocardiographic effects of hypercalcemia include

- Shortening of the QT_c interval due to an abbreviation of the ST segment
- Minor effects on the P- and T-wave morphology

Important Considerations

The electrocardiogram is very insensitive to acute or chronic elevation of serum calcium levels and cannot be reliably used to gauge the severity of hypercalcemia.

Hypocalcemia (Fig. 15–1)

The electrocardiographic effects of hypocalcemia include

- Lengthening of the QT_c interval due to prolongation of the ST segment
- Lower amplitude or, occasionally, inversion or slight peaking and elevation of the T wave. Significant T-wave inversion simulating ischemia may occur in the right precordial leads

Important Considerations

- The QT_c interval prolongation rarely exceeds 140 percent of the normal.
- The prolonged QT_c interval of hypocalcemia differs from most other causes of QT_c prolongation since the T-wave duration is unaffected.
- A prolonged QT_c interval with a narrow, peaked T wave suggests hypocalcemia plus hyperkalemia in a patient with uremia.

Other Electrolytes

Hyper- and hypomagnesemia have been associated with electrocardiographic changes, but the changes are usually insignificant and nonspecific. Changes in sodium concentration do not affect the electrocardiogram.

Central Nervous System Disorders (Figs. 9–26, 15–4)

A variety of electrocardiographic changes may occur with subarachnoid hemorrhage, ischemic or hemorrhagic cerebral infarction, brain tumor, or head trauma. These changes include

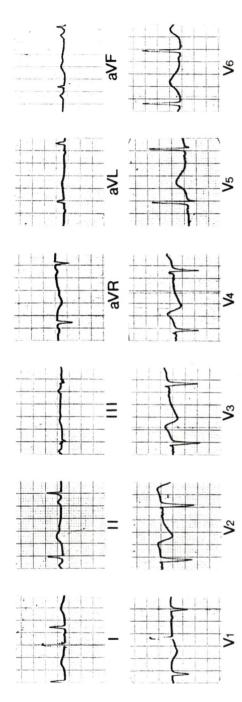

FIG. 15–4. Central nervous system disease. The electrocardiogram is from a 51-year-old female with a subarachnoid hemorrhage. A prolonged QT interval, a broad T wave with a bizarre configuration, and possibly a negative U wave in V_2 to V_4 are seen.

- Large, tall, pointed, notched, or inverted T waves
- ST-segment elevation or depression
- Prominent U waves
- QT_c interval prolongation
- Tall, peaked, or broad P waves
- Abnormal Q waves (rare)
- Arrhythmias, including sinus bradycardia, sinus arrhythmia, premature atrial and ventricular complexes, atrial fibrillation, ventricular tachycardia, asystole, and AV block

Important Considerations

- Electrocardiographic changes are common, occurring in 40 to 80 percent of studies. The most characteristic finding is a prolonged QT_c interval with a bizarre-appearing T wave that may be very large, pointed, or inverted.
- Myocardial infarction may be simulated by the ST-segment elevation, T-wave inversion, or the rare development of Q waves.

Digitalis

Digitalis Effect *(Figs. 9–25, 15–5 to 15–7)*

Digitalis exerts multiple, complex effects on the electrocardiogram by accelerating ventricular repolarization, increasing vagal tone on the heart, and improving contractility. The electrocardiographic changes include

- Prolongation of the PR interval. This is due to a vagotonically-induced slowing of conduction at the AV node
- Slowing of the sinus rate of discharge
- Rotation of the ST vector opposite to the mean QRS vector. Under the influence of digitalis, part of the repolarization occurs so quickly that repolarization forces are manifest during the ST segment. These forces proceed from endocardium to epicardium, opposite in direction from normal. Accordingly, a mean ST vector representing early repolarization develops which is oriented 180° away from the mean QRS vector
- Decrease in magnitude of the T-wave vector. The T wave becomes smaller while retaining its normal orientation parallel to the mean QRS vector. In some patients the T wave is incorporated into the end of an abbreviated, depressed ST segment imparting a diphasic (negative, then positive) appearance. At times the digitalis effect may be so marked that all of repolarization takes place during the ST segment; no T waves can be seen or the T wave becomes inverted
- Shortening of the QT interval due to an enhanced cellular repolarization

Important Considerations

- The term *digitalis effect* refers to the combination of a shortened QT interval, a small or diphasic T wave, and ST-segment depression in leads with an upright QRS.
- The degree of ST-segment deviation and T-wave changes may vary from unnoticeable to marked in different individuals, tending to be more pronounced when heart disease is present. The reason for this is unclear. Physiologic stresses, particularly exercise, may accentuate the digitalis effect even if no changes are seen on the baseline tracing. For this reason evaluation of the ST segment for the purposes of an exercise test is invalid in a patient taking digitalis.
- The ST-T changes of the digitalis effect may closely resemble subendocardial injury, subendocardial ischemia, or the secondary effects of left ventricular hypertrophy. In each of these situations the mean ST vector is directed relatively opposite to the mean QRS vector, and the electrocardiogram cannot reliably differentiate among these possibilities.
- The electrocardiogram is not helpful in judging the serum level of digitalis—minimal changes may be pres-

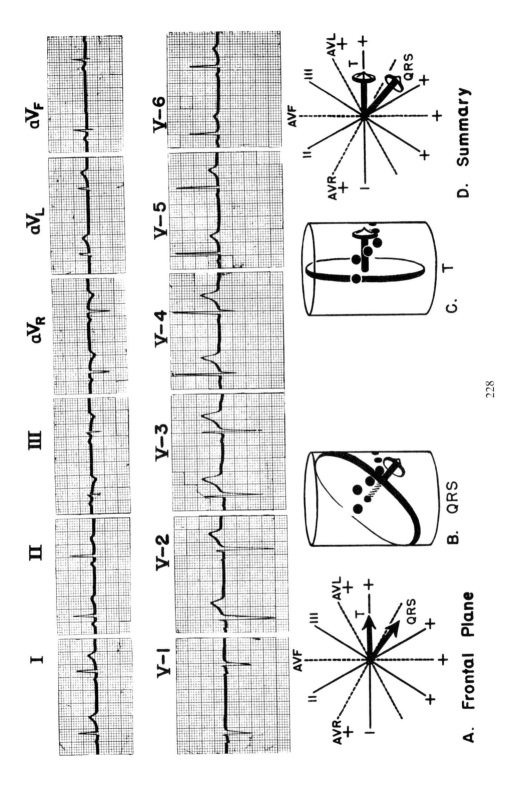

FIG. 15–5A. The electrocardiogram of a normal subject, 29 years of age, made prior to digitalis medication.

(A) The frontal plane projection of the mean spatial QRS and T vectors.

(B) The mean QRS vector is tilted 30° posteriorly because the transitional pathway passes between electrode positions V_3 and V_4.

(C) The mean T vector is tilted 10° anteriorly because the transitional pathway passes through electrode position V_1.

(D) Final summary figure showing the spatial arrangements of the mean QRS and T vectors. This electrocardiogram is normal and is presented for contrast with the next figure.

ent at toxic levels or marked changes may be seen at levels considered to be normal or low.

Digitalis-Induced Arrhythmias

Virtually any rhythm disturbance can be caused by digitalis. The following arrhythmias are more commonly associated with digitalis:

- Premature atrial complexes. These may be uniform, multiform, or blocked
- Premature ventricular complexes (PVCs). Digitalis is particularly implicated when the PVCs are multiform, in a bigeminal pattern, paired, or showing a varying morphology
- Atrial or ventricular tachycardia. Atrial tachycardia with AV block is especially characteristic
- Accelerated junctional rhythm
- Bidirectional tachycardia—alternation of the direction of the complexes
- Sinus node or AV node Wenckebach
- Sinus node arrest
- Complete AV block
- Ventricular fibrillation

Important Considerations

- The combination of an excitant effect, such as an accelerated junctional rhythm or atrial tachycardia, associated with slowing of the sinus rate or the development of AV block, should be strongly suspected as being caused by digitalis.
- Slight PR interval prolongation may be due to digitalis effect and is not a sign of toxicity.
- Atrial flutter and atrial fibrillation are relatively uncommon expressions of digitalis toxicity but can occur.
- All of the arrhythmias listed can also occur in the absence of digitalis or be unrelated to the presence of digitalis.

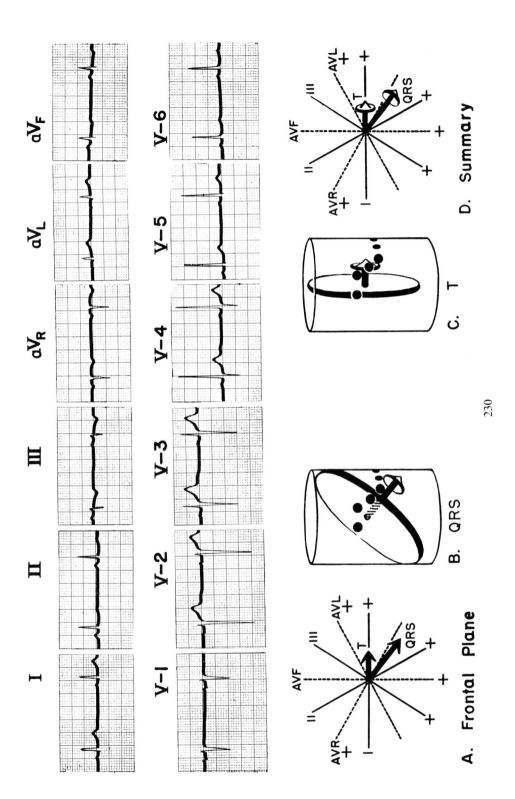

FIG. 15–5B. The electrocardiogram of the same subject shown in Fig. 15–5A made after 2 mg of digoxin were given orally over a 24-h period.

(A) The frontal plane projection of the mean spatial QRS and T vectors. Note that the QRS vector has not been altered by digitalis medication. The mean T vector has not changed in direction but is smaller in magnitude after digitalis medication.

(B) The mean QRS vector is tilted 30° posteriorly because the transitional pathway passes between electrode positions V_3 and V_4.

(C) The mean T vector is tilted 10° anteriorly because the transitional pathway passes through electrode position V_1.

(D) Final summary figure showing the spatial arrangement of the mean QRS and T vectors. The only significant change following digitalis medication is the decrease in magnitude of the T vector, while the direction of the mean T vector remains the same. The Q-T interval has not been altered significantly in this particular instance following digitalis medication.

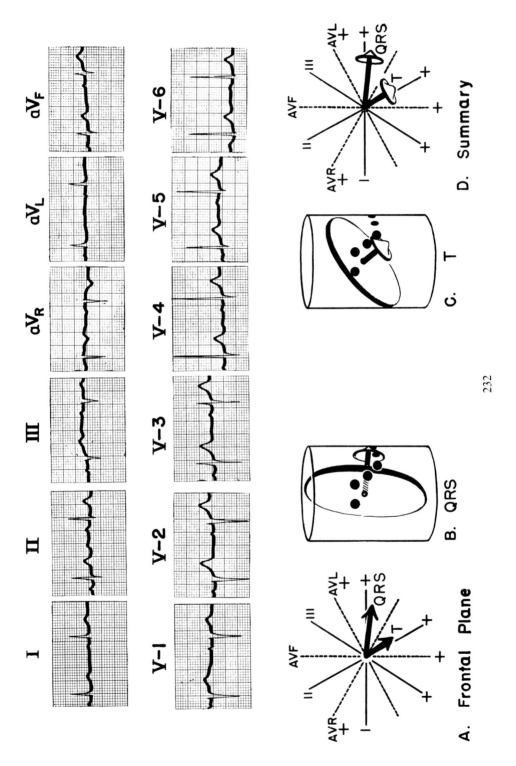

FIG. 15–6. The electrocardiogram of a hypertensive patient, 77 years of age, made prior to digitalis medication.

(A) The frontal plane projection of the mean spatial QRS and T vectors.

(B) The mean QRS vector is tilted 30° posteriorly because the transitional pathway passes between electrode positions V_3 and V_4.

(C) The mean T vector is tilted at least 15° anteriorly because all the precordial leads record upright T waves.

(D) Final summary figure showing the spatial arrangement of the mean QRS and T vectors. This is a normal electrocardiogram and is presented for contrast with the next figure.

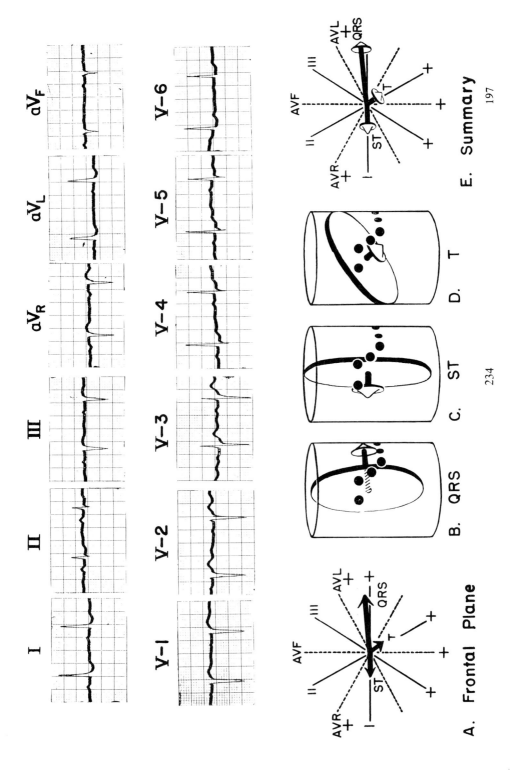

FIG. 15–7. The electrocardiogram of the same subject shown in Fig. 15–6 made after digitalis medication.

(A) The frontal plane projection of the mean QRS, ST, and T vectors. Note that the T waves are extremely small and difficult to identify. The ST segment displacement is greatest and negative in lead I and smallest in lead aV_F. Accordingly, the mean ST vector is perpendicular to lead aV_F and is directed toward the negative pole of lead I.

(B) The mean QRS vector is tilted 30° posteriorly because the transitional pathway passes between electrode positions V_3 and V_4.

(C) The mean ST vector is tilted 15° anteriorly because the transitional pathway passes between electrode positions V_2 and V_3. Note that this will produce elevated ST segments in V_1 and V_2 and depressed ST segments in V_3, V_4, V_5, and V_6.

(D) The mean T vector has not changed its position since the previous tracing, but it is a great deal smaller after digitalis medication.

(E) Final summary figure showing the spatial arrangements of the vectors. As the T vector becomes smaller, an ST vector becomes prominent and is directed opposite to the mean QRS vector. The QT interval prior to digitalis medication was 0.36 s and after digitalis medication is 0.29 s. These findings are characteristic of digitalis effect.

Chapter 16

Summary

The direction of the electrical forces of the heart can be determined by simple inspection of the routine electrocardiographic leads and represented by spatial vectors. By this method, normal electrocardiograms and their variants can be easily recognized and abnormal electrocardiograms can be more easily interpreted. In Fig. 16–1 the spatial vector arrangements for the common electrocardiographic syndromes are illustrated.

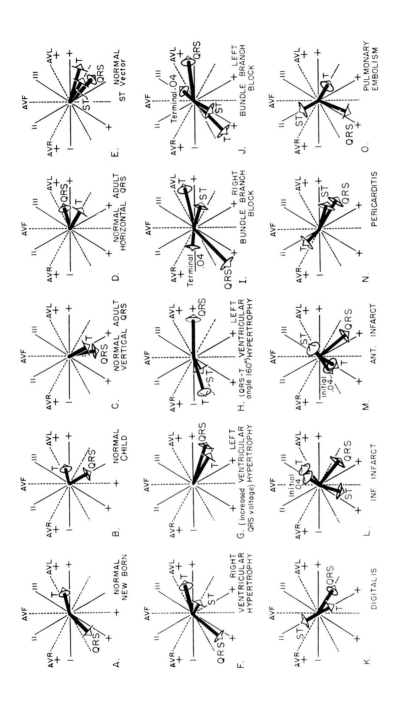

FIG. 16–1. The diagrams above illustrate the spatial vector arrangements for most of the electrocardiographic syndromes commonly observed in clinical practice.

Part Four
Cardiac Arrhythmias

Chapter 17
Introduction to Arrhythmias

Abnormalities of cardiac rhythm and conduction are common. They may be discovered either subjectively by the patient or during a physical examination by the physician, or they may go unnoticed. In any event, the diagnosis of the exact nature of the rhythm disturbance almost always is dependent upon the electrocardiogram. A rational approach to the accurate electrocardiographic analysis of cardiac rhythms requires (1) knowledge of the physiology of cardiac impulse formation and conduction (Fig. 17–1), (2) proper selection and length of the electrocardiographic leads to be studied, and (3) an organized system of analysis.

Physiology of Cardiac Impulse Formation and Conduction

The two physiologic properties of the heart of primary importance in rhythm disturbances are *automaticity* and *conduction*.

Automaticity is the physiological term denoting the process of impulse formation. It also implies "rate" of impulse formation. Automaticity is a function of the highly specialized pacemaker cells. Most electrically active cells maintain a steady charge across their cell membranes when they are in the resting state. This charge is called the *resting transmembrane potential*. The potential does not change until an impulse arrives and lowers the membrane potential to a level known as the *threshold potential*. When the threshold potential is reached, the cell membrane rapidly and completely depolarizes. After this, the cell repolarizes to the original resting potential. The charge remains steady until the arrival of the next impulse. However, the *pacemaker cells* of the heart possess some unique features. Instead of remaining at a steady resting transmembrane potential following repolarization, they spontaneously discharge slowly until the threshold potential is reached, at which point complete, rapid depolarization occurs. Thus, the most significant difference between the pacemaker cell and ordinary electrically active cells is the ability of the pacemaker cell to undergo spontaneous depolarization, allowing impulses to be formed de novo. Once formed, these impulses can be conducted through the rest of the heart. Any influence which (1) changes the transmembrane potential at the end of repolarization, (2) changes the threshold potential, or (3) changes the rate of the slow, spontaneous depolarization phase will change the frequency of depolarization of the automatic cells. In addition, the pacemaker cells in the various areas of the heart have markedly different inherent rates of impulse formation (see Fig. 17-1).

The automatic pacemaker cells in the sinus node, which normally initiate the cardiac electrical impulse, have a physiologic periodicity of 60 to 100 impulses per minute. The automatic cells at the AV junctional level (i.e., the atrial margin of the AV node, portions of the AV node itself, and the bundle of His) have a periodicity of 40 to 60 impulses per minute, while those at the ventricular level have an inherent rate of 20 to 40 impulses per minute. This arrangement of decreasing inherent rate of lower levels allows the next lower level to assume pacemaker function should a higher center fail, but prevents the lower centers from usurping pacemaker function under physiologic conditions. Several cell types which ordinarily do not manifest automaticity under normal conditions become automatic as a result of pharmacologic or pathologic influences.

Conduction is the term denoting the ability to propagate the formed impulse throughout the heart. This property permits the conduction system to rapidly propagate an impulse to all parts of the myocardium in an orderly physiologic sequence. Conduction may be altered or blocked (1) by physiologic stimuli, (2) by a number of pathologic states, and (3) by pharmacologic agents.

The Sequence of Cardiac Excitation

The cardiac electrical impulse is normally initiated in the automatic cells of the sinus node (Fig. 17-1). The impulse then passes into the surrounding atrial tissue

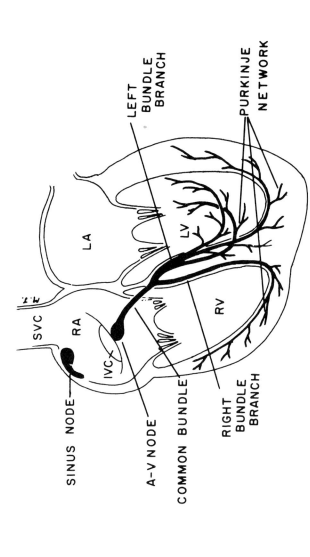

FIG. 17–1. The impulse-forming and -conducting system of the heart. The cardiac impulse is normally formed in the *sinus node*, located at the junction between the superior vena cava (SVC) and the right atrium (RA). From the site of impulse formation, the impulse enters the right atrial tissue (across the so-called SA junction, which probably is no more than a physiological junction whose existence becomes apparent only in disease states) and courses through the right atrium toward the *AV node* and to the left atrium (LA). The passage of the impulse is delayed at the AV node and after this delay passes into the *common bundle* (the bundle of His). The impulse then moves into the *left bundle branch* and the *right bundle bunch*. Depolarization of the septum, with the wave of depolarization moving from left to right, occurs while the impulse continues to be propagated through the distal ramifications of the two bundle branches. The impulse continues into the intramyocardial conduction system, the *Purkinje network*. The wave of myocardial depolarization spreads through the apex of the heart and then up the free walls of the right ventricle (RV) and the left ventricle (LV). Finally, the wave spreads around to the posterior basal portion of the heart.

(Legend for Fig. 17–1 continued on page 244)

(Legend for Fig. 17–1 continued from page 243)
The normal rate of impulse formation in the sinus node is 60 to 100 impulses per minute. Under some circumstances, however, it may form impulses much more rapidly or more slowly. Pacemaker activity is also present in other areas of the heart and may take over either (1) by increasing their rate of impulse formation *above* that of the sinus node cells or (2) by the sinus node cells decreasing their rate of impulse formation *below* that of the other sites (junctional area) of impulse formation. Cells in the area of the AV node have pacemaker function and normally form impulses at the rate of 40 to 60 per minute. Pacemaker cells in the ventricles normally form impulses at the rate of 20 to 40 per minute. The descending inherent rate of impulse formation at the lower levels provides a safety mechanism whereby a lower center may pace the heart if the higher centers fail; but the lower centers will not take over the pacemaker function unnecessarily, since their inherent rate is slower than that of the higher pacemaker.

and is conducted through the atria to the AV node. The impulse passes through the AV node and the common bundle of His to the left and right bundle branches (Fig. 17–1). The impulse is then conducted to the left and right ventricular muscle cells through the ramifications of the Purkinje network.

General Mechanisms of Arrhythmias

Arrhythmias may be attributable to disorders of automaticity, disorders of conduction, or a combination of both. Automaticity may be either *increased* or *decreased*. Abnormal conduction generally means a *decreased* conductivity, but rarely rhythm disturbances may result from impulses during the phase of *supernormal conduction*.

Any stimulus which causes the automatic cells in any location to increase their rate of impulse formation is said to have increased the automaticity of these cells. For instance, increased automaticity of the cells of the sinus node results in sinus tachycardia, and increased automaticity of a pacemaker focus in the ventricle may result in a form of ventricular tachycardia.

Electrocardiographic Lead Selection and Length of Tracing

The analysis of most arrhythmias and conduction disturbances requires the recognition of the relationship between P waves and the QRS complexes, and a lead which records both clearly is often essential. Usually standard lead II or lead V_1 will suffice. However, even in these leads, the P waves may be small or obscured by QRS complexes or by T waves. Therefore, special techniques may be required to demonstrate P waves. Such techniques may include an exploratory chest electrode, an esophageal electrode, or a transvenous right atrial electrode.

In most instances, a length of electrocardiographic tracing equivalent to 15 or 30 s will be sufficient to analyze the events of the cardiac rhythm. Occasionally, however, tracings of 60 to 120 s duration or more will be necessary.

General Versus Specific Diagnoses

In an emergency situation, it is often necessary to make a quick general diagnosis of the rhythm disturbance (such as differentiating between supraventricular and ventricular tachycardia), rather than attempt to elucidate the specific mechanisms involved. The rapid initiation of appropriate therapy in such cases may be lifesaving. Under other circumstances, however, it is desirable to develop the habit of attempting to define the precise mechanism of each abnormal rhythm, using a standard and orderly approach. These habits, fully developed, will assist in making the rapid general diagnosis in the emergency situation much easier and more accurate.

Chapter 18
The AV Diagram

The more obvious arrhythmias are easily and accurately identified by pattern recognition. However, this method of analysis lacks the precision and order of a systematic approach and makes the diagnosis of more complex arrhythmias difficult or impossible.

The AV Diagram

This is also called AV ladder, laddergram, or Lewis lines. The AV diagram was devised to demonstrate graphically the sequence of events in an arrhythmia. It is a simple and precise method of depicting the time relationships of cardiac electrical events.

The only direct rhythm information available from the electrocardiogram is the occurrence of atrial muscular depolarization (P wave) and ventricular muscular depolarization (QRS complex). All else is inferred from the relationships between the P waves, the QRS complexes, and the PR intervals. Thus, the need for an orderly approach to study these relationships is obvious. The AV diagram, properly used, can provide the necessary method.

The AV diagram (Fig. 18–1) is mounted (or drawn) below the electrocardiogram to be analyzed. The *A* level represents atrial depolarization (P waves), and the *V* level represents ventricular depolarization (QRS complexes). The *AV* level is used to represent conduction, and sometimes impulse formation, in the AV conduction system, or junction, i.e., in the conduction pathway between the atria and the ventricles.

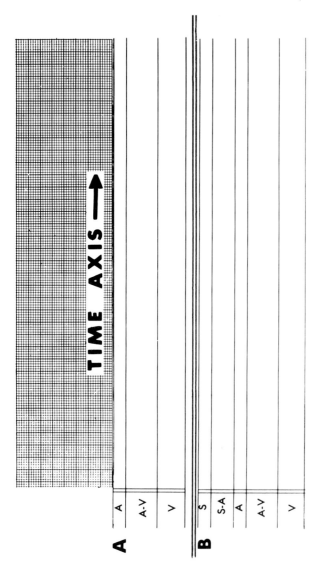

FIG. 18-1. (A) The usual AV diagram for analysis of arrhythmias. The A level of the diagram is used to represent atrial depolarization (the P wave); the V level is used to demonstrate ventricular depolarization (the QRS complex); and the AV level is used to analyze and represent AV conduction.

(B) Diagram used in the special situation where an abnormality of sinoatrial conduction (i.e., conduction from the site of impulse formation in the sinus node to the atrial musculature) is suspected. In addition to the standard A, V, and AV levels, an S level for sinus impulse formation and an SA level for conduction from the site of impulse formation to the atrial musculature are included.

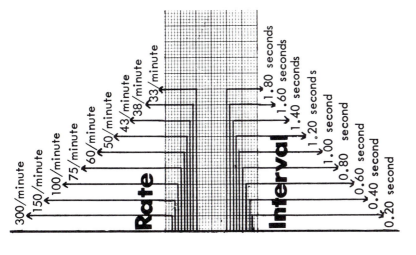

Rate

All intervals—PP, RR, PR, and others when necessary—are carefully measured and noted on the diagram. When measuring intervals always measure from the *beginning* of one event to the *beginning* of the next, e.g., from the beginning of one P wave to the beginning of the next or from the beginning of the P wave to the beginning of the QRS complex. Measurements are best made with a pair of fine-point calipers, several types of which are available commercially.

It is useful to remember the rate-interval relationships for the more common intervals (Fig. 18–2). An interval of 0.20 s occurs when the rate is 300 per minute, 0.40 s equals 150 per minute, 0.60 s equals 100 per minute, and 1.00 s equals 60 per minute.

The A Level

The P waves should be first identified on the electrocardiogram, if possible, and represented in the *A* level of the diagram. Since atrial depolarization is not an

FIG. 18–2. Rate-interval relationship. When the rate of a cardiac event is 300 times per minute, the interval of time occurring between the events is 0.20 s or one large square on the ECG paper. When the event is occurring 150 times per minute, the interval is 0.40 s or two large squares. The diagram demonstrates some of the rate-interval relationships in the more common range. A table giving more complete rate-interval information is in the Appendix. Just as the horizontal axis from left to right indicates time on the electrocardiogram, it also indicates time on the AV diagram.

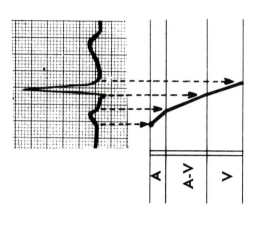

FIG. 18-3. Representation of a normal P-QRS complex on the AV diagram. The beginning of the P wave is represented on the top line of the A level of the diagram, and the end of the P wave is noted on the line between the A and AV levels. The two points are connected, giving a sloped line which represents both the direction and duration of the P wave. The beginning of the QRS complex is noted as a point on the line between the AV and V levels, and the end of the QRS is noted on the bottom line of the V level. Again, the two points are connected, giving a sloping line in the V level. Finally, the end point of the P wave and the beginning point of the QRS complex are connected to represent the normal AV conduction.

instantaneous event (the P wave has a measurable duration), and since the horizontal axis of the diagram indicates time, P-wave duration is indicated by sloping the P-wave representation on the diagram so as to indicate time. If the atrial impulse is normally conducted from the sinus node to the AV node (anterograde conduction) and is therefore upright in standard lead II, the slope representing atrial depolarization time is directed from above downward (Fig. 18-3). If atrial depolarization occurs retrograde from the AV node or ventricle backward (P wave inverted in lead II), the slope is drawn from below upward along the time axis (Fig. 18-4). Atrial *fusion complexes* occur when the timing between an anterograde impulse and a retrograde impulse, is such that each depolarizes part of the atrial myocardium. They are represented by the anterograde and retrograde lines meeting in the middle of the A level (Fig 18-4).

The V Level

After the P waves have been represented on the A level of the diagram—or before this if the P waves are obscure and difficult to identify—the QRS complexes are represented on the V level of the diagram. The same rules determine the representation of time and the site of impulse origin. Figure 18-3 demonstrates the QRS representation of a normally conducted ventricular impulse. Figure 18-5 demonstrates the proper method to indicate the QRS complex on the AV diagram for a

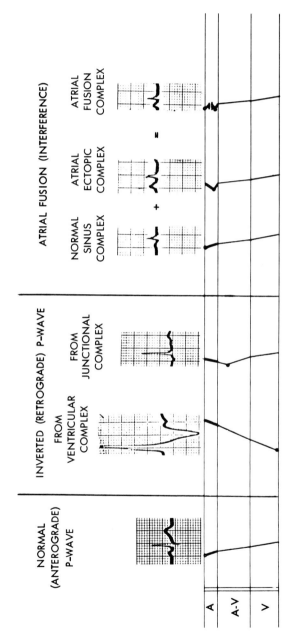

FIG. 18-4. Representation of P wave on the AV diagram. (All complexes from lead II and impulse origins represented by dots.) The first complex is normal and shows normal P-wave representation. The second and third complexes show retrograde P waves (conducted through the atria from an impulse originating below them). The slope of the line is now from the bottom of the A level to the top along the time axis, indicating clearly that the impulse which depolarizes the atria came from below. The last three complexes demonstrate atrial fusion. When two sites of impulse formation can each function independently of each other, each may depolarize part of the atria when the timing is correct, and a P wave intermediate between the two independent forms results. This is represented as shown in the last complex.

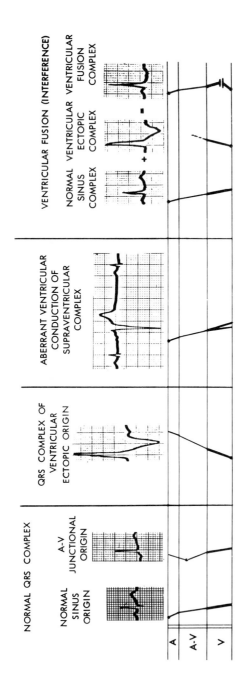

FIG. 18-5. Representation of QRS complexes on the AV diagram. All complexes resulting from normal conduction of supraventricular impulses, whatever the site of impulse formation (sinus, ectopic atrial, or nodal), are represented by the normal QRS notation as demonstrated in the first two complexes. If, however, an impulse of supraventricular origin is conducted through the ventricles along an aberrant pathway of conduction, the AV diagram notation is as shown in the fourth complex. An impulse of ectopic ventricular origin is represented by noting the *beginning* of the QRS complex at the *bottom* of the *V* level and the *end* at the *top*, as shown in the third complex. Finally, fusion complexes at the ventricular level are approached and represented by essentially the same technique as at the atrial level, as shown by the last three complexes on the illustration.

252

A-V DIAGRAM NOTATIONS OF A-V CONDUCTION

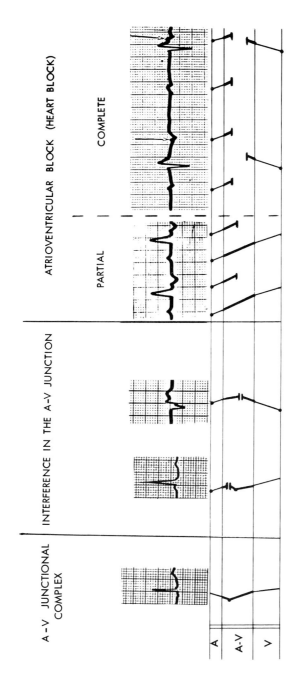

FIG. 18–6. Representation of events in the AV junction on the AV diagram. When an impulse originates in the AV junction, conduction may occur anterograde to the ventricles and retrograde to the atria. An arbitrary point is chosen on the AV diagram time axis to indicate the time of impulse formation, and this point must precede any of the electrical events of the complex (P wave and QRS complex). Then the retrograde P wave, if present, and the anterograde QRS complex are noted in the standard manner. The representation is completed as shown in the first complex. The phenomenon of interference between two impulses coming at each other from different directions in the AV junction (and thus blocking each other's passage) is represented in the second and third complexes. In essence, this phenomenon is the same as fusion complexes, but since it is occurring in the AV junction, there is no direct electrocardiographic representation of it other than physiological block of further conduction of both impulses. Pathological block representation is shown in the last two sequences of complexes in the figure. The first group of complexes is from a tracing showing 2:1 AV block, and the second group is from a case of complete heart block.

253

FIG. 18–7. An electrocardiogram showing normal sinus rhythm demonstrates the sequence of steps in the construction of an AV diagram.

(A) The diagram is mounted or drawn below the electrocardiogram and the P waves identified and represented at the A level. The PP intervals are measured and recorded.

(B) The QRS complexes are identified and represented at the V level. The RR intervals are measured and recorded. Intervals are measured from the *beginning* of one QRS complex to the *beginning* of the next. The same rule applies to the PP intervals.

(C) The final step is the representation of AV conduction at the AV level. This step is often the most difficult, and frequently the most important, and will be discussed later in more detail.

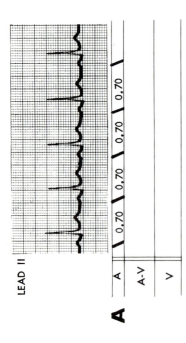

junctional complex, a ventricular complex, aberrant ventricular conduction, and ventricular fusion complexes.

The AV Level

After all identifiable P waves and QRS complexes have been represented on the diagram, AV conduction is represented. The distal end of the P-wave line is connected to the proximal end of the QRS line. The AV line slope thus indicates AV conduction duration (Fig. 18–3.) Figure 18–6 demonstrates the method of representing various types of events in the AV junction. AV block with a dropped complex (for example, 2:1 AV block in which only one of every two atrial impulses can be conducted through the conduction system to discharge the ventricular myocardium) is represented by a line extending partway down the AV level (Fig. 18–6). Anterograde and retrograde conduction of an impulse formed in the AV junction tissue is represented as shown in Fig. 18–6.

Interference, which occurs when two impulses approach each other from different directions and thus prevent each other's passage, is also demonstrated in Fig. 18–6.

The use of the AV diagram in diagramming specific abnormalities of impulse formation and/or conduction will be presented in more detail later. Figure 18–7 demonstrates the sequence used in the construction of the complete diagram, using a normal sinus rhythm as an example.

Chapter 19
Variations in Sinus Node Rhythms and Atrial Arrhythmias

Sinus Arrhythmia and Wandering Pacemaker

Not all variations of sinus node impulse formation are abnormal, and two common mechanisms which fall into the category of normal variants are *Sinus arrhythmia* and *wandering pacemaker*.

Sinus arrhythmia is common in childhood and tends to disappear with advancing age, but may also be seen in normal adults. It is often, but not always, related to the respiratory cycle. Characteristic of sinus arrhythmia is a normal sinus pacemaker which alternately slows and speeds up. Normal atrial depolarization pattern (i.e., normal P waves), normal AV conduction (i.e., normal PR interval), and normal QRS configuration are present. This arrhythmia involves only the rate of impulse formation by cells of the sinus node. Thus, the PP and RR intervals are equally affected in each cycle and of equal duration in any given cycle (Fig. 19–1). The minimal variation in cycle length between the shortest cycle and the longest cycle in a sinus arrhythmia is 0.12 s.

A *wandering pacemaker within the sinus node* (Fig. 19–2) is characterized electrocardiographically by rate changes as seen in ordinary sinus arrhythmia plus P-wave variations and minor PR interval changes with rate. The P waves tend to be taller and PR intervals longer with a faster rate. It also may be *phasic* (i.e., related to the respiratory cycle) or *nonphasic*. A wan-

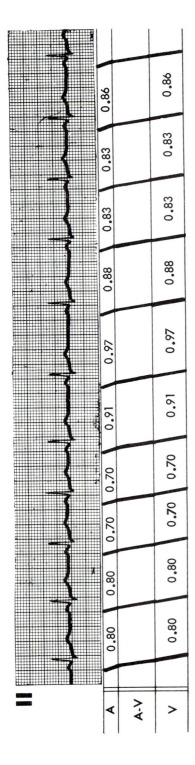

FIG. 19-1. Sinus arrhythmia. There is a normal sinus node mechanism of impulse formation, normal conduction, and a normal ventricular response. There is a variation in the rate of sinus node impulse formation which is greater than 0.12 s between the longest and shortest cycles (longest cycle = 0.97 s, shortest cycle = 0.70 s; therefore, variation = 0.27). The lack of variation in P-wave morphology and in PR interval differentiates sinus arrhythmia from a wandering pacemaker.

dering pacemaker within the SA node does not, in itself, indicate disease. A *wandering atrial pacemaker* (wandering between the sinus node and AV node) can be diagnosed when the rate changes of sinus arrhythmia are associated with more marked P wave and PR interval variations (such as biphasic or inverted P waves in lead II). The P waves, which are intermediate between the upright sinus node complexes and the inverted retrograde AV junctional P waves, are usually atrial fusion complexes. (See Chapter 24).

Sinus Bradycardia

Sinus bradycardia is defined as a heart rate of less than 60 complexes per minute with a normal sinus mechanism. It is a normal variant in well-conditioned athletes at rest, and in normal sleep in healthy individuals. It may also be caused by increased parasympathetic tone of any cause and may occur in acute inferior myocardial infarction. The electrocardiographic findings include a normal P wave, normal QRS configuration, and

258

a normal PR interval with a PP and RR interval of greater than 1.00 s (Fig. 19-3).

Sinus Tachycardia

Sinus tachycardia is defined as a heart rate greater than 100 impulses or beats per minute, with a normal sinus mechanism of impulse formation. It occurs frequently in both cardiac and noncardiac disease states, as well as in normal adaptive physiologic responses to exercise, fright, or other sympathetic stimuli. Rapid sinus tachycardia in adults usually does not exceed 150 to 160 impulses or beats per minute, although it occasionally occurs with rates as fast as 170 to 180 per minute. Further, in a few individuals, it may reach or exceed 200 per minute under conditions of extreme exercise. In young children, on the other hand, sinus tachycardia not uncommonly may exceed 200 impulses or beats per minute. With slower rates of sinus tachycardia, normal P waves and normal QRS complex duration and configuration and normal PR intervals are the rule and are easily recognized (Fig. 19-4). However, when the rate increases to the point where the P waves may be buried in the preceding T waves and the rate approaches that seen in ectopic tachycardias (e.g., paroxysmal atrial tachycardia), the recognition of sinus tachycardia becomes more difficult (Fig. 19-5). In this latter situation, diagnostic clues favoring sinus tachycardia include gradual slowing of the rate over a period of minutes to hours and the response to carotid sinus pressure (slowing, followed by a gradual return to the original rate in a few seconds to a minute). These points will be discussed further in the section on the differential diagnosis of tachycardias.

Paroxysmal Supraventricular Tachycardia

Paroxysmal supraventricular tachycardia is a rapid regular tachycardia characterized by normal QRS complexes, inverted (retrograde) P waves in leads II, III, and aV_F, and a heart rate in the range of 140 to 240 (usually 170 to 220) impulses or beats per minute (Fig. 19-6). The most common mechanism of paroxysmal supraventricular tachycardia is AV nodal reentry in a patient with dual AV nodal pathways. Dual AV nodal pathways can only be identified with intracardiac electrophysiologic studies; but, functionally, the AV node behaves as though there are rapidly conducting and slowly conducting pathways having different refractory periods. The refractory period of the fast pathway is longer; and, therefore, a premature atrial impulse may block in the fast pathway and conduct in the slow pathway. On the electrocardiogram one therefore sees abrupt prolongation of the PR interval with an appropriately timed premature atrial impulse; and, if the timing characteristics are proper, the impulse will go down the slow pathway, reenter the fast pathway in a retrograde direction, and set up a circus movement tachy-

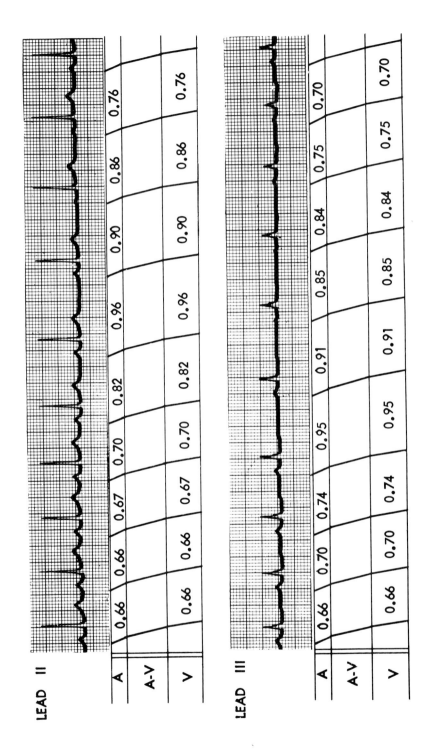

FIG. 19–2. Wandering pacemaker. There is a rhythmic slowing and speeding of the heart rate as in sinus arrhythmia. However, the P waves tend to be taller and the PR intervals slightly longer when the PP interval shortens (i.e., when the heart rate increases). Conversely, the P waves are shorter and the PR intervals shorter when the heart rate decreases. This is characteristic of so-called *wandering pacemaker within the sinus node*. If the shortening of the P waves in lead II progresses to the point of inversion of the P waves, a *wandering atrial pacemaker* would be diagnosed (i.e., wandering to the AV node). Inversion of the P wave in lead III alone does not have the same significance since this may occur from respiratory influences alone–in the absence of a wandering pacemaker.

cardia. The second most common clinical setting for paroxysmal supraventricular tachycardia is the Wolff-Parkinson-White (W-P-W) syndrome. The bypass tract (Kent bundle) in W-P-W usually has a longer refractory period than the AV node; and, therefore, a premature atrial impulse may block entering the bypass tract, conduct down the normal pathway, and then reenter the bypass tract in the retrograde direction. If this sequence is sustained, paroxysmal supraventricular tachycardia can result. True paroxysmal supraventric-

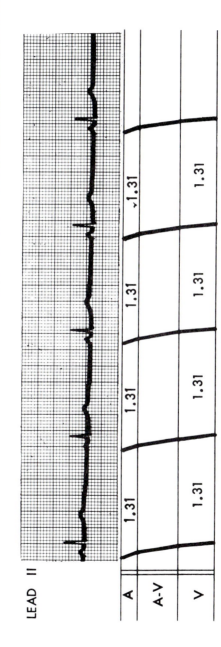

FIG. 19–3. Sinus bradycardia. The rhythm is regular, the mechanism is of normal sinus origin, and the rate is less than 60 per minute. In this tracing the PP and RR intervals are 1.31 s; the rate therefore is 46 per minute. An RR interval of 1.00 s represents a rate of exactly 60 per minute; thus an interval greater than 1.00 s indicates a rate of less than 60 per minute.

ular tachycardia is characterized by a 1:1 relationship between atrial activity and ventricular activity. In paroxysmal supraventricular tachycardia due to AV nodal reentry, the retrograde P waves are usually hidden in the QRS complex and not visible on the standard electrocardiogram. In paroxysmal supraventricular tachycardia due to W-P-W, the retrograde P waves usually follow the QRS complex.

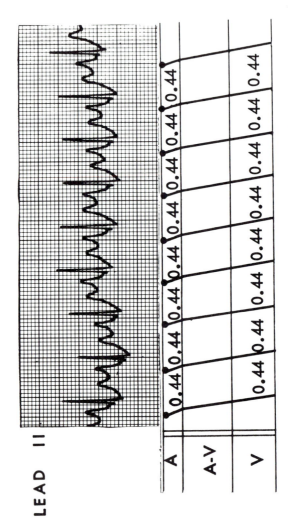

FIG. 19–4. Sinus tachycardia. The PP and RR intervals are 0.44 s, indicating a heart rate of 136 per minute. The PR intervals are normal, indicating normal conduction from atria to ventricles. Thus, this tracing demonstrates a moderate sinus tachycardia.

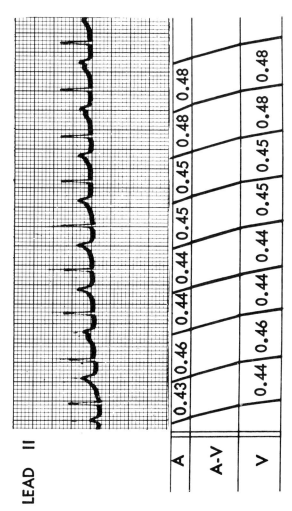

FIG. 19-5. Sinus tachycardia. The fourth, fifth, sixth, and seventh P waves would be difficult to distinguish from the T waves of the preceding complexes were it not for the slight variation in heart rate which separates the P waves from the T waves in the first, third, eighth, and ninth complexes. P waves are not ordinarily obscured by T waves at this rate (133 per minute); however, the first-degree heart block (prolonged PR interval) in this case is responsible for the obscured P waves. Slight rhythmic variation in the rate of a supraventricular tachycardia tends to favor the diagnosis of sinus tachycardia, rather than paroxysmal atrial tachycardia or atrial flutter. The rate variation in atrial fibrillation is usually erratic, rather than rhythmic.

Ectopic Atrial Tachycardia

An ectopic atrial focus firing at a rapid rate can result in a narrow QRS regular tachycardia similar to paroxysmal supraventricular tachycardia. However, there are important differences in that ectopic atrial tachycardia is often due to an automatic focus in the atrium, and the impulses formed in the atrium by this mechanism must be conducted across the AV conducting system. The rate range for this tachycardia is similar to paroxysmal supraventricular tachycardia, but the electrocardiogram differs in that P waves are usually visible prior to each QRS complex, although the P waves may have a different morphology than the normal sinus P waves. They may be diminutive in voltage, and may have a different vector than the sinus P waves. In addition, AV nodal conduction may not always keep pace with the rate of atrial impulse formation, and 2:1 conduction across the AV node may occur. Carotid sinus massage also may result in varying degrees of AV conduction impairment, in contrast to paroxysmal supraventricular tachycardia, in which carotid sinus massage causes abrupt cessation of the rhythm disturbance (see below).

Atrial Flutter

Atrial flutter is generally categorized as a regular arrhythmia (such as sinus tachycardia or paroxysmal atrial tachycardia) because of its effect on atrial and ven-

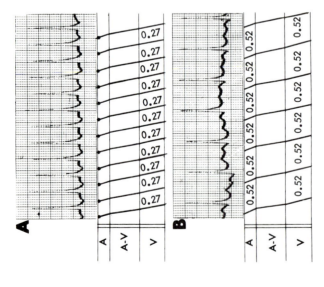

FIG. 19-6. Paroxysmal supraventricular tachycardia.
(A) A short strip obtained during an attack of paroxysmal supraventricular tachycardia, demonstrating a heart rate of 222 beats per minute (RR interval = 0.27 s). The P waves cannot be discerned because of the extremely rapid rate.
(B) After abrupt conversion to a normal sinus mechanism, the heart rate is 115 beats per minute (RR interval = 0.52 s). The P waves are now easily seen.

tricular electrocardiographic events, but conduction may become irregular due to Wenckebach conduction across the AV node. The precise mechanism of atrial flutter remains somewhat controversial, but it is probably not due to a discrete focus in the atrium. A circus movement or multiple reentry mechanism seems likely.

The *atrial rate* in atrial flutter is usually between 250 and 350 per minute and commonly approximates 300 per minute. Since even a normal AV node can rarely conduct at this rate and atrial flutter is most frequently associated with organic disease, flutter is almost always accompanied by some degree of AV conduction disturbance, such as 2:1 conduction. Thus, the *rate of ventricular response* in atrial flutter does not often exceed 150 to 160 impulses or beats per minute. In fact, any time a rate of 150 per minute is seen, atrial flutter with 2:1 conduction should be considered unless P waves are easily identifiable. Since the rate of flutter tends to remain relatively constant and the degree of AV block varies from time to time, the ventricular rate in this arrhythmia may vary erratically between 150 (2:1 conduction), 100 (3:1 conduction), and 75 (4:1 conduction); or, on the other hand, it may remain constant at 150, 100, or 75 per minute.

The diagnosis is very simple when typical sawtooth flutter waves and a high degree of AV block are present (Fig. 19–7). However, when the ventricular rate is rapid (Fig. 19–8) or the flutter waves atypical, differentiation from other tachycardias may be difficult. Carotid sinus pressure, when effective, may help in this situation, since it increases the degree of AV block, decreasing the ventricular response and allowing the flutter waves to become obvious. Occasionally, carotid sinus pressure speeds up the flutter rate or rarely even converts it to atrial fibrillation.

Atrial Fibrillation

As in the case of atrial flutter, the precise mechanism responsible for atrial fibrillation remains obscure. Several theories have been proposed, but none has been conclusively proved. Among the causes of atrial fibrillation are coronary artery disease, mitral valve disease, and thyrotoxicosis.

Electrocardiographically, atrial activity in atrial fibrillation is represented by irregular waves, which may be coarse or fine, at a rate which is usually well over 400 per minute. Sometimes the fibrillatory waves may be so fine as to be unrecognizable on the clinical electrocardiogram. In this situation, only the QRS-T complex appears on the electrocardiogram, without obvious atrial activity. At the other extreme, the fibrillatory waves may be extremely coarse and relatively regular, resembling atrial flutter waves.

The characteristic ventricular response pattern in atrial fibrillation is a grossly irregular rhythm with a normal QRS duration and contour (Fig. 19–9). With digitalis intoxication and/or disease of the AV con-

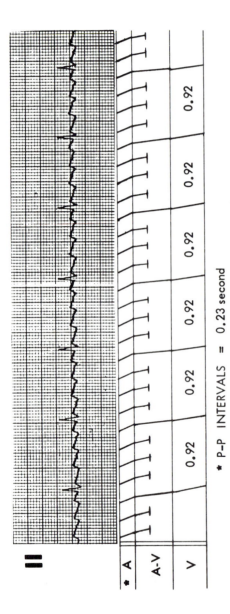

FIG. 19-7. Atrial flutter with 4:1 AV conduction. Typical sawtooth flutter waves and the high degree of AV block with consequent paucity of QRS complexes make the flutter pattern simple to recognize. The atrial flutter rate is 260 per minute (PP interval = 0.23 s) and the ventricular rate is 65 per minute (RR interval = 0.92 s). Only one of each four flutter waves is conducted through the AV junction to depolarize the ventricles—hence the term 4:1 AV conduction.

ducting system, the ventricular response in atrial fibrillation may be regular (Fig. 19-10) because of a high-grade AV block and a junctional pacemaker. On the other hand, with very rapid ventricular response in atrial fibrillation, the rhythm may appear to be regular.

The ventricular rate in untreated atrial fibrillation is usually 140 to 200 impulses or beats per minute, but may sometimes be extremely rapid (up to but rarely exceeding 250 impulses or beats per minute), especially at its onset. With the less rapid ventricular rates, the atrial fibrillatory waves and the gross irregularity of rhythm are easily recognizable on the electrocardiogram. With digitalis therapy administered to decrease the ventricular response toward a normal heart rate, the electrocardiographic characteristics of atrial fibrillation become even more obvious (Fig. 19-9). As mentioned earlier, digitalis intoxication or disease of the AV node may make the ventricular rhythm regular

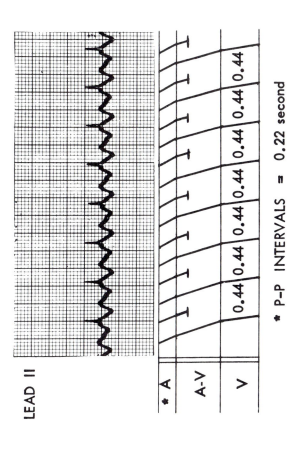

FIG. 19–8. Atrial flutter with 2:1 AV conduction. The atrial flutter rate is 272 per minute (PP interval = 0.22 s), and the ventricular rate is 136 per minute (RR interval = 0.44 s). Sawtooth flutter waves may be less obvious in the presence of the more rapid ventricular response. As the atrial flutter rate increases and/or the ventricular response increases, atrial flutter becomes more difficult to recognize.

because of complete heart block with a junctional or ventricular pacemaker. In these instances, the representation of atrial activity on the electrocardiogram does not change.

Carotid sinus pressure may be helpful in the diagnosis of a very rapid tachycardia due to atrial fibrillation. As in the case of atrial flutter, carotid sinus pressure may cause a transient decrease in the ventricular response, allowing the otherwise obscured atrial fibrillatory waves to be seen between the QRS complexes.

In summary, the differential diagnosis of rapid atrial

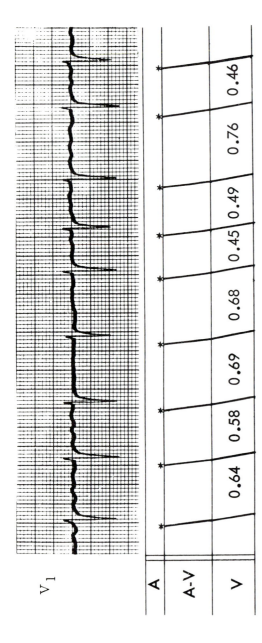

FIG. 19-9. Atrial fibrillation. There is a grossly irregular ventricular response, with RR intervals varying from 0.76 to 0.45 s. The baseline shows fibrillatory wave activity with some variation in the depth of the waves.

arrhythmias includes sinus tachycardia, paroxysmal supraventricular tachycardia, atrial flutter, and atrial fibrillation. While the rate of the tachycardia may occasionally be useful (at least in a statistical sense), its primary value is a negative one. For example, if discrete atrial activity is seen at a relatively slower tachycardia (120 to 140), atrial fibrillation is excluded and atrial flutter may also be excluded. Constant electrocardiographic monitoring during carotid sinus pressure is an extremely helpful technique. Sinus tachycardia will slow and then gradually speed up again after carotid sinus pressure. Paroxysmal supraventricular tachycardia is either uninfluenced by carotid sinus pressure or will abruptly revert to a normal sinus rhythm; and atrial flutter and fibrillation exhibit a decrease in ventricular response, often rendering flutter or fibrillatory waves obvious during the slower rate. This is a temporary response; the rate rapidly returns to its prior level.

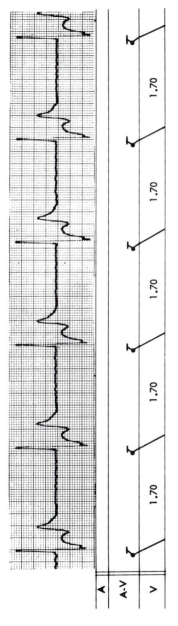

FIG. 19–10. Atrial fibrillation with complete heart block. The baseline demonstrates fine atrial fibrillation. However, instead of the expected gross irregularity and normal or rapid heart rate, the ventricular response is slow (36 per minute) and perfectly regular. The precise pacemaker location is difficult to determine in this case, but it is probably junctional, rather than ventricular. Atrial fibrillation with a slow and regular ventricular response indicates the presence of a high degree of heart block, which may be either pathologic or drug-induced.

Atrial Premature Complexes

These are common and occur both with and without identifiable heart disease. Frequent (often multiform) premature atrial complexes often precede the onset of atrial tachycardia or atrial flutter or fibrillation. On the other hand, occasional uniform atrial premature complexes are often seen in the absence of heart disease, sometimes being precipitated by excesses of caffeine, tobacco, or alcohol or by fatigue.

Electrocardiographically, the premature atrial complex is recognized as an early P wave, frequently different in configuration from the normal P wave (Fig. 19–11). Conduction of the premature impulse, with a resulting QRS complex, may or may not occur.

The premature P-QRS is followed by a pause. There are two types of pauses that occur after premature complexes—the *compensatory pause* and the *noncompensatory pause*. If the time duration between the P-QRS preceding the premature complex and the P-QRS following the premature complex is equal to two normal cycles, the pause is fully *compensatory*. This occurs when the premature impulse does not interfere

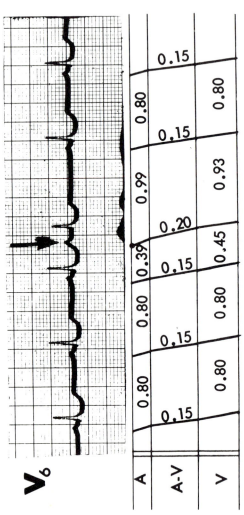

FIG. 19–11. Premature atrial complex. The fourth QRS is early and of the same configuration as the other complexes. The differential diagnosis lies between premature atrial complex and premature junctional complex. There is an abrupt upward deflection at the end of the T wave of the complex preceding the premature beat. This deflection is not present in the T waves of the other complexes on the tracing and is the representation of the superimposed P wave of the premature atrial complex. The pause following the premature complex is noncompensatory (less than two full cycle lengths from the P wave before the early P wave to the P wave after it—see text). The PR interval of the premature atrial complexes is prolonged because of residual refractoriness in parts of the AV conduction system at the time of the early complex.

node and discharges it early, thus interrupting the sinus cycle. *A noncompensatory pause is the rule following a premature atrial complex, although compensatory pauses do occur rarely* (Fig. 19–12).

When a premature impulse is conducted the resulting

with the sinus node cycle. When the time duration between the P-QRS preceding and the P-QRS following the premature complex is less than two normal sinus cycles, the pause is *noncompensatory*. This occurs when the premature impulse travels retrogradely to the sinus

270

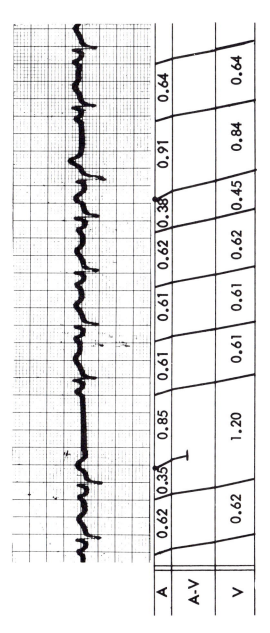

FIG. 19–12. Premature atrial complexes, conducted and nonconducted. The T waves of the second and sixth QRS complexes on the tracing are slightly deformed by the P waves of two premature atrial complexes. The first premature atrial impulse is not conducted to the ventricles; thus, there is no QRS complex following it. The second premature atrial impulse is conducted, and a QRS complex with slight aberration of conduction (Chapter 21) follows the early P wave. It is noteworthy that both premature atrial complexes are followed by fully compensatory pauses, rather than the noncompensatory pause which usually follows premature atrial complexes.

ventricular complex either may be perfectly normal in configuration or may be aberrantly conducted, with an abnormal configuration. (See Chapter 21 for discussion of aberrant ventricular conduction.) When the premature atrial complex occurs close enough to the preceding complex or when there is some degree of AV block present, the atrial impulse may not be conducted to the ventricles (Fig. 19–12). Thus, an early abnormal P wave, not followed by the QRS, is seen on the electrocardiogram, and a pause follows which is usually noncompensatory. A premature atrial complex may occur during the inscription of the T waves of the preceding complex, and the abnormal P wave may be difficult or impossible to recognize; and the differentiation of the premature atrial complex from a junctional premature complex or from a ventricular premature complex (if aberrant ventricular conduction has occurred) may be difficult. Frequently, however, the P wave obscured by the T wave sufficiently deforms the T wave to make its presence identifiable (Fig. 19–11). For this reason, when premature atrial complexes are suspected, but P waves cannot be identified, careful study of the T-wave contour of the preceding and subsequent complexes may reveal the diagnosis.

When an inverted early P wave is present in lead II and is followed by a normal QRS with PR interval of 0.12 s or longer, differentiation between a lower atrial premature complex and a junctional premature complex with anterograde delay of conduction (see Chapter 20) may be impossible.

Chapter 20
AV Junctional Rhythm Disturbances

AV Junctional Pacemaker Function

The AV junction is equipped with its own pacemaker function, at an intrinsic rate of 40 to 60 impulses or beats per minute. Teleologically, this provides a safety mechanism that will take over the pacing function of the heart should the higher (SA nodal or atrial) centers fail. Conversely, since the normal AV junctional rate is slower than the normal sinus rate, the junctional pacemaker function will not disturb the physiological pattern of impulse formation and conduction under normal circumstances. In the presence of pathological or pharmacological abnormalities, however, there may be inappropriate usurping of pacemaker function by this mechanism.

Junctional Escape Complexes

When the normal sinus mechanism slows sufficiently or fails completely, the AV junction will escape and pace the heart—unless, of course, the AV junction is diseased or suppressed to the extent that it cannot function in this capacity. Activation of this escape mechanism may occur in the absence of disease, as in the well-trained athlete whose physiologic bradycardia may become slow enough that junctional escape beats occur. Excessive vagal tone due to pharmacologic effects may also induce junctional escape. Among diseases associated with junctional escape mechanisms are sinus bradycardia in the course of acute inferior myocardial infarction and any degenerative or inflammatory lesion which may interfere with sinus node or atrial pacemaker function.

The electrocardiographic representation of AV junctional escape is easily recognized (Fig. 20–1). Since the pathway of conduction of the impulse through the ventricles is usually normal, the QRS complexes of junctional escape complexes are usually identical (or nearly so) to the normally conducted sinus complexes on the tracing. In addition to a normal QRS configuration, the junctional escape complex characteristically has a long pause (at least 1.00 s) preceding the escape; and sinus bradycardia, or sinus arrest, is usually present. Junctional rhythm in the presence of complete heart block may be considered an escape mechanism. However, junctional rhythm is unusual with complete heart block because the disease of the AV junction causing heart block is often extensive enough to destroy pacemaker function or to block conduction of a junctional impulse.

Premature Junctional Complexes

Inflammatory, ischemic, pharmacologic, or "idiopathic" lesions of the AV node or His bundle may be associated with premature junctional complexes. The complexes often have an identical configuration as those of the normal sinus complexes. However, instead of following a pause or occurring in association with sinus bradycardia or sinus arrest, junctional extrasystoles may occur at any heart rate and occur early (i.e., a short interval preceding the junctional complex).

Careful search for P waves should be made if junctional premature complexes are suspected. When a normal anterograde P wave (with a normal or long PR interval) is seen to precede an early complex, the early complex is a premature atrial complex rather than a premature junctional complex. When an inverted P wave (lead II, III, or V_F) occurring less than 0.08 s before the premature QRS is associated with the premature complex of normal configuration, it is usually positive evidence of a junctional premature complex (Figs. 20–2 and 20–3). The inverted P wave may precede or follow the QRS complex, or it may be buried in the QRS complex and be unidentifiable on the standard electrocardiogram.

It may be difficult or impossible to differentiate a premature junctional complex conducted with ventricular aberration from a ventricular premature complex.

However, an inverted P wave in a lead normally having upright P waves (lead II or aV_F) preceding a QRS complex of abnormal configuration with a PR interval of less than 0.08 s makes the diagnosis of junctional premature complex with aberration probable. The atria would not be discharged before the ventricles by an impulse originating in the ventricles.

274

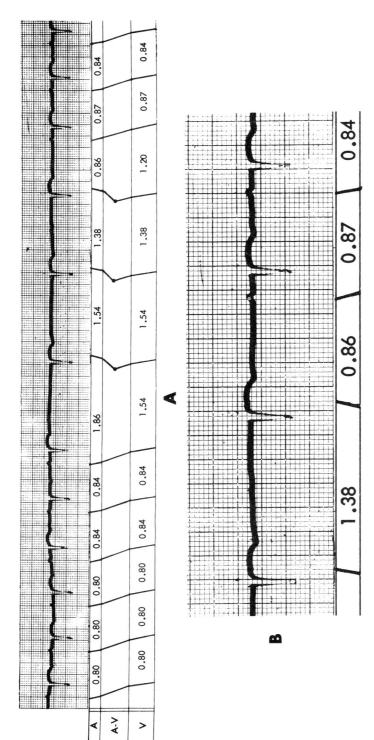

FIG. 20-1. Sinus pause or arrest with junctional escape.

(A) The first six complexes show normal sinus rhythm. A long pause (1.54 s) follows the sixth complex, and the pause is terminated by an *escape* complex. The junction escapes twice more before a normal sinus mechanism returns. The escape complexes have the same QRS configuration as the sinus complexes.

(B) The top of the T wave of each junctional complex is slightly deformed by a very small negative deflection not present on the T waves of the normally conducted sinus complexes. This negative deflection is an inverted P wave conducted retrograde from the junctional pacemaker.

275

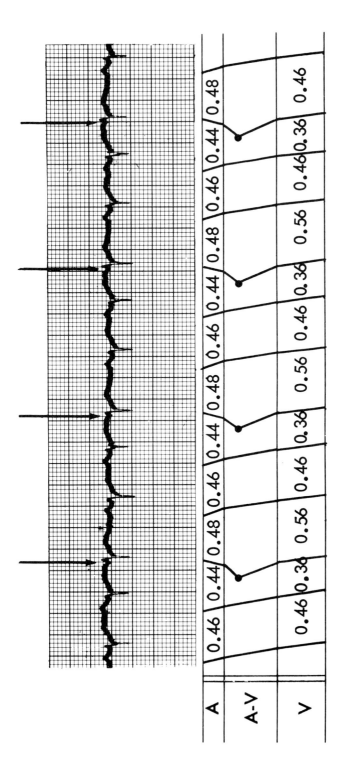

FIG. 20–2. Junctional premature complexes with fixed coupling intervals. Every third complex is premature (the third, sixth, ninth, and twelfth complexes). These occur *early* and have the same configuration as the QRS of the sinus complexes. In addition, the premature complexes are *preceded by inverted P waves* (arrows) beginning *0.04 s before the QRS*. Since the PR interval is less than 0.12 s, it may be concluded that the P waves are conducted retrograde from the focus of the junctional pacemaker. The PR intervals of the sinus complexes are constant at 0.14 s, and the premature junctional complexes are followed by a fully compensatory pause.

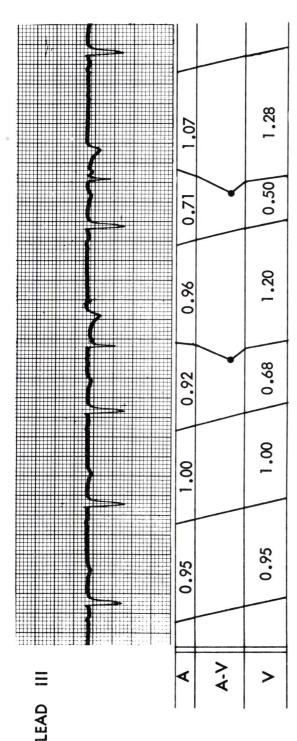

FIG. 20-3. Junctional extrasystoles. The fourth and sixth complexes occur early and are similar to the normally conducted complexes. The sixth complex is followed by an inverted P wave buried in the ST segment, and the fourth complex is deformed at the ST junction by another inverted P wave. The AV diagram demonstrates that the junctional extrasystoles have both anterograde and retrograde conduction, with the retrograde conduction being responsible for the inverted P waves. The variable coupling interval between the normal complexes and the extrasystoles (0.68 and 0.50 s) suggests that junctional parasystolic activity (see Chapter 24).

Junctional Tachycardia

If a junctional pacemaker usurps the pacing function of the heart at a rate in excess of 100 impulses or beats per minute, junctional tachycardia is present. However, if the rate is between 60 and 100 impulses or beats per minute, tachycardia is not present by definition, but as the normal intrinsic rate of the junctional pacemaker is below 60 impulses or beats per minute, a junctional rate between 60 and 100 per minute is abnormally rapid for this pacemaker. Thus, this rhythm should be considered as an *accelerated junctional rhythm*, which implies an abnormality but not a *tachycardia*.

The electrocardiographic criteria for junctional tachycardia are the same as those for premature junctional complexes insofar as QRS morphology and PR relationships are concerned. The heart rate must exceed 100 impulses or beats per minute. Persistent junctional tachycardia presents no problem of definition. Intermittent groups of junctional premature complexes do pose a problem in terminology, however, and different authorities accept several different numbers of consecutive complexes as constituting a burst of junctional tachycardia. Whether three, four, five or more consecutive junctional complexes constitute the minimum for diagnosis of a "burst of junctional tachycardia," is not critical, as long as the significance of their presence is understood.

AV Dissociation

Much of the confusion regarding AV dissociation is due to conflicting terms and definitions. Our definition is chosen for its simplicity, but different terms and definitions are presented by others (see discussion of topic by Marriott).

AV dissociation usually occurs by one, or by a combination, of two mechanisms—either by an abnormal slowing of the sinus node to a rate below the intrinsic AV junctional rate or by an increase of the intrinsic AV junctional rate above the sinus node pacemaker rate. In both instances, the common denominator is a junctional rate faster than the sinus rate (Fig. 20–4). Two different pacemakers thus drive the heart—a sinus pacemaker controls the atria and an AV junctional pacemaker controls the ventricles. While the junctional pacemaker is the faster, the rates of the two pacemakers are usually fairly close. Were this not true, the junctional pacemaker would drive both the ventricles *and* atria and a junctional rhythm with retrograde atrial activation would be present. However, when the rates are close together, the sinus impulses conducted into the AV tissue interfere with retrograde conduction of the junctional impulses, and thus the two pacemakers continue to function (Fig. 20–4). When concomitant partial AV block is also present, however, the rates of the two pacemakers may be more divergent.

The rhythm in AV dissociation is basically regular, but the regularity is interrupted by *capture beats*. Remembering that AV dissociation is not, in itself, a form of *heart block* and that AV conduction is therefore usually potentially normal, a P wave occurring at a time when the conducting tissue is no longer refractory from the preceding junctional impulse, and before the next junctional impulse occurs, may be conducted and depolarize the ventricles. This is called a *capture beat* and is recognized as an early complex, preceded by a

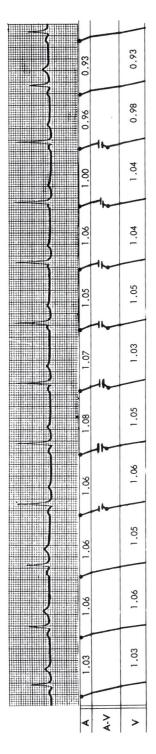

FIG. 20-4. AV dissociation due to sinus bradycardia and junctional escape. The first three complexes are normal sinus beats with normal AV conduction. The heart rate is just below 60 per minute. The fourth complex is a junctional escape with a slightly different QRS morphology and shorter interval between the onset of the P wave and the onset of the QRS complex than the preceding sinus complexes. The sinus node rate slows a little more during the next few cycles and the junctional escape rate remains relatively constant, perpetuating the AV dissociation. As the sinus rate then increases, the P waves emerge from the QRS complexes and finally *recapture* the ventricles (last two complexes). The atrial (higher) pacemaker is slower than the junctional (lower) pacemaker during the period of dissociation, permitting the AV dissociation to occur.

P wave, which occurs beyond the refractory period of the preceding QRS complex. The PR interval of a capture beat is normal unless (1) the P wave occurs in the relative refractory period of the preceding complex or (2) first-degree heart block coexists with the AV dissociation.

It should be clearly understood that, while the atria and ventricles are hemodynamically and pathologically "dissociated" in complete heart block, the term *AV dissociation*, as we are using it refers to a physiologic dissociation which occurs when a lower pacemaker has a higher rate than a higher pacemaker. Heart block may or may not coexist with AV dissociation, but heart block is not an essential feature of it. To avoid confusion, we feel that the term *AV dissociation* should be reserved for the physiologic dissociation described and should not be used in reference to the dissociation of complete heart block.

Chapter 21
Ventricular Arrhythmias

Ventricular Pacemaker Function

If all the higher pacemakers fail to function, the intrinsic pacemaker activity of the ventricles will pace the heart at a spontaneous discharge rate of 20 to 40 impulses or beats per minute. Again, therefore, a lower pacemaker is present with a slower intrinsic rate than the higher level pacemakers, and the slower rate prevents the lower pacemaker from usurping pacemaker function under normal conditions.

Ventricular Escape Complexes

Ventricular escape complexes occur most commonly in complete heart block (see Chapter 23). In this situation, even though the higher and faster atrial pacemaker may be intact and functioning, none of the impulses reach the ventricles because of the AV block. Thus, the dominant rhythm becomes a ventricular escape rhythm or idioventricular rhythm. Ventricular escape complexes also occasionally occur during carotid sinus pressure for reversion of paroxysmal atrial tachycardia. Other than these two situations, ventricular escape complexes are uncommon, as the faster AV junctional pacemaker tends to escape during a sinus pause.

Premature Ventricular Complexes

Premature ventricular complexes are extremely common in all age groups, both with and without demonstrable organic heart disease. The patient may be completely asymptomatic or may experience only annoying symptoms such as palpitations. Or the premature complexes may be a cause for serious concern to both patient and physician—depending upon the setting in which they occur and upon their frequency.

Electrocardiographically, the characteristics of premature ventricular complexes are (1) early complexes which (2) have a QRS duration greater than 0.12 s and bizarre contour and (3) are followed by a fully compensatory pause (Fig. 21–1). The fully compensatory pause is due to the fact that the sinus node rhythm is not interrupted by retrograde conduction from the premature complex. Thus, two full sinus cycles enclose the premature ventricular complex.

Another type of premature ventricular complex (Fig. 21–2) is the *interpolated* complex. The interpolated premature ventricular complex occurs between two consecutive normal sinus complexes and does not interrupt the basic sinus rhythm. Thus, there is no pause and this is truly an "extra" systole. The interpolated premature ventricular complex usually occurs in the setting of a relatively slow sinus rate, because with a rapid sinus rate, the ventricles and/or conducting system would be refractory to the first sinus impulse following the premature complex (Fig. 21–2).

A simple premature ventricular complex is usually related to the preceding sinus complex by *fixed coupling*; that is, each premature complex on a given electrocardiogram occurs at a constant time interval from the onset of the sinus complex immediately preceding it. On the other hand, when the coupling interval is variable, a parasystole may be the mechanism of the premature complexes (see Chapter 24).

Differentiation of Premature Ventricular Complexes from Premature Supraventricular Complexes with Aberrant Ventricular Conduction

A premature atrial or premature AV junctional complex occurring soon enough after the preceding sinus complex may reach the ventricular conducting tissue before it has fully recovered from the preceding complex. Since recovery is not perfectly uniform, some areas of the ventricular conducting system may be partially refractory, while other areas of the system may be able to conduct normally. The activation impulse may thus take an aberrant pathway through the ventricles, rather than follow the normal pathway and sequence of depolarization. Electrocardiographically, this presents as a bizarre, widened QRS complex (Fig. 21–3), often of a right bundle branch block type of configuration. The aberration is an inversely variable function of the time since the last depolarization, and so there may be anything from a minimal change in QRS duration to a completely bizarre complex which mimics premature ventricular activity. Differentiation of premature atrial or junctional complexes with marked aberration from premature ventricular complexes may

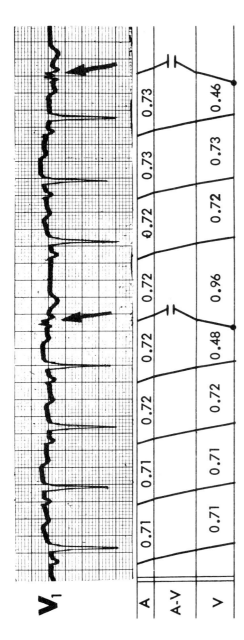

FIG. 21-1. Premature ventricular complexes. There is a normal sinus rhythm, with the fifth and ninth complexes (arrows) occurring early and having a markedly different configuration from that of the normal sinus complexes. They have a QRS duration in excess of 0.12 s and are not preceded by discernible P waves. Both premature complexes are followed by a fully compensatory pause; that is, the two sinus cycles from the second to the fourth complex measure 1.43 s and the two cycles from the fourth to the sixth complex (which includes the abnormal fifth) measure 1.44 s. All these characteristics favor the diagnosis of premature ventricular complexes. Finally, it can be positively demonstrated that the sinus node cycle is not interrupted. The PP interval of the cycle preceding the first premature complex measures 0.72 s in duration. If one measures 0.72 s from the P wave of the fourth complex, it is seen to coincide with the inverted wave at the beginning of the ST segment of the premature complex, which exactly matches the configuration of the normal P waves in this lead. Thus, the P wave originates in the sinus node and discharges the atria but is not conducted to the ventricles. The AV diagram indicates the interference at the AV level. Finally, measuring from the P wave at the end of the premature beat to the next P wave demonstrates the expected 0.72 s length of the cycle.

283

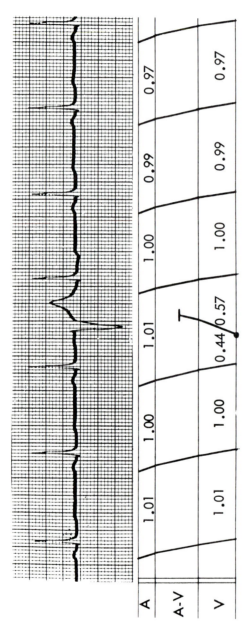

FIG. 21–2. Interpolated premature ventricular contractions. The P waves and QRS complexes on the tracing are quite constant at a rate of about 60 per minute. There is a wide, abnormally configured premature QRS between the third and fourth sinus complexes, and the premature complex does not interrupt the sinus rhythm. The P wave of the fourth complex (the one following the premature complex) is difficult to identify in the descending limb of the T wave of the premature complex, but its presence can be inferred from the fact that the complex following the premature complex is normal in configuration and does not break the sinus cycle sequence (as indicated in the AV diagram). Finally, note the phenomenon of postextrasystolic T-wave inversion in the first normal complex after the premature complex.

be difficult or sometimes impossible. If a premature atrial complex is seen preceding the early, bizarre QRS, aberration is the cause. However, premature atrial complexes are often difficult to identify because they may be small and fall in the T waves of preceding complexes. In addition, aberrant conduction often occurs in the presence of atrial fibrillation. Therefore, it is frequently necessary to rely upon other criteria, based for the most part on QRS morphology and certain time relationships (see Marriott), to make the differentiation.

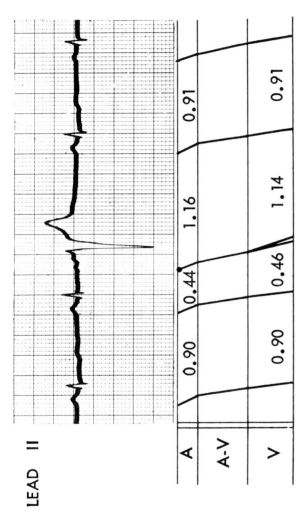

FIG. 21-3. Premature atrial impulse with aberrant ventricular conduction. The first two complexes on the tracing are sinus. The P waves, QRS complexes, and PR intervals are normal, and the rate is 67 per minute. The T wave of the second complex is deformed by an abnormal, biphasic, early P wave which is followed by a QRS complex of distinctly abnormal configuration. Because of the presence of the premature P wave coupled to the abnormal QRS complex by a normal PR interval, the diagnosis of premature atrial impulse with aberration of ventricular conduction may be made. This occurs because of refractoriness in parts of the AV junction at the time when the premature impulse arrives, causing an abnormal pathway of conduction. In the case of a premature AV *junctional* complex with aberrant conduction, the differentiation from premature ventricular complex may be more difficult or impossible—depending on the P-wave relationship.

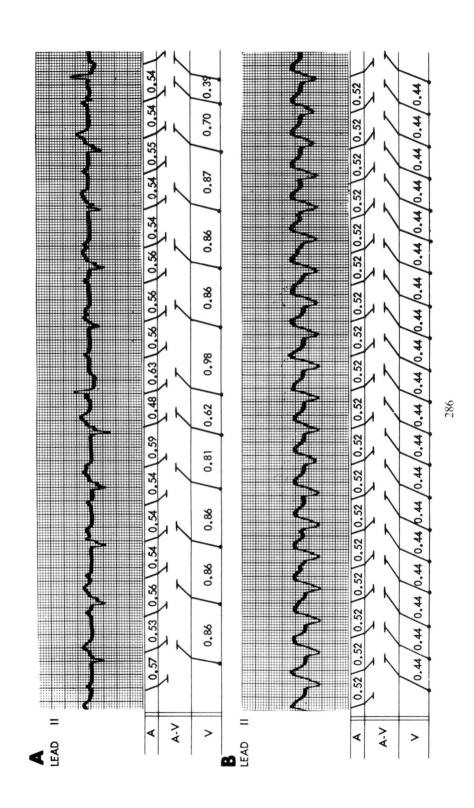

Fig. 21-4. Ventricular tachycardia.

(A) Complete heart block is present, as manifested by the absence of any relationship between the P waves and QRS complexes and an idioventricular rhythm. The rate of the idioventricular rhythm, however, is much more rapid than the normal escape rate of a ventricular pacemaker (PR interval of basic rhythm = 0.86 s, rate = 70 per minute). Therefore, even though the rate does not conform to the usual definition of tachycardia (rate = 100), it is an abnormal rate for this pacemaker and is therefore called an *accelerated ventricular rhythm*. Note, too, the irregular extrasystolic activity present. (B) Ventricular tachycardia with a rate of 136 per minute is present. Complete heart block is still present and a number of the P waves are easily seen. Since the PP intervals are quite constant, the presence of the other P waves is inferred. The P waves and QRS complexes are completely independent of each other because of the complete heart block.

Ventricular Tachycardia and Ventricular Flutter

Ventricular tachycardia is one of the most serious of the arrhythmias, in terms of both its immediate hemodynamic alterations and its prognostic significance. It occurs most frequently with coronary artery occlusion or as a manifestation of digitalis intoxication and/or electrolyte disturbances. Sustained ventricular tachycardia generally requires prompt therapy.

Various authorities require different numbers of con-

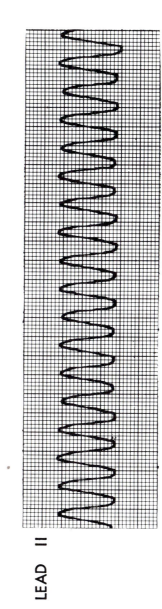

Fig. 21-5. Ventricular flutter. This rhythm forms a clinical bridge between ventricular tachycardia and ventricular fibrillation. There are very smooth, regular waveforms at a rate of 207 per minute. The patient still had a cardiac output at the time of this event, but it was markedly reduced. This rhythm rarely lasts more than a few seconds to a minute, tending to progress rapidly to ventricular fibrillation or to revert to ventricular tachycardia or other rhythms.

secutive ectopic ventricular complexes for the diagnosis of ventricular tachycardia. These requirements begin at three consecutive complexes and increase. We feel that the specific number of ectopic ventricular complexes is less important than the recognition of the clinical setting of the arrhythmia and an understanding of its prognostic implications. The electrocardiographic representation of a burst of ventricular tachycardia (see Fig. 21-4) is a cluster of wide (greater than 0.12 s), bizarre QRS complexes interrupting the basic cardiac rhythm. A paroxysm of sustained ventricular tachycardia may sometimes be difficult to recognize. The complexes are wide and bizarre, but differentiation from supraventricular tachycardia with aberrant ventricular conduction may be difficult or impossible.

The rate of ventricular tachycardia may be as fast as 180 to 200, but may also be much slower. The same problem of definition exists with ventricular rhythms as with junctional rhythms when the heart rate is less than 100, but greater than the intrinsic rate of the ventricular pacemaker (i.e., greater than 40 per minute). It is best to reserve the term *tachycardia* for instances when the rate is greater than 100 per minute and to use the term *accelerated ventricular rhythm* for rates between 40 and 100.

Ventricular tachycardia commonly occurs at a rate of 130 to 180 per minute, which places it in the same range of rates as most supraventricular tachycardias. The rhythm of ventricular tachycardia may be somewhat irregular, but the degree of irregularity is often minimal, similar to the slight irregularity occasionally seen in some of the supraventricular tachycardias. P waves may be of help in the differential diagnosis if they can be identified (Fig. 21-4).

Ventricular flutter probably is not a distinct entity, but an extreme end of the spectrum of ventricular tachycardia, bridging it with ventricular fibrillation. Ventricular flutter is characterized by very regular and smooth ventricular waveforms at a rate of 200 to 300 per minute (Fig. 21-5). P waves are not evident.

Ventricular Fibrillation

Ventricular fibrillation is incompatible with life, since it is an uncoordinated depolarization of the ventricular musculature which does not result in an effective cardiac output. Now that effective electrical defibrillation devices are available, it is often a treatable arrhythmia if cardiac output is maintained by external cardiac massage until defibrillation can be performed.

The electrocardiogram shows irregular waveform activity (Fig. 21-6). The waves may range from quite coarse to very fine, the latter approaching a straight line. More coarse waves tend to be seen at the onset, with fine waves preceding the cessation of all electrical

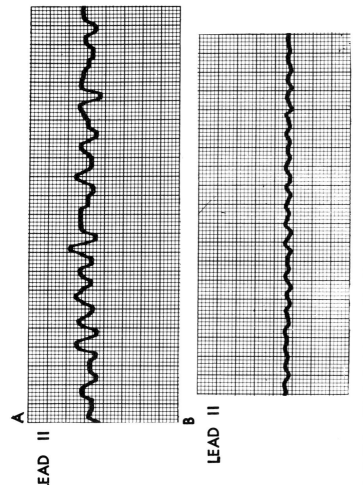

FIG. 21-6. Ventricular fibrillation. This rhythm is incompatible with life since it represents uncoordinated ventricular activity with no cardiac output. It is, however, frequently treatable, the success of treatment depending on the setting in which it occurs.

(A) *Coarse ventricular fibrillation.* Note the irregular waveform activity.

(B) *Fine ventricular fibrillation.* This type of pattern frequently precedes the complete cessation of electrical activity at the time of biological death of the heart and is very difficult to defibrillate.

activity at the time of biological death of the cardiac muscle cells.

Ventricular fibrillation should be differentiated from *cardiac standstill*, in which no identifiable ventricular activity is seen. In cardiac standstill the electrocardiogram is simply a straight line or occasionally a straight line with P waves. Ventricular fibrillation probably accounts for most sudden deaths in the course of acute myocardial infarction, whereas cardiac standstill is probably more common in long-standing degenerative or ischemic heart disease without identifiable acute precipitating cause of death and also in acute anoxic states.

Chapter **22**

The Differential Diagnosis of a Tachycardia

It is common to be confronted with the problem of the differential diagnosis of a tachycardia. Accuracy is important since the various tachycardias are treated differently and have different prognostic significance. Often the diagnosis is clear immediately upon examining the patient or briefly studying the electrocardiogram. On the other hand, however, it may occasionally be almost impossible to make a definitive conclusion about the nature of a tachycardia—even with the use of the most sophisticated techniques available. Nevertheless, with the careful application of a few general rules, most of the tachycardias can be identified.

Differentiation between Supraventricular and Ventricular Tachycardias

When the supraventricular tachycardias (sinus tachycardia, paroxysmal atrial tachycardia, atrial flutter with 2:1 ventricular response, atrial fibrillation with rapid ventricular response, and AV nodal tachycardia) have normal conduction through the ventricles, distinction between them (as a group) and ventricular tachycardia is usually simple, since the QRS morphology will be normal. In ventricular tachycardia, however, the QRS complex is always widened beyond 0.12 s and is of

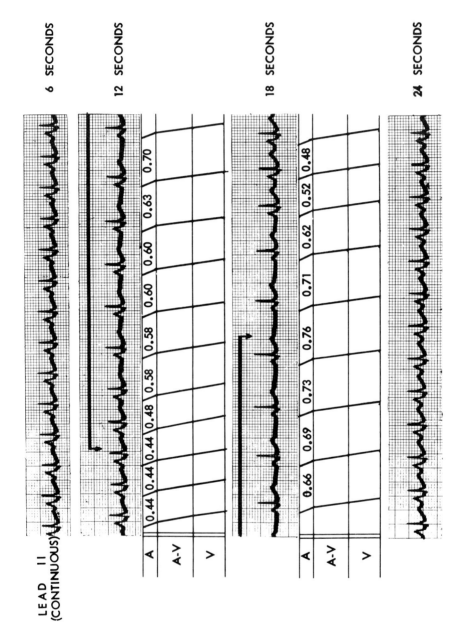

FIG. 22–1. Sinus tachycardia with carotid sinus pressure. The first 6 s (top tracing) of the electrocardiogram demonstrates a typical sinus tachycardia at a rate of 136 per minute. The PP and RR intervals are constant at 0.44 s, and the PR interval is constant. When carotid sinus pressure is applied at the time of the first arrow (second strip of the tracing), the rate slows progressively. When the carotid sinus pressure is stopped at the time of the second arrow (third strip of the tracing), the rate progressively increases until it reaches the original rate of 136 per minute at the end of the fourth strip of the electrocardiogram. Note also the shortening of the P waves and PR intervals as the rate decreases and the return to their original voltage and duration after the release of pressure. This pattern of events is the same as seen in wandering pacemaker and is seen occasionally in sinus tachycardia with carotid sinus pressure.

abnormal configuration. But when supraventricular tachycardia with coexistent bundle branch block occurs or when supraventricular tachycardia is accompanied by ventricular aberration, QRS morphology is of little help in making the distinction. Thus, a normal QRS complex indicates supraventricular tachycardia, whereas a wide, abnormal QRS may be seen with either supraventricular or ventricular tachycardia.

P-wave characteristics may aid in diagnosis. Upright P waves in leads II, III, and aV_F with a 1:1 relationship to QRS complexes indicate a supraventricular (sinus or atrial) tachycardia, and inverted P waves in these leads (which precede the QRS) also indicate supraventricular tachycardia (low atrial or AV junctional). Inverted P waves following a QRS complex are characteristic of both supraventricular and ventricular tachycardia. Upright P waves without fixed relationship to the QRS complexes are of limited value, since dissociation between the P waves and QRS complexes may occur in both supraventricular (junctional) and ventricular tachycardias.

The rhythm is frequently of value. Ventricular tachycardia may be somewhat irregular; however, the degree of this irregularity is often small and may occur to almost the same extent with some of the supraventricular tachycardias. Nevertheless, a tachycardia with wide, bizarre QRS complexes and some irregularity and with no fixed PR relationship strongly favors ventricular tachycardia over supraventricular tachycardia. When no P waves are seen, with a somewhat irregular tachycardia and wide QRS complexes, atrial fibrillation with aberrant conduction or bundle branch block may be present. This is especially difficult to differentiate from ventricular tachycardia when the rate is rapid.

The range of rates of ventricular and supraventricular tachycardias overlap, making rate of limited value in the differential diagnosis. Carotid sinus pressure, which usually has no effect on the rate of ventricular tachycardia, but does affect rate in most of the supraventricular tachycardias, may aid in the differential diagnosis.

The differentiation of supraventricular tachycardia

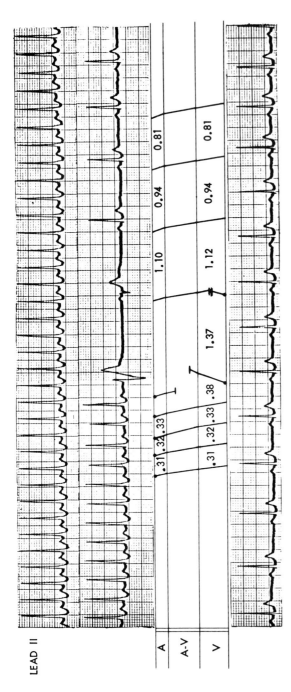

FIG. 22–2. Paroxysmal supraventricular tachycardia with carotid sinus pressure. This is a continuous tracing (lead II) recorded during a typical attack of supraventricular tachycardia in a 9-year-old girl without evidence of organic heart disease. In the upper strip, the rate is over 200 per minute and P waves are not identifiable. QRS duration and morphology are normal. In the middle strip of the tracing, an abrupt termination of the paroxysmal supraventricular tachycardia with carotid sinus pressure occurs. An extrasystole (see Chapter 21) follows the last beat of the tachycardia. This is followed by a pause terminated by a *fusion* complex (fusion between a conducted sinus beat and an escape complex—see Chapter 24). A normal sinus mechanism then resumes as seen in the rest of the second strip and in the third strip of the tracing.

with bundle branch block or with aberrant conduction from ventricular tachycardia is very important and frequently impossible with standard electrocardiography. In this setting, some of the more sophisticated diagnostic techniques, such as an esophageal or transvenous right atrial lead, are indicated. These leads will reveal P waves that are not identifiable on the standard electrocardiogram and thus make it possible to study the relationships between the P waves and the QRS complexes.

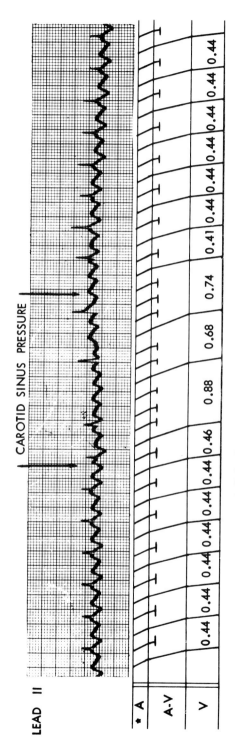

FIG. 22–3. Atrial flutter with 2:1 conduction and carotid sinus pressure. The effect of carotid sinus pressure in the presence of atrial flutter is demonstrated. Before carotid pressure is applied (first arrow), the interval between successive flutter waves is 0.22 s. The atrial rate speeds up slightly (interval about 0.20 s) during the application of pressure. Decrease in AV conduction is present with consequent *temporary* slowing of the ventricular response as a result of the increased vagal tone. The decrease in conduction is frequently a whole-number multiple of the basic flutter wave intervals. During the period of slower ventricular rate, the flutter pattern becomes more obvious.

295

Differentiation of the Various Supraventricular Tachycardias

When ventricular tachycardia is ruled out on clinical and electrocardiographic evidence, the various supraventricular tachycardias must next be differentiated. Many differential points have already been listed (Chapter 19). When the clinical picture, rate, and presence and nature of P-wave activity are not diagnostic, the use of carotid sinus pressure is indicated. This procedure should always be performed under constant electrocardiographic monitoring, since the effect of carotid sinus pressure on rate may be so subtle that it cannot be picked up by palpation or auscultation, and because this procedure is attended by a small but real danger of inducing more serious arrhythmias or even

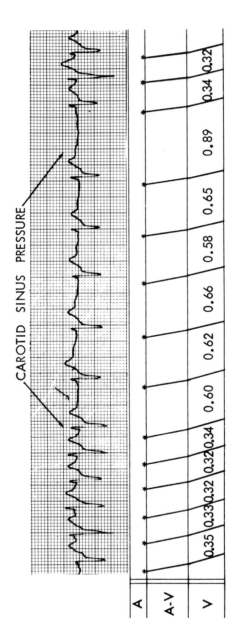

FIG. 22-4. Atrial fibrillation (rapid) with carotid sinus pressure. The tracing, standard lead II, was recorded while attempting to make a diagnosis on a patient with a tachycardia. The first six QRS complexes on the electrocardiogram demonstrates a rate of about 180 per minute with slight irregularity. No P waves are visible and atrial fibrillation with rapid ventricular response was suspected. Carotid sinus massage was performed, and the rate slowed markedly to the range of 90 to 100 per minute. Irregular ventricular response and the absence of P waves is evident during the period of slower rate. Very soon after the carotid sinus pressure is stopped, the rate returns to about 180 per minute.

cardiac arrest. Carotid massage should not be performed in patients with diseased carotid arteries or with known cerebrovascular disease and should be used only under extremely strong indications in patients with recent myocardial infarction. An alternative to the use of carotid sinus pressure is the use of the drug edrophonium (Tensilon), 10 mg intravenously. This will often be as effective as carotid pressure in terms of parasympathetic effect.

Sinus tachycardia responds to carotid stimulation by a temporary decrease in rate, followed by a gradual return to the prestimulation rate (Fig. 22–1).

Paroxysmal supraventricular tachycardia responds in one of two ways: (1) either there is no effect at all (rarely slight slowing) or (2) there is an abrupt cessation of the tachycardia and resumption of a normal sinus rhythm (Fig. 22–2). When ectopic atrial tachycardia with *varying block* (usually seen in digitalis intoxication) is present, the diagnosis is usually obvious without the use of carotid sinus pressure, since (1) the varying block permits the P waves to be seen and (2) the rhythm is irregular.

When *atrial flutter with 2:1 conduction* is present, carotid sinus pressure usually induces an increase in the degree of block, the increase being in whole-number multiples of the rate. Thus, the conduction may become 3:1, 4:1, etc. (rate of approximately 100, 75, etc.). This increase in block is transient, and a return to the original rate fairly rapidly is the rule (Fig. 22–3).

Atrial fibrillation similarly responds to carotid sinus pressure with an increased degree of block (Fig. 22–4), and the slowing may make obscure fibrillatory waves demonstrable. In addition, the ventricular response will have the typical irregular response of atrial fibrillation—unless complete block with junctional rhythm is temporarily induced, resulting in a regular response. It is not uncommon, however, for atrial fibrillation to fail to respond to carotid sinus pressure.

297

Chapter **23**

Abnormalities of Conduction and Heart Block

Disease or pharmacologic agents may affect the conduction system of the heart, causing a variable degree of conduction impairment. When the impairment becomes clinically recognizable, the condition is referred to as *block*. The most easily recognized site of block clinically is in the AV junction, because the AV junction is the electrical bridge between the P wave and the QRS complex. However, block may occur anywhere that conducting tissue is present. When it occurs in the conducting tissue distal to the bundle of His, the QRS pattern of right or left bundle branch block, or of intraventricular block, results (see Chapter 7).

Three degrees of AV block may occur—designated first, second, and third (complete). First-degree AV block involves a simple prolongation of conduction time; second-degree AV block is intermittent failure of conduction; and third-degree AV block is complete failure of conduction. Again, it should be emphasized that these various degrees of block are most easily recognized in the AV junction, but each may theoretically occur in a number of areas where conduction tissue is present—although not all are demonstrable by clinical electrocardiography.

First-Degree AV Block *(Fig. 23–1)*

This is a prolongation of the conduction time across the AV junction and is manifested electrocardiographically as a constant prolongation of the PR interval in all complexes, as measured from the onset of the P wave to the first deflection of the QRS complex. The upper limit of normal for the PR interval varies somewhat with age and with heart rate. (See Appendix, Table 1.) The upper limit of normal in the adult patient is 0.20 s and is lower in children. The upper limit of normal also varies with heart rate, tending to be shorter with more rapid rates in normal persons.

Second-Degree AV block

This occurs in two forms: the *Wenckebach type* (the more common form) and the *intermittent block type*. Both types have in common the characteristic of dropped beats, i.e., supraventricular impulses (P waves) which are not conducted through the AV junction to discharge the ventricle.

The Wenckebach phenomenon is characterized by groups of complexes ("periods") having progressively increasing PR intervals until conduction fails completely and a complex is dropped. The dropped ventricular complex terminates each Wenckebach period (Fig. 23–2). The greatest PR interval *increment* (i.e., increase in PR interval from one complex to the next) occurs between the first and second complexes of the period, and the *increment* progressively *decreases* thereafter. The RR intervals of each cycle in the Wenckebach period progressively *decrease concomitant with the decreasing PR interval increment* as the period continues. The pause associated with the dropped complex is less than twice the length of the last or shortest cycle in the period. A minimum of three atrial

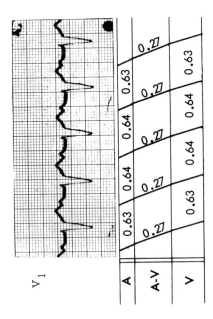

FIG. 23–1. First-degree AV block. The PR interval is constant and prolonged to 0.27 s. When the heart rate is rapid in the presence of first-degree heart block, the P waves may be buried in the T waves of the preceding complexes. In this situation, the recognition of the pacemaker site may be difficult (see Chapter 19, Fig. 19–5), and carotid sinus pressure may aid in diagnosis.

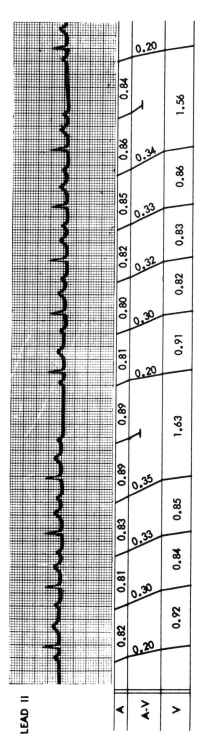

FIG. 23–2. Second-degree AV block, *type I* (the Wenckebach phenomenon). The characteristics of a Wenckebach phenomenon are (1) *progressively increasing* PR intervals with (2) *progressively decreasing* RR intervals and (3) *a pause due to a dropped complex*, the pause being less than twice the length of the last RR interval before the pause (usually the shortest) in the period. The greatest increment of PR interval occurs between the first and second complexes of any period, and the *increment progressively decreases* through the period. Thus, in the first Wenckebach period on the electrocardiogram, the first PR interval is 0.20 s and the second PR interval is 0.30 s, giving an increment of 0.30 − 0.20 = 0.10; the next increment is 0.33 − 0.30 = 0.03 s; and the last increment is 0.35 − 0.33 = 0.02 s. The RR intervals decrease from 0.92 to 0.84 s. Then the last RR interval before the pause should also decrease but does not do so in this case because of the presence of the concomitant sinus rate variation. The duration of the pause due to the dropped complex is 1.63 s, which is less than twice the RR interval of the last cycle of the period (0.85 × 2 = 1.70).

complexes with two ventricular complexes is required for diagnosis of a Wenckebach phenomenon. This is called a 3:2 Wenckebach period. When four atrial complexes and three ventricular complexes are present, the period is termed 4:3 Wenckebach; and a 5:4 Wenckebach period consists of five P waves and four QRS complexes.

==Intermittent type of second-degree AV block (*Mobitz type II block*) is characterized by fixed PR intervals with dropped complexes (Fig. 23–3). There may be a fixed and constant ratio of atrial to ventricular complexes==, such as every other atrial complex blocked (2:1 block) or three of four atrial complexes blocked (4:1 block); or more commonly, the block is irregularly

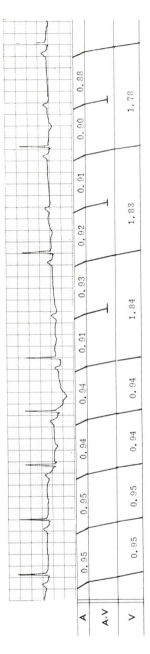

FIG. 23-3. Second-degree AV block, *type II*. The first five complexes on the tracing represent normal sinus rhythm at a rate of approximately 65 per minute. The sixth P wave is abruptly blocked, and the seventh is conducted with a normal PR interval. The patient then continues in 2:1 block to the end of the strip. Note that the PR intervals prior to the first dropped beat are constant, as opposed to the progressive prolongation prior to the dropped complex in *type I* block (the Wenckebach phenomenon).

intermittent with blocked complexes occurring variably on the tracing, without fixed pattern.

Complete AV Block

This is complete interruption of the electrical bridge between atria and ventricles. Both the atria and the ventricles have their own pacemaker, and the electrocardiogram, therefore, shows P waves and QRS complexes that are independent of each other and occurring at different rates. The ventricular rhythm is regular (Fig. 23-4). Since most cases of complete heart block are associated with an idioventricular pacemaker, the ventricular rate is usually in the range of 30 to 40 complexes per minute. Less commonly, complete heart block is present with a junctional pacemaker rhythm with a rate of 40 to 60 impulses or beats per minute. The atrial rate is usually normal or may be increased. When an electrical pacemaker is implanted, the ventricular rate is set by the physician as desired, often in the range of 60 to 80. The pacemaker artifact precedes each ventricular complex (Fig. 23-5). The rhythm is regular.

Sinoatrial (SA) Block

Evidence from the studies of certain arrhythmias suggests that the sinus node may be separated from the

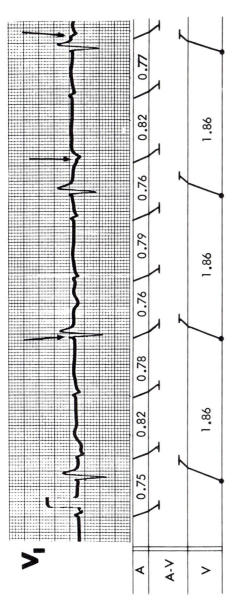

FIG. 23–4. Complete AV block. The ventricular rate is 32 per minute and the ventricular rhythm is regular. There is no fixed relationship between the P waves and QRS complexes. The arrows indicate some of the P waves that fall within the QRS complexes or T waves and may be difficult to discern. There is some variation in the PP intervals. The P-wave irregularity has a definite pattern; namely, the PP interval tends to be shorter when a QRS complex falls between the two P waves and to be longer when the two P waves fall between two QRS complexes. Thus, the PP intervals between the first and second, sixth and seventh, and eighth and ninth P waves are 0.75, 0.76 and 0.77 s, respectively; and the PP intervals between the second and third, fifth and sixth, and seventh and eighth P waves are 0.82, 0.79, and 0.82 s, respectively. This phenomenon is called *ventriculophasic sinus arrhythmia*, a common finding in complete heart block with normal atrial activity.

atrial musculature by a "bridge" (at least functional, if not anatomic) analogous to the AV junction. There is normally a minimal delay between sinus node impulse formation and the beginning of P-wave inscription on the electrocardiogram. If this "bridge" (the SA junction) becomes diseased, block in the SA junction may occur.

First-degree SA block cannot be recognized clinically because there is no effect on the absolute or relative pattern of P waves and QRS complexes; and, of

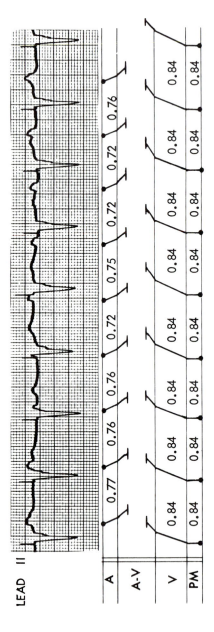

FIG. 23–5. Complete heart block with a permanent implanted artificial pacemaker. Each QRS complex is preceded by a sharp upright spike which is very narrow and occurs about 0.02 to 0.03 s before the QRS. This spike is caused by the artificial pacemaker activity and is called the *pacemaker artifact*. The RR intervals are precisely 0.84 s, giving a rate of 71 beats per minute. Other than the presence of the pacemaker artifact and the rate, the tracing fulfills the criteria for complete heart block.

course, the sinus node impulse does not appear on the clinical electrocardiogram.

Second-degree SA block may be recognized by inference under certain circumstances. For example, *SA Wenckebach phenomenon* is recognizable because the same Wenckebach manifestations seen below the level of block in AV nodal Wenckebach (i.e., the effect on the RR intervals) are seen below the level of block in SA junction Wenckebach (i.e., the effect on the PP intervals). Thus, SA Wenckebach phenomenon is characterized by progressive *shortening* of the PP intervals, followed by a pause, with a duration less than twice the last or shortest cycle in the period (Fig. 23–6). Since the AV junction is not involved in SA Wenckebach phenomenon, the QRS complexes maintain a normal relationship to the P waves with a constant PR interval. Therefore, the RR interval pattern of variation matches that of the PP intervals.

The intermittent type of second-degree SA block is manifested by dropped P waves, just as intermittent

LEAD II

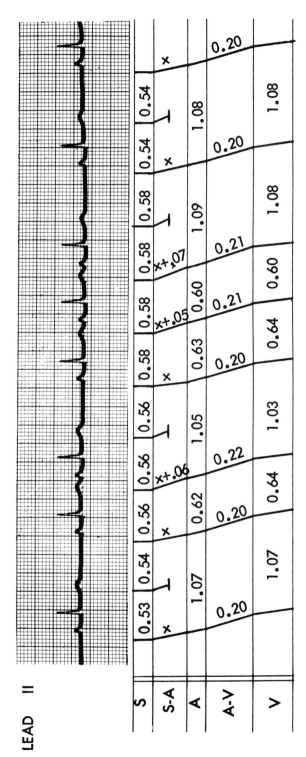

FIG. 23-6. Second-degree SA block, Wenckebach type. The QRS complexes and PR intervals are normal, so that it is immediately evident that the ventricles are discharged by an impulse from above conducted through the AV node. The P waves are normal in contour; so a sinus mechanism may be assumed. However, there is some irregularity of the PP intervals which does not demonstrate the smooth slowing and speeding up of a sinus arrhythmia. There is also some group beating evident. Looking now at the group of three complexes in the middle of the tracing, it is evident that the interval between the first two P waves in the group is longer (0.63 s) than the interval between the second and third P waves in the group (0.60 s). A pause then occurs and the length of the pause is less than twice the PP interval between the second and third beat (pause = 1.09 s, whereas $2 \times 0.60 = 1.20$ s). Thus, these P waves are behaving in the same manner as the QRS complexes in a typical AV Wenckebach period, i.e., the complexes below the area of the block. With this clue, one should think of the possibility of a Wenckebach type of block *above* the P waves in this group of beats, i.e., in the SA junction. Since the sinus node impulse formation itself is not indicated on the electrocardiogram, further investigation of this hypothesis must be by indirect evidence. Since the impulse above the area of block in a Wenckebach phenomenon is normal and occurs one more time in any period than the complex below it (because of the dropped beat),

(Legend for Fig. 23-6 continued on page 306)

(Legend for Fig. 23-6 continued from page 305) it is assumed that in this period of the three P waves there are four sinus node impulses generated, the last being nonconducted. Thus the interval between the first P wave in the group and the first P wave after the pause is measured and divided into four parts (2.32 s ÷ 4 = 0.58 s). We do not know precisely how long before the onset of the first P wave the sinus impulse occurs; therefore we choose an arbitrary value (say 0.08 s) and call it x. Now measuring 0.58 s from that point we find that the interval between the time of impulse formation of the second impulse and the second P wave is $x + 0.05$ s or an increment of 0.05 s. The next interval between site of impulse formation and onset of P wave is $x + 0.07$ s, or an increment of 0.02 s. There is no P wave following the next sinus node impulse (blocked), and the following sinus impulse falls x second before the first P wave following the pause. Putting all these observations together, we have a lengthening SA interval with the *increment* of lengthening decreasing (0.05→0.02 s), a pause less than twice the PP interval of the last cycle before the pause, and progressive shortening of the PP intervals before the pause (0.63→0.60 s). These features are exactly analogous to a 4:3 Wenckebach phenomenon in the AV node. Note also on this tracing the 3:2 period preceding the group of three complexes and the intermittent 2:1 SA block at the end of the tracing.

second-degree AV block is manifested by dropped QRS complexes. However, when it occurs in a fixed form, such as constant 2:1, 3:1, 4:1, it is unrecognizable in the clinical electrocardiogram because the rhythm remains constant. But when the block is irregularly intermittent (Fig. 23-7), a pause occurs which bears a whole-number relationship to the sinus cycle and is therefore recognizable. A long pause, not related numerically (as a multiple of the sinus rate) to the sinus cycle length, is referred to as sinus pause or sinus arrest, rather than SA block.

Third-degree, or complete, SA block is not recognizable clinically.

In summary, for SA block to be identifiable on the clinical electrocardiogram, it must be of the Wenckebach type or of the intermittent type of second-degree block (type II).

Special Terms Used to Describe Block

So far, we have been discussing only block of the forward-conducted impulse (that is, block of the impulse originating above and moving toward the ventricles), or *anterograde block*. Conversely, when a primary pacemaker of the heart is present at a junctional or ventricular level (as in junctional or ventricular tachycardia), block in the reverse direction—or *retrograde block* from ventricle or AV node to atria, across the AV junction—may occur. The cases in which block in one direction is absent while block in the other direction is present demonstrates that *unidirectional block* may occur. It is a complex and poorly understood pathophysiological phenomenon. The concept of unidirectional block is very important in the understanding of reciprocal rhythm (Chapter 24).

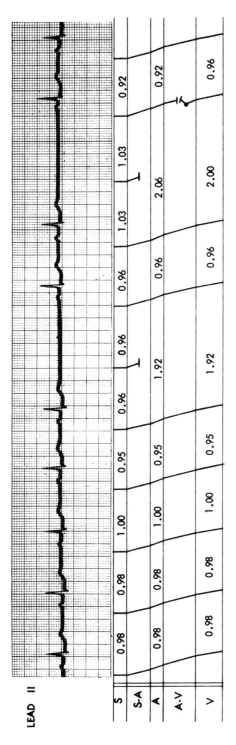

FIG. 23–7. Intermittent second-degree sinoatrial (SA) block (type II). The first five complexes on the tracing are normal sinus impulses at a rate of approximately 60 per minute. This is followed by a pause approximately equal to two cycle lengths. No P wave is seen during this pause. Since the pause is equal to two cycle lengths, it is inferred that the normal pacemaker function of the sinus node has not been interrupted and that the block, therefore, must have occurred between the sinus node and the atrial tissue (SA junction). The second pause (between the seventh and eighth beats) is terminated by a junctional escape beat, because this pause is long enough to allow escape of the intrinsic junctional pacemaker. The clue to the escape mechanism is the short PR interval of the eighth complex, indicating that the AV node escaped before the atrial impulse could be conducted through the AV node.

307

Chapter 24

Arrhythmic Patterns Due to Various Interacting Mechanisms

Group Beating

It is frequently possible to identify a regular or recurring pattern in an arrhythmia. Complexes may occur in pairs followed by a pause (bigeminy), in groups of three followed by a pause (trigeminy), or in groups of four (quadrigeminy) or more. The nature and cause of the group beating may be suggested by the clinical history and physical examination, but electrocardiographic confirmation is usually necessary.

The most common causes of bigeminal rhythm are premature atrial (Fig. 24–1) or premature ventricular (Fig. 24–2) complexes. The electrocardiogram is characterized by a normal sinus complex followed closely by an early atrial or an early ventricular complex. The group is followed by a noncompensatory pause after a premature atrial complex or by a fully compensatory pause after a premature ventricular complex. The coupling interval (i.e., the time between the onset of the QRS complex or P wave of the normal complex and the onset of the QRS complex or P wave of the premature complex) in these types of bigeminy is constant, giving rise to the concept that in some way *the premature complex is triggered by and dependent upon the normal complex.* This type of premature complex

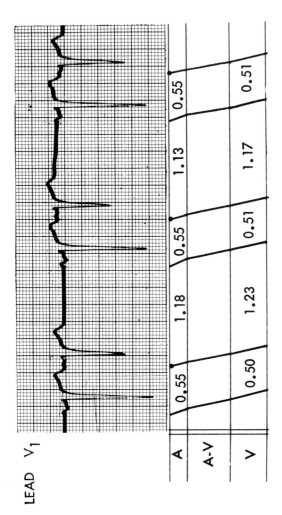

FIG. 24-1. Atrial bigeminy. The first, third, and fifth P-QRS complexes on the tracing are normal sinus impulses. Each is followed by a premature atrial complex with slightly aberrant conduction, and there is a pause after each premature complex. Therefore, the characteristic feature is groups of two complexes—one normal and one premature—followed by a pause.

only occurs after the complex to which it is coupled and does not occur during a pause. Various theories proposed to explain this relationship are summarized by Katz and Pick and by Massie and Walsh.

Bigeminy may occur between any two pacemakers.

The *coupling interval*, the interval between the sinus P wave and the ectopic P wave, is constant at 0.55 s. The pattern is designated as *atrial* bigeminy because the coupled ectopic complexes are atrial in origin.

Thus, there may be sinus-ventricular bigeminy, sinus-atrial bigeminy (commonly called atrial bigeminy), ventricular-ventricular bigeminy (i.e., bigeminy due to two separate ventricular foci, one being the primary pacemaker of the heart and the other being the coupled

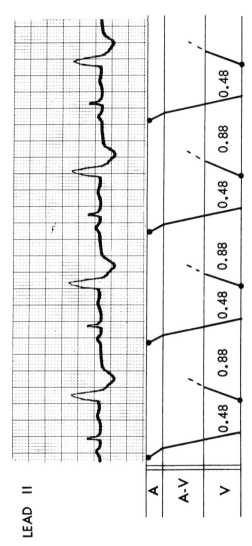

FIG. 24–2. Ventricular bigeminy. The first, third, fifth, and seventh complexes on the electrocardiogram are normal sinus impulses. Each of these is followed by an ectopic complex of abnormal configuration and prolongation beyond 0.12-s. No P waves precede these ectopic complexes. (Note: The positive deflections preceding the ectopic complexes are the T waves of the preceding sinus beats.) The ectopic complexes are coupled to the preceding sinus by a *fixed coupling interval* of 0.48 s, as measured from the onset of the sinus QRS to the onset of the ectopic QRS. A pause then occurs, and therefore the complexes are occurring in groups of two, or bigeminy. Since the ectopic complexes fulfill the criteria for *ventricular ectopics* and since the pattern is groups of two complexes, the rhythm is called *ventricular bigeminy*.

focus), junctional-ventricular bigeminy (AV nodal primary pacemaker and ventricular ectopic), and other combinations.

Trigeminy is the occurrence of complexes in groups of three. It may present as two sinus complexes followed by one ectopic complex or as one sinus complex followed by two consecutive ectopic complexes. The subsequent pause causes the pattern of the triple rhythm.

Any group beating may be caused by *conduction disturbances* (*especially the Wenckebach phenomenon*), without any ectopic activity occurring. For example, a 3:2 Wenckebach phenomenon will produce

311

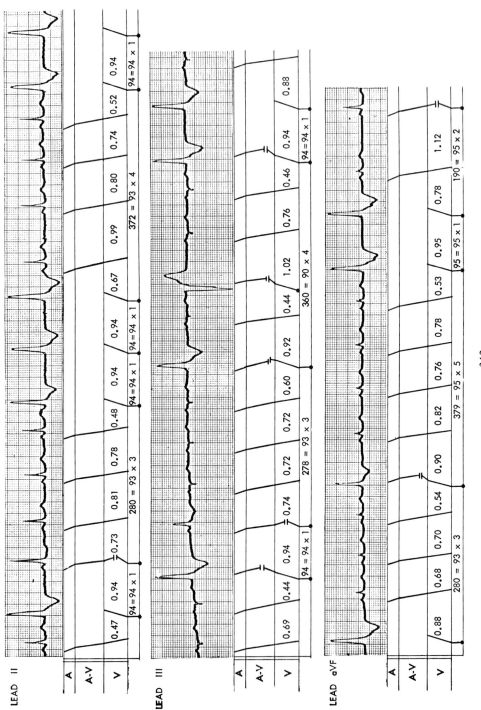

FIG. 24-3. Ventricular parasystole. Three leads from an electrocardiogram demonstrating ventricular parasystole are shown. The basic mechanism is a normal sinus rhythm. However, numerous ventricular extrasystoles are present.

The coupling interval between the normal sinus complexes and the extrasystoles is studied first. If the extrasystoles were the ordinary type of dependent premature ventricular complexes (as demonstrated in Figs. 21-1 and 21-2, and in this chapter, Fig. 24-2), the coupling interval between the extrasystole and the normal sinus preceding it would tend to be constant. However, on this tracing, the coupling intervals are variable and range from 0.44 (first extrasystole in lead III) to 0.60 s (between the seventh and eighth complexes in lead III). If the coupling intervals of the three fusion complexes (third complex on lead II, fourth complex on lead III, and last complex on lead aV$_F$) are included, the range of coupling intervals is extended to 0.44 to 1.12 s. The presence of *variable coupling intervals* and *fusion complexes* is strong evidence for the presence of parasystole.

Next, the *interectopic intervals* are studied. The purpose of this is to determine the frequency of discharge of the ectopic pacemaker and to demonstrate that it is relatively constant. It should also demonstrate that the ectopic discharge depolarizes the ventricles whenever they are not refractory. The frequency of ectopic impulse formation should be independent of the rate of sinus impulse formation. Note that the sinus rate is somewhat variable in the range of 75 to 80 per minute. The interectopic intervals on the tracing should be carefully measured, since a common denominator of these intervals can be calculated to determine the rate of the automatic ectopic pacemaker. This tracing is particularly simple in this regard because automatic complexes are occurring in pairs at several places, and this gives the ectopic frequency directly. Thus, in lead II, the interval between the seventh and eighth, between the eighth and ninth, and between the last two complexes on the tracing is 0.94 s. This makes the automatic rate 64 impulses per minute. Note that the interval between the second complex in lead II (ectopic complex) and the third complex (fusion complex) is also 0.94 s. If the pairs of ectopic complexes were not present (as frequently happens), the ectopic pacemaker rate could be determined in another way. When the intervals between nonpaired ectopic complexes are measured, a series of numbers which have common denominators is obtained. For instance, in lead II, the interval between the third complex (fusion complex) and the seventh complex (ectopic complex) is 2.80 s; the interval between the ninth complex and the fourteenth complex is 3.72 s. Therefore, since 2.80 s is approximately 3×0.93 s and 3.72 s is 4×0.93 s, the largest common denominator is 0.93 s. Calculating through the rest of the tracing in this manner, the common denominator remains in the range of 0.93 to 0.95 s.

If 0.94 s is measured from the onset of the third complex in lead II, it becomes evident that the next ectopic impulse falls in the refractory period of the fourth complex and does not, therefore, discharge the ventricles. The same holds true for the next ectopic impulse. But the one following the latter falls beyond the refractory period and discharges the ventricles. The shortest coupling interval on the tracing is 0.44 s (between the second and third complexes in lead III). This appears to be the shortest time from the onset of the QRS of a normal sinus complex in which an ectopic impulse can discharge the ventricles. Using this critical interval of 0.44 s, it should be demonstrable that no impulse occurring earlier than this will discharge the ventricles and no impulse occurring later than this will fail to discharge the ventricles.

The tenth complex on lead III is a premature complex from another focus and is not part of the parasystolic mechanism.

In summary, this electrocardiogram demonstrates a normal sinus rhythm at a rate of about 75 to 80 per minute, interrupted by a second, automatic focus of impulse formation firing at a rate of about 64 per minute. The secondary focus discharges the ventricles whenever they are not refractory from the primary focus. The ectopic complexes do not show fixed coupling to the sinus complexes preceding them, and several fusion complexes are present.

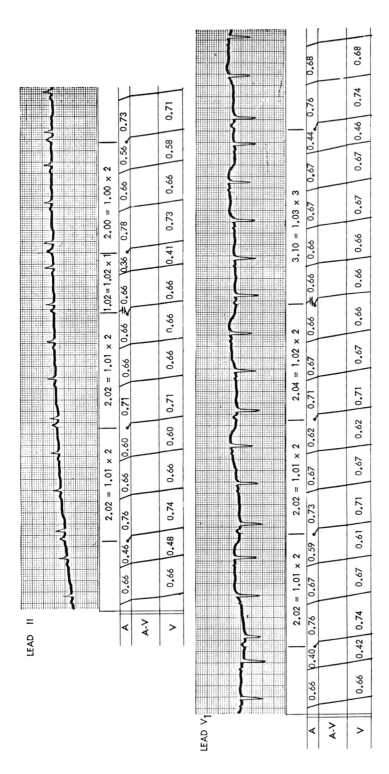

FIG. 24–4. Atrial parasystole. In atrial parasystole, two independent foci are competing. In this case, however, both sites of impulse formation are supraventricular. Therefore, the QRS complexes are of the same configuration whether they are due to ectopic focus discharge or to sinus node discharge.

Varying coupling intervals are again characteristic, as are *fusion complexes*; but in atrial parasystole, the fusion complexes are atrial fusions (P waves) rather than ventricular. Note that there are three P-wave configurations present on the tracing: (1) the short P waves of sinus node origin as in the first complexes in both leads; (2) the tall P waves of ectopic origin as in the third complexes of both leads; and (3) the P waves of intermediate configuration (fusion complexes) as in the ninth complex on lead II and the twelfth complex on lead V_1).

The coupling intervals vary from 0.36 (from the onset of the tenth P wave on lead II to the onset of the eleventh P wave) to 0.66 s (between the eleventh and twelfth P waves on lead V_1).

The shortest interectopic interval is 1.02 s. All other interectopic intervals are approximate whole-number multiples of 1.0 to 1.02 s. Thus, the independent ectopic rate of impulse formation is about 60 per minute. The sinus rate is about 90 per minute. (See Fig. 24–3 for method of calculation of independent ectopic discharge rate.)

In summary, there is a sinus mechanism at a rate of 90 per minute interrupted by an independent ectopic mechanism at a rate of 60 per minute. The independent ectopic impulse discharges the atria anytime that it occurs 0.36 s or more beyond the onset of the preceding sinus P wave.

perceptible bigeminy of the pulse and a 4:3 Wenckebach will produce trigeminy. These are easy to differentiate from ventricular bigeminy and trigeminy on the electrocardiogram and sometimes may be distinguished clinically as well.

The Parasystoles

Parasystole is characterized by a primary cardiac pacemaker and another automatic pacemaker which is *independent* of the primary pacemaker (i.e., one is not required to trigger the other as is the case with ectopic complexes with fixed coupling intervals). The most common form of parasystole is *ventricular parasystole*. In this arrhythmia, a sinus node pacemaker drives the heart, while a second automatic pacemaker in the ventricles (which is protected from, and thus not discharged by, the descending sinus impulse because of a form of block) is intermittently discharging the ventricles (Fig. 24-3). The ventricular pacemaker is normally slower than the sinus pacemaker. When the ventricular pacemaker is faster it usurps the primary function of the heart and a ventricular tachycardia results.

The electrocardiographic features of ventricular parasystole are *ventricular ectopic complexes not coupled to the preceding sinus complexes by fixed intervals* (i.e., the interval between the onset of the preceding sinus QRS and the onset of the parasystolic QRS is *not constant*) and showing no fixed pattern of variability. The *parasystolic complexes are related to each other* in a definite mathematical relationship. The interectopic interval (from the onset of one ectopic QRS to the onset of the next) is a multiple of a common denominator, as demonstrated in Fig. 24–3. Whenever the parasystolic impulse occurs while the ventricles are still refractory from the previous complex, the parasystolic focus does not discharge the ventricles and the automatic complex does not occur. If an automatic complex fails to occur following an impulse outside of the refractory period of the previous complex, however, *exit block* is proposed. Exit block is a form of conduction disturbance, rather than a physiological refractoriness, and it prevents the automatic impulse from exiting from its site of origin.

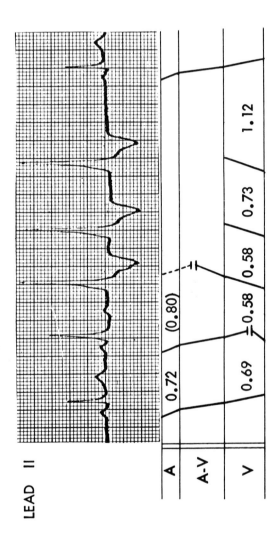

FIG. 24–5. Fusion complex. The first and last complexes on the tracing are normal sinus complexes. The third, fourth, and fifth complexes are of ventricular origin. Note, however, the second beat. It is intermediate between the first and third complex in (1) voltage, (2) QRS duration, (3) QRS configuration, and (4) T-wave configuration. In addition, the RR interval between it and the third complex is the same as between the third and fourth complex. Finally, the PR interval of the fusion complex is shorter than the PR intervals of the sinus complexes—a phenomenon which may also occur with fusion.

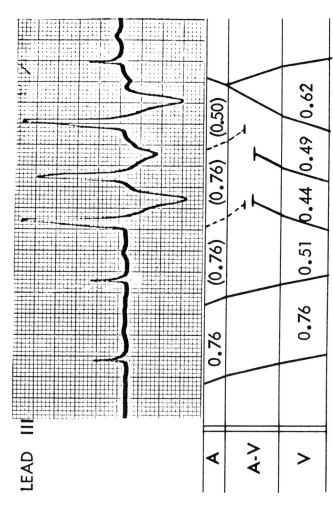

FIG. 24-6. Reciprocal beat. The last complex of ventricular origin on the tracing (fifth QRS complex) is followed by an inverted P wave (at the end of the T wave). The inverted P wave is then coupled to a normal QRS complex by a PR interval of about 0.22 s. As shown in the AV diagram, the impulse originates in the ventricles and is conducted retrogradely through the AV junction. It then discharges the atria retrogradely, as well as reenters the AV junction to discharge the ventricles again.

Ventricular parasystole is the most common form of parasystole, but parasystole may occur between the sinus pacemaker and an ectopic atrial focus (Fig. 24-4) or the sinus pacemaker and an ectopic AV junctional focus or, very rarely, between any other two automatic centers, one being the primary pacemaker of the heart and the other the parasystolic pacemaker.

Fusion Complexes

When two pacemakers discharge at such time that each is able to depolarize part of the ventricular musculature before they physiologically interfere with each other, a ventricular *fusion complex* results. Electrocardiographically, the fusion QRS-T complex is intermediate in contour between the configuration of the QRS complexes of each of the pacemakers (Fig. 24-5). The two foci can often be demonstrated to discharge very closely to each other. Atrial fusion complexes also occur by the same mechanisms as ventricular fusion complexes. Fusion complexes are common in parasystoles.

Reciprocal Rhythm

A reciprocal ventricular beat is a QRS complex which is caused by an impulse that originates in the ventricle, or AV junction, leaves it, and then returns to discharge it a second time. The impulse from the original ventricular complex travels retrogradely through part of the AV junction. Upon reaching the junction between atria and AV node, the impulse enters another part of the AV junction anterogradely to discharge the ventricles once again (Fig. 24-6). Two unusual pathophysiological states are proposed to explain reciprocal rhythm: (1) unidirectional block and (2) longitudinal dissociation in the AV junction. In unidirectional block, conducting tissue is able to function in one direction but not in the other; and longitudinal dissociation means that an impulse can pass through one part of the AV junction without affecting another part (Katz and Pick). Thus, in reciprocal rhythm, one part of the AV junction conducts the retrograde impulse and the other part blocks the impulse (unidirectional block).

While the part with retrograde block is able to conduct anterogradely, the longitudinal dissociation "insulates" that part from the passing impulse, and the impulse does not enter until it reaches the top of the AV junction. Then it enters that part of the junction and reenters the ventricular conducting system.

The electrocardiogram reveals an ectopic AV junctional or ventricular complex followed by an inverted P wave, which is in turn followed by a normal (anterograde) QRS complex.

Reciprocal atrial complexes also occur, but they are very rare and often difficult to identify with any degree of certainty.

Appendix

Table 1

Upper Limits of the Normal PR Intervals (Duration in Seconds)

Rate	Below 70	71–90	91–110	111–130	Above 130
Large adults	0.21	0.20	0.19	0.18	0.17
Small adults	0.20	0.19	0.18	0.17	0.16
Children, ages 14–17	0.19	0.18	0.17	0.16	0.15
Children, ages 7–13	0.18	0.17	0.16	0.15	0.14
Children, ages $1\frac{1}{2}$–6	0.17	0.165	0.155	0.145	0.135
Children, ages 0–$1\frac{1}{2}$	0.16	0.15	0.145	0.135	0.125

Source: The authors express appreciation to Dr. Richard Ashman, Dr. Edgar Hull, and The Macmillan Company for permitting us to use Tables 1 and 2 shown in the Appendix.

Table 2
Normal Q-T Intervals and the Upper Limits of the Normal

Cycle lengths, s	Heart rate per min	Men and children, s	Women, s	Upper limits of normal	
				Men and children, s	Women, s
1.50	40.0	0.449	0.461	0.491	0.503
1.40	43.0	0.438	0.450	0.479	0.491
1.30	46.0	0.426	0.438	0.466	0.478
1.25	48.0	0.420	0.432	0.460	0.471
1.20	50.0	0.414	0.425	0.453	0.464
1.15	52.0	0.407	0.418	0.445	0.456
1.10	54.5	0.400	0.411	0.438	0.449
1.05	57.0	0.393	0.404	0.430	0.441
1.00	60.0	0.386	0.396	0.422	0.432
0.95	63.0	0.378	0.388	0.413	0.423
0.90	66.5	0.370	0.380	0.404	0.414
0.85	70.5	0.361	0.371	0.395	0.405
0.80	75.0	0.352	0.362	0.384	0.394
0.75	80.0	0.342	0.352	0.374	0.384
0.70	86.0	0.332	0.341	0.363	0.372
0.65	92.0	0.321	0.330	0.351	0.360
0.60	100.0	0.310	0.318	0.338	0.347
0.55	109.0	0.297	0.305	0.325	0.333
0.50	120.0	0.283	0.291	0.310	0.317
0.45	133.0	0.268	0.276	0.294	0.301
0.40	150.0	0.252	0.258	0.275	0.282
0.35	172.0	0.234	0.240	0.255	0.262

Source: The authors express appreciation to Dr. Richard Ashman, Dr. Edgar Hull, and The Macmillan Company for permitting us to use Tables 1 and 2 shown in the Appendix.

References

GENERAL READING

Beckwith, J. R.: *Grant's Clinical Electrocardiography*, 2d ed., McGraw-Hill Book Company, New York, 1970.

Chou, T.: *Electrocardiography in Clinical Practice*, Grune & Stratton, New York, 1979.

Chou, T., Helm, R. A., and Kaplan, S.: *Clinical Vectorcardiography*, 2d ed., Grune & Stratton, New York, 1979.

Cooksey, J. D., Dunn, M., and Massie, E.: *Clinical Vectorcardiography and Electrocardiography*, 2d ed., Year Book Medical Publishers, Chicago, 1977.

Silverman, M. E., and Silverman, B. D.: The diagnostic capabilities and limitations of the electrocardiogram, in J. W. Hurst (ed.), *Update I: The Heart*, McGraw-Hill Book Company, New York, 1979, p. 13.

Surawicz, B., Uhley, H., and Task Force: Standardization of terminology and interpretation. *Am. J. Cardiol.*, 1978; 41:131.

BASIC CONCEPTS OF ELECTROCARDIOGRAPHY

Fozzard, H. A., and Gibbons, W. R.: Action potential and contraction of heart muscle. *Am. J. Cardiol.*, 1973; 31:182.

Grant, R. P.: Spatial vector electrocardiography: A method for calculating the spatial electrical vectors of the heart from conventional leads. *Circulation*, 1950; 2:676.

Grant, R. P.: The relationship of unipolar chest leads to the electrical field of the heart. *Circulation*, 1950; 1:878.

Sheffield, L. T., Prineas, R., Cohen, H. C., et al.: Quality of electrocardiographic records. *Am. J. Cardiol.*, 1978; 41:146.

THE INTERPRETATION OF THE ELECTROCARDIOGRAM

Ashman, R.: The normal duration of the Q-T interval. *Am. Heart J.*, 1942; 23:522.

Bachman, S., Sparrow, D., and Smith, L. K.: Effect of aging on the electrocardiogram. *Am. J. Cardiol.*, 1981; 48:513.

Herbert, W. H., and Sobol, B. D.: "Normal" atrioventricular conduction times. *Am. J. Med.*, 1970; 48:145.

Johnson, J. C., Horan, L. G., and Flowers, N. C.: Diagnostic accuracy of the electrocardiogram, in A. N. Brest (ed.), *Clinical Electrocardiographic Correlations, Cardiovascular Clinics*, Vol. 8, F. A. Davis Company, Philadelphia, 1977, p. 25.

Kilty, S. E., and Lepeschkin, E.: Effect of body build on the QRS voltage of the electrocardiogram in normal men. *Circulation*, 1965; 31:77.

Nemati, M., Doyle, J., McCaughan, D., et al.: The orthogonal electrocardiogram in normal women. Implications of sex differences in diagnostic electrocardiography. *Am. Heart J.*, 1978; 95:12.

Selzer, A.: The Bayes theorem and clinical electrocardiography. *Am. Heart J.*, 1981; 101:360.

Simonson, E.: *Differentiation between Normal and Abnormal in Electrocardiography*, The C. V. Mosby Company, St. Louis, 1961.

Simonson, E., Blackburn, H., Puchner, T. C., et al.: Sex differences in the electrocardiogram. *Circulation*, 1960; 22:598.

THE NORMAL ELECTROCARDIOGRAM

Abildskov, J. A., Burgess, M. J., Millar, K., et al.: New data and concepts concerning the ventricular gradient. *Chest*, 1970; 58:244.

Ashman, R., Byer, E., and Bayley, R. H.: The normal human ventricular gradient; Factors which affect its direction and its relation to the mean QRS axis, with an appendix on notation. *Am. Heart J.*, 1943; 25:16.

Grant, R. P., Estes, E. H., Jr., and Doyle, J. T.: Spatial vector electrocardiography; The clinical characteristics of the ST and T vectors. *Circulation*, 1951; 3:182.

Kossmann, C. E.: The normal electrocardiogram. *Circulation*, 1953; 8:920.

Kossmann, C. E.: The primary "T" wave of the electrocardiogram, in J. W. Hurst (ed.), *Update IV: The Heart*, McGraw-Hill Book Company, New York, 1981.

Parisi, A. F., Bechmann, C. H., and Lancaster, M. C.: The spectrum of ST segment elevation of the electrocardiograms of healthy adult men. *J. Electrocardiol.*, 1971; 4:137.

Sreenivasan, V. V., Fisher, B. J., Liebman, J., and Downs, T. D.: Longitudinal study of the standard electrocardiogram in the healthy premature infant during the first year of life. *Am. J. Cardiol.*, 1973; 31:57.

Strong, W. B., Downs, T. D., Liebman, J., et al.: The normal adolescent electrocardiogram. *Am. Heart J.*, 1972; 83:115.

ALTERED ANATOMIC OR ELECTROPHYSIOLOGIC DISTURBANCES OF THE ELECTROCARDIOGRAM

Beach, C., Kenmure, A. C. F., and Short, D.: Electrocardiogram of pure left ventricular hypertrophy and its differentiation from lateral ischaemia. *Br. Heart J.*, 1981; 46:285.

Benditt, D. G., Pritchett, E. L. C., Smith, W. M., et al.: Characteristics of atrioventricular conduction and the spectrum of arrhythmias in Lown-Ganong-Levine syndrome. *Circulation*, 1978; 57:454.

Denes, P., Pick, A., Miller, R. H., et al.: A characteristic precordial repolarization abnormality with intermittent left bundle branch block. *Ann. Intern. Med.*, 1978; 89:55.

Dolgin, M., Fisher, V. J., Shah, A., et al.: The electrocardiographic diagnosis of left ventricular hypertrophy: Correlation with quantitative angiography. *Am. J. Med. Sci.*, 1977; 237:301.

Gallagher, J. J., Pritchett, E. L. C., Sealy, W. C., et al.: The preexcitation syndromes. *Prog. Cardiovasc. Dis.*, 1978; 20:285.

Goodwin, J. F., and Abdin, Z. H.: The cardiogram of congenital and acquired right ventricular hypertrophy. *Br. Heart J.*, 1959; 21:523.

Havelda, C. J., Sohi, G. S., Flowers, N. C., et al.: The pathologic correlates of the electrocardiogram: Complete left bundle branch block. *Circulation*, 1982; 65:445.

Josephson, M. E., Kastor, J. A., and Morganroth, J.: Electrocardiographic left atrial enlargement. *Am. J. Cardiol.*, 1977; 39:967.

Moller, J. H., White, R. D., Anderson, R. C., et al.: Significance of the $S_1S_2S_3$ electrocardiographic pattern in children. *Am. J. Cardiol.*, 1965; 16:524.

Perloff, J. K., Roberts, N. K., and Cabeen, W. R. Jr.: Left axis deviation: A reassessment. *Circulation*, 1979; 60:12.

Ray, C. T., Horan, L. G., and Flowers, N. C.: An early sign of right ventricular enlargement. *J. Electrocardiol.*, 1970; 3:57.

Roman, G. T., Walsh, T. J., and Massie, E.: Right ventricular hypertrophy. *Am. J. Cardiol.*, 1961; 7:481.

Romhilt, D. W., Bove, K. E., Conradi, S., et al.: Morphologic significance of left atrial involvement. *Am. Heart J.*, 1972; 83:322.

Romhilt, D. W., Bove, K. E., and Norris, R. J.: A critical appraisal of the electrocardiographic criteria for the diagnosis of left ventricular hypertrophy. *Circulation*, 1969; 40:185.

Romhilt, D. W., and Estes, H. E.: A point-score system for the ECG diagnosis of left ventricular hypertrophy. *Am. Heart J.*, 1968; 75:752.

Rosenbaum, M. B., Elizari, M. V., Lazzari, J. O., et al.: Intraventricular trifascicular blocks. Review of the literature and classification. *Am. Heart J.*, 1969; 78:450.

Scott, R. C.: The electrocardiographic diagnosis of right ventricular hypertrophy: Correlation with anatomic findings. *Am. Heart J.*, 1960; 60:659.

Scott, R. C.: Left bundle branch block—A clinical assessment. Part I. *Am. Heart J.*, 1965; 70:535.

Scott, R. C.: Ventricular hypertrophy. *Cardiovas. Clin.*, 1973; 5:220.

Sokolow, M., and Lyon, T. P.: The ventricular complex in left ventricular hypertrophy as obtained by unipolar precordial and limb leads. *Am. Heart J.*, 1949; 37:161.

Termini, B. A., and Lee, Y.: Echocardiographic and electrocardiographic criteria for diagnosing left atrial enlargement. *South. Med. J.*, 1975; 68:161.

CORONARY ARTERY DISEASE

Abbott, J. A., and Scheinman, M. M.: Nondiagnostic electrocardiogram in patients with acute myocardial infarction. *Am. J. Med.*, 1973; 55:608.

Bayley, R. H.: The electrocardiographic effects of injury at the endocardial surface of the left ventricle. *Am. Heart J.*, 1946; 31:677.

Burns-Cox, C. J.: The occurrence of a normal electrocardiogram after myocardial infarction. *Am. Heart J.*, 1968; 75:512.

Chou, T., van der Bel-Kahn, J., Allen, J., et al.: Electrocardiographic diagnosis of right ventricular infarction. *Am. J. Med.*, 1981; 70:1175.

Gardin, J. M., and Singer, D. H.: Atrial infarction. *Arch. Intern. Med.*, 1981; 141:1345.

Goldberger, A. L.: Recognition of ECG pseudo-infarct patterns. *Mod. Concepts Cardiovas. Dis.*, 1980; 49:13.

Helfant, R. H.: Q waves in coronary heart disease: Newer understanding of their clinical implications. *Am. J. Cardiol.*, 1976; 38:662.

Hilsenrath, J., Hamby, R. I., and Hoffman, I.: Pitfalls in the prediction of coronary artery disease from the electrocardiogram or vectorcardiogram. *J. Electrocardiol.*, 1973; 6:291.

Horan, L. G., Flowers, N. C., and Johnson, J. C.: Significance of the diagnostic Q waves of myocardial infarction. *Circulation*, 1971; 43:428.

Hurd, H. P. II, Starling, M. R., Crawford, M. H., et al.: Comparative accuracy of electrocardiographic and vectorcardiographic criteria for inferior myocardial infarction. *Circulation*, 1981; 63:1025.

Kishida, H., Cole, J. S., Surawicz, B.: Negative U wave: A highly specific but poorly understood sign of heart disease. *Am. J. Cardiol.*, 1982; 49:2030.

Martinez-Rios, M. A., Da Costa, B., Cencena-Seldner, F. A., et al.: Normal electrocardiogram in the presence of severe coronary artery disease. *Am. J. Cardiol.*, 1970; 25:320.

Merrill, S. L., and Pearce, M. L.: An autopsy study of the accuracy of the electrocardiogram in the diagnosis of recurrent myocardial infarction. *Am. Heart J.*, 1971; 81:48.

Mills, R. M., Young, E., Gorlin, R., et al.: Natural history of S-T segment elevation after acute myocardial infarction. *Am. J. Cardiol.*, 1975; 35:609.

Perloff, J. K.: The recognition of strictly posterior myocardial infarction by conventional scalar electrocardiography. *Circulation*, 1964; 30:706.

Pipberger, H. V., and Lopez, E. A.: "Silent" subendocardial infarcts: Fact or fiction? *Am. Heart J.*, 1980; 100:597.

Pruitt, R. D.: The electrocardiogram in acute subendocardial myocardial infarction, in J. W. Hurst (ed.), *Update IV: The Heart*, McGraw-Hill Book Company, New York, 1981.

Rahim, A., Parameswaran, R., and Goldberg, H.: Electrocardiographic changes during chest pain in unstable angina. *Br. Heart J.*, 1977; 39:1340.

Redy, K., Hamby, R. I., Hilsenrath, J., et al.: Severity and distribution of coronary artery disease in patients with normal resting electrocardiograms. *J. Electrocardiol.*, 1974; 7:115.

Savage, R. M., Wagner, G. S., Ideker, R. E., et al.: Correlation of postmortem anatomic findings with electrocardiographic changes in patients with myocardial infarction. *Circulation*, 1977; 55:279.

Shettigar, U. R., Hultgren, H. N., Pfeifer, J. F., et al.: Diagnostic value of Q-waves in inferior myocardial infarction. *Am. Heart J.*, 1974; 88:170.

Short, D.: Value and limitations of electrocardiogram in diagnosis of slight and subacute coronary attacks. *Br. Med. J.*, 1968; 4:673.

Sullivan, W., Vlodaver, Z., Tuna, N., et al.: Correlation of electrocardiographic and pathologic findings in healed myocardial infarction. *Am. J. Cardiol.*, 1978; 42:724.

Williams, R. A., Cohn, P. F., Vokonas, P. S., et al.: Electrocardiographic, arteriographic and ventriculographic correlations in transmural myocardial infarction. *Am. J. Cardiol.*, 1973; 31:595.

LUNG DISEASE

Fowler, N. O., Daniels, C., Scott, R. C., et al.: The electrocardiogram in cor pulmonale with and without emphysema. *Am. J. Cardiol.*, 1965; 16:500.

Graham, J. H., Barrett, P. A., Barnaby, P. F., et al.: Diagnosis of old anterior myocardial infarction in emphysema with poor R wave progression in anterior chest leads. *Br. Heart J.*, 1981; 45:522.

Kamper, D., Chou, T., Fowler, N. O., et al.: The reliability of electrocardiographic criteria of chronic obstructive lung disease. *Am. Heart J.*, 1970; 80:445.

Littmann, D.: The electrocardiographic findings in pulmonary emphysema. *Am. J. Cardiol.*, 1960; 5:339.

Oram, S., and Davies, P.: The electrocardiogram in cor pulmonale. *Prog. Cardiovasc. Dis.*, 1967; 9:341.

Phillips, J. H., and Burch, G. E.: Problems in the diagnosis of cor pulmonale. *Am. Heart J.*, 1963; 66:818.

Spodick, D. H.: Electrocardiographic responses to pulmonary embolism. *Am. J. Cardiol.*, 1972; 30:659.

Stein, P. D., Dalen, J. E., McIntyre, K. M., et al.: The electrocardiogram in acute pulmonary embolism. *Prog. Cardiovasc. Dis.*, 1975; 17:247.

The urokinase-pulmonary embolism trial. *Circulation* 1973; 47(suppl.):2.

Walston, A., Brewer, D. L., Kitchens, C. S., et al.: The electrocardiographic manifestations of spontaneous left pneumothorax. *Ann. Intern. Med.*, 1974; 80:375.

Zema, M. J., and Kligfield, P.: ECG poor R-wave progression. *Arch. Intern. Med.*, 1982; 142:1145.

PERICARDITIS

Ginzton, L. E., and Laks, M. M.: The differential diagnosis of acute pericarditis from the normal variant: New electrocardiographic criteria. *Circulation*, 1982; 65:1004.

McGregor, M., and Baskind, E.: Electric alternans in pericardial effusion. *Circulation*, 1955; 11:837.

Spodick, D. H.: Diagnostic electrocardiographic sequences in acute pericarditis. *Circulation*, 1973; 48:575.

Spodick, D. H.: Electrocardiogram in acute pericarditis. *Am. J. Cardiol.*, 1974; 33:470.

Spodick, D. H.: Differential characteristics of the electrocardiogram in early repolarization and acute pericarditis. *N. Engl. J. Med.*, 1976; 295:523.

Surawicz, B., and Lasseter, K. C.: Electrocardiogram in pericarditis. *Am. J. Cardiol.*, 1970; 26:471.

Unverferth, D. V., Williams, T. E., Fulkerson, P. K.: Electrocardiographic voltage in pericardial effusion. *Chest*, 1979; 75:157.

CARDIOMYOPATHY

Bahl, O. P., and Massie, E.: Electrocardiographic and vectorcardiographic patterns in cardiomyopathy. *Cardiovasc. Clin.*, 1972; 4:95.

Chen, C. H., Nobuyoshi, M., and Kawai, C.: ECG pattern of left ventricular hypertrophy in nonobstructive hypertrophic cardiomyopathy: The significance of the mid-precordial changes. *Am. Heart J.*, 1979; 97:687.

Hollister, R. M., and Goodwin, J. F.: The electrocardiogram in cardiomyopathy. *Br. Heart J.*, 1963; 25:357.

McMartin, D. E., and Flowers, N. C.: Clinical electrocardiographic correlations in diseases of the myocardium. *Cardiovasc. Clin.*, 1977; 8:191.

Savage, D. D., Seides, S. F., Clark, C. E., et al.: Electrocardiographic findings in patients with obstructive and nonobstructive hypertrophic cardiomyopathy. *Circulation*, 1978; 58:402.

Stapleton, J. F., Segal, J. P., and Harvey, W. P.: The electrocardiogram of myocardiopathy. *Prog. Cardiovasc. Dis.*, 1970; 13:217.

AORTIC AND MITRAL VALVULAR DISEASE

Bentivoglio, L. G., Uricchio, J. F., Waldow, A., et al. An electrocardiographic analysis of sixty-five cases of mitral regurgitation. *Circulation*, 1958; 28:572.

Cabrera, E., and Monroy, J. R.: Systolic and diastolic loading of the heart. II. *Am. Heart J.*, 1952; 43:669.

Gooch, A. S., Calatagud, J. B., Rogers, P. A., et al.: Analysis of the P wave in severe aortic stenosis. *Chest*, 1966; 49:459.

Malcolm, A. D., Boughner, D. R., Kostuk, W. J., et al.: Clinical features and investigative findings in presence of mitral leaflet prolapse. *Br. Heart J.*, 1976; 38:244.

Morris, J. J., Estes, H. E., and Whalen, R. E.: P-wave analysis in valvular heart disease. *Circulation*, 1964; 29:242.

Segal, J., Harvey, W. P., and Hufnagel, C.: A clinical study of one hundred cases of severe aortic insufficiency. *Am. J. Med.*, 1956; 21:200.

Semler, H. J., and Pruitt, R. D.: An electrocardiographic estimation of the pulmonary vascular obstruction in 80 patients with mitral stenosis. *Am. Heart J.*, 1960; 59:541.

Shah, P. M.: Clinical-electrocardiographic correlations: Aortic valve disease and hypertrophic subaortic stenosis. *Cardiovasc. Clin.*, 1977; 8:151.

Rios, J. C., and Goo, W.: Electrocardiographic correlates of rheumatic valvular disease. *Cardiovasc. Clin.*, 1973; 5(2):247.

Rios, J. C., and Leet, C.: Electrocardiographic assessment of valvular heart disease. *Cardiovasc. Clin.*, 1977; 8:161.

CONGENITAL HEART DISEASE

Bender, S. R., Dreifus, L. S., and Downing, D.: Anatomic and electrocardiographic correlation of Fallot's tetralogy—A study of 100 proved cases. *Am. J. Cardiol.*, 1961; 7:475.

Bentivoglio, L. G., Maranhao, V., and Downing, D. F.: The electrocardiogram in pulmonary stenosis with intact septa. *Am. Heart J.*, 1960; 59:347.

Burchell, H. B., Dushane, J. W., and Brandenburg, R. O.: The electrocardiogram of patients with atrioventricular cushion defects. *Am. J. Cardiol.*, 1960; 6:575.

Campbell, M., and Reynolds, G.: Significance of the direction of the P wave in dextrocardia and isolated levocardia. *Br. Heart J.*, 1952; 14:481.

DePasquale, N. P., and Burch, G. E.: The electrocardiogram, vectorcardiogram, and ventricular gradient in the tetralogy of Fallot. *Circulation*, 1961; 24:94.

Ellison, R. C., Freedom, R. M., Keane, J. F., et al.: Indirect assessment of severity of pulmonary stenosis. *Circulation*, 1977; 56(suppl. 1):14.

Gaum, W. E., Chou, T. C., and Kaplan, S.: The vectorcardiogram and electrocardiogram in supravalvular aortic stenosis and coarctation of the aorta. *Am. Heart J.*, 1972; 84:620.

Gooch, A. S., and Kini, P. M.: Electrocardiogram in adults with congenital heart disease. *Cardiovasc. Clin.*, 1977; 8:171.

Lee, Y. C., and Scherlis, L.: Atrial septal defect: Electrocardiographic, vectorcardiographic, and catheterization data. *Circulation*, 1962; 25:1024.

Perloff, J. K.: *The Clinical Recognition of Congenital Heart Disease*, 2d ed., W. B. Saunders, 1978, Philadelphia.

Rao, P. S.: Dextrocardia: Systematic approach to differential diagnosis. *Am. Heart J.*, 1981; 102:389.

Schiebler, G. L., Adams, P., Jr., Anderson, R. C., et al.: Clinical study of twenty-three cases of Ebstein's anomaly of the tricuspid valve. *Circulation*, 1959; 29:165.

Scott, R. C.: The electrocardiogram in ventricular septal defect. *Am. Heart J.*, 1961; 62:842.

Vince, D. J., and Keith, J. D.: The electrocardiogram in ventricular septal defect. *Circulation*, 1961; 23:225.

Weidman, W. H., Gersony, W. M., Nugent, E. W., et al.: Indirect assessment of severity in ventricular septal defect. *Circulation*, 1977; 56(suppl. 1):24.

Witham, A. C., and McDaniel, J. S.: Electrocardiogram, vectorcardiogram, and hemodynamics in ventricular septal defect. *Am. Heart J.*, 1970; 79:335.

MISCELLANEOUS ELECTROCARDIOGRAPHIC ABNORMALITIES

Bronsky, D., Dubin, A., Kushner, D. S., et al.: Calcium and the electrocardiogram, III. The relationship of the intervals of the electrocardiogram to the level of serum calcium. *Am. J. Cardiol.*, 1961; 7:843.

Bronsky, D., Dubin, A., Waldstein, S. S., et al.: Calcium and the electrocardiogram, I. The electrocardiographic manifestations of hypoparathyroidism. *Am. J. Cardiol.*, 1961; 7:823.

Bronsky, D., Dubin, A., Waldstein, S. S., et al.: Calcium and the electrocardiogram, II. The electrocardiographic manifestations of hyperparathyroidism and of marked hypercalcemia from various other etiologies. *Am. J. Cardiol.*, 1961; 7:833.

Ettinger, P. O., Regan, T. J., and Oldewurtel, H. A.: Hyperkalemia, cardiac conduction, and the electrocardiogram: A review. *Am. Heart J.*, 1974; 88:360.

Fisch, C., Knoebel, S. B., Feigenbaum, H., et al.: Potassium and the monophasic action potential, electrocardiogram, conduction and arrhythmias. *Prog. Cardiovasc. Dis.*, 1966; 8:387.

Hammer, W. J., Luessenhop, A. J., and Weintraub, A. M.: Observations on the electrocardiographic changes associated with subarachnoid hemorrhage with special reference to their genesis. *Am. J. Med.*, 1975; 59:427.

Rumancik, W. M., Denlinger, J. K., Nahrwold, M. L., et al.: The QT interval and serum ionized calcium. *JAMA*, 1978; 240:366.

Surawicz, B.: Relationship between electrocardiogram and electrolytes. *Am. Heart J.*, 1967; 73:814.

Weaver, W. F., and Burchell, H. B.: Serum potassium and the electrocardiogram in hypokalemia. *Circulation*, 1960; 21:505.

Wortsman, J., and Frank, S.: The QT interval in clinical hypercalcemia. *Clin. Cardiol.*, 1981; 4:87.

Yamour, B. J., Sridharan, M. R., Rice, J. F., et al.: Electrocardiographic changes in cerebrovascular hemorrhage. *Am. Heart J.*, 1980; 99:294.

CARDIAC ARRHYTHMIAS

Bellet, S.: *Clinical Disorders of the Heart Beat*, Lea and Febiger, Philadelphia, 1971.

Castellanos, A., ed.: *Cardiac arrhythmias: Mechanisms and Management*, F. A. Davis, Philadelphia, 1980.

Gallagher, J. J.: Mechanisms of arrhythmias and conduction abnormalities, in J. W. Hurst (ed.), *The Heart*, McGraw-Hill Book Company, New York, 1982.

Harrison, D. C., ed.: *Cardiac Arrhythmias: A Decade of Progress*, G. K. Hall, Medical Publishers, Boston, 1981.

Josephson, M. E., and Seides, S. F.: *Clinical Cardiac Electrophysiology: Techniques and Interpretation*, Lea and Febiger, Philadelphia, 1979.

Katz, L. N., and Pick, A.: Clinical electrocardiography, Part I. *The Arrhythmias*, Lea and Febiger, Philadelphia, 1956.

Marriott, H. J. L., and Myerburg, R. J.: Recognition of arrhythmias and conduction abnormalities, in J. W. Hurst (ed.), *The Heart*, McGraw-Hill Book Company, New York, 1982.

Narula, O. S., ed.: *Cardiac Arrhythmias: Electrophysiology: Diagnosis and Management*, Williams & Wilkins, Baltimore, 1979.

Schamroth, L.: *The Disorders of Cardiac Rhythm*, Blackwell Scientific Publications, Oxford, 1980.

Scherf, D., and Schott, A.: *Extrasystoles and Allied Arrhythmias*, 2nd ed., Year Book Medical Publishers, Chicago, 1973.

Wellens, H. J. J., Lie, K. I., and Jansse, M. J.: *The Conduction System of the Heart: Structure, Function, and Clinical Implications*, Stenfort Croese, Leiden, 1976.

Glossary

Aberrant conduction An abnormal pathway of conduction through the heart due to physiologic refractoriness of part of the conducting system.

Action potential The curve of the sequential changes in electrical voltage occurring across the membrane of a single cell during depolarization and repolarization.

Anterograde conduction Conduction in the normal forward pathway between the sinus node and ventricular myocardium.

Arrhythmia An abnormality or variation of the cardiac rhythm.

Automaticity The property of the heart responsible for impulse formation.

AV diagram A horizontal line diagram used to demonstrate rhythm events.

AV dissociation Independent activity of the atria and ventricles.

AV junction The specialized tissue forming the electrical "bridge" of conduction between the atria and ventricles. The AV junction is largely responsible for the normal delay between atrial depolarization and ventricular depolarization.

Bifascicular block Block of the right bundle branch plus one of the divisions of the left bundle branch.

Bigeminy Complexes occurring in pairs.

Bipolar leads Leads I, II, and III. These leads consist of a positive and a negative pole, both of which measure electrical potential. The resultant electrical potential is the difference between the two electrodes.

Block A pathologic state in the conducting system causing the propagation of an impulse to be slowed or stopped.

Bradycardia A heart rate of less than 60 complexes per minute.

Bundle branch block A delay or block of conduction in the left or right branch of the bundle of His.

Central (indifferent) terminal The negative pole of a unipolar lead. This pole is always at zero potential.

Conduction The property of impulse transmission.

Coupling interval The interval between a sinus complex and a premature complex or between any two complexes occurring in pairs.

Delta wave Slurred initial portion of the QRS complex due to myocardial conduction via a bypass tract.

Depolarization The electrical process in which the cell membrane becomes permeable to an inward flux of sodium ions resulting in a less negative transmembrane potential difference.

Dipole A facing pair of positive and negative charges across the cell membrane.

Ectopic complex A complex caused by an impulse originating in an area other than the sinus node.

Escape complex A complex originating in one of the lower pacemaker centers of the heart with a slower intrinsic rate. The escape complex is due to failure of the faster sinus node pacemaker to discharge.

Fascicular block A partial or complete delay in the

333

conduction through one or more of the three divisions of the ventricular conducting pathways.

Fibrillation Uncoordinated, irregular activity of cardiac muscle, ineffective for pumping blood.

Fusion complex A complex intermediate in configuration between complexes of two different origins due to simultaneous discharge of parts of the myocardium by each of the two sites of impulse formation.

Hypertrophy Enlargement due to increase in mass.

Interference Two impulses traveling toward each other from different directions and preventing each other's passage.

Interpolated complex An extra complex occurring between two sinus complexes without affecting the sinus cycle or ventricular cycle.

Interval The time between two electrocardiographic events.

Intrinsic pacemaker rate The rate at which a pacemaker focus spontaneously discharges.

Inverted wave A complex (especially P waves or T waves) whose major deflection is below the isoelectric line.

Myocardial infarction The death of cardiac muscle due to anoxia.

P wave The electrocardiographic representation of atrial depolarization.

Pacemaker cells Those specialized cells responsible for the initiation of a cardiac impulse.

Parasystole A rhythm in which the heart is being paced by two independent pacemakers.

Paroxysmal tachycardia A tachycardia of sudden onset and sudden end.

Pause A delay between consecutive impulses.

Pericarditis An inflammation of the pericardium surrounding the heart.

Potential The energy of an electric charge due to its position in an electric field.

PP interval The period of time between the onset of one P wave and the onset of the next P wave.

PR interval The duration of time between the onset of the P wave (atrial depolarization) and the onset of the QRS complex (ventricular depolarization).

Preexcitation Early activation of a portion of the ventricles due to the presence of a bypass tract.

Premature complex An early complex not in the normal sequence of cardiac impulses.

Purkinje network The terminal ramifications of the conducting system in the ventricular myocardium.

Q wave A negative electrocardiographic deflection occurring at the onset of ventricular depolarization.

QRS complex The electrocardiographic representation of ventricular depolarization.

QRS loop The sequential connection of the instantaneous vectors of ventricular depolarization.

QRS-T angle The spatial angle between the mean QRS vector and the mean T wave vector.

QT interval The duration of time between the onset of the QRS complex (ventricular depolarization) and the end of the T wave (ventricular repolarization).

R wave The first upward electrocardiographic deflection of ventricular depolarization whether or not a Q wave is present.

Reciprocal complex A complex triggered by an impulse which has left and then reentered its area of origin.

Refractory period, absolute The period of the cardiac electrical cycle after a discharge, during which the electrically active tissue cannot transmit or respond to an impulse.

Refractory period, relative That period of the cardiac electrical cycle after the absolute refractory period during which the electrically active tissue can transmit, or respond to, an impulse only to a subnormal extent.

Repolarization The electrical process in which the transmembrane potential difference is restored to a fully polarized state.

Resting transmembrane potential difference The electrical difference between the inside and outside of the fully repolarized cell before the onset of depolarization. This is normally about 90 mV.

Retrograde conduction Conduction backward in the conducting system along a pathway from the ventricles or the AV node to the atria.

RP interval The period of time between the onset of a QRS complex and the onset of the following P wave.

RR interval The period of time between the onset of one QRS complex and the onset of the next QRS complex.

S wave Electrocardiographic deflection below the isoelectric line during ventricular depolarization.

SA junction The physiologic "bridge" between the site of impulse formation in the sinus node and the atrial myocardium.

Spontaneous depolarization The slow, automatic depolarization of a pacemaker cell. Spontaneous depolarization is critical in impulse formation.

ST segment The portion of the ECG between the end of the QRS complex and the beginning of the T wave.

Standstill, cardiac The complete cessation of electrical and mechanical activity of the heart.

Supraventricular Pertaining to a complex or run of complexes whose site of impulse formation is above the ventricular level.

T wave The electrocardiographic representation of ventricular repolarization.

Ta wave The atrial T wave; the wave of repolarization associated with the P wave.

Tachycardia A heart rate of greater than 100 complexes per minute.

Trifascicular block Block in the right bundle branch, one division of the left bundle branch, and delayed conduction in the second division of the left bundle branch.

Trigeminy Complexes occurring in groups of three.

U wave A deflection of uncertain origin which follows the T wave but is not always evident.

Unipolar leads Leads aV_R, aV_L, aV_F, and V_1 to V_6. These leads consist of a positive (exploring) electrode and a negative (indifferent) electrode. Since the negative electrode is always at zero potential, the positive electrode equals the potential difference between the two electrodes.

Vector, electrocardiographic The representation of the direction in space and the magnitude of the electrical activity of the heart.

Vector, instantaneous The spatial direction and magnitude of an electrocardiographic representation of a cardiac electrical event at an instantaneous point in time.

Vector, mean The average direction and magnitude of an electrocardiographic representation of a cardiac electrical event, e.g., mean QRS vector, mean T wave vector.

Zero potential plane A plane of zero potential which is always perpendicular to the direction of the electrical forces.

INDEX

Index

Page numbers followed by "f" or "t" refer to figures and tables, respectively.

Aberrant conduction, 252f, 282, 284, 284f, 288, 293
   of premature atrial complexes, 269–272
   of premature AV junctional complexes, 274, 276f
Accelerated rhythms:
   AV junctional, 277, 278
   ventricular, 286f, 288
Action potential, 6
   ECG correlation, 7
   transmembrane, 6, 7f
   phases 0–4, 7
Age, influence of, 48
Amyloid heart disease, 200
Angina pectoris (*see* Myocardial ischemia)
Aortic regurgitation, 203
   ECG findings in, 202f, 203
Aortic stenosis, 201
   ECG findings in, 90f, 201, 203
Arrhythmias, 241–318
Asymmetric septal hypertrophy (*see* Cardiomyopathy, hypertrophic)
Asystole (*see* Ventricular arrhythmia, standstill)
Atrial abnormality, 85–88
   biatrial, 87
      ECG criteria for, 87
      in patent ductus arteriosus, 213

Atrial abnormality (*Cont.*):
   in cardiomyopathy, 197
   definition of, 85, 86
   important considerations in, 87
   left, 86, 86f, 87, 198f
      in aortic regurgitation, 203
      in aortic stenosis, 201
      in coarctation of aorta, 219
      ECG criteria for, 87, 88t
      in hypertension, 200
      in hypertrophic cardiomyopathy, 199
      in left ventricular hypertrophy, 99
      in mitral regurgitation, 205
      in mitral stenosis, 203
      in ostium primum defect, 211
      in patent ductus arteriosus, 213
      in pericarditis, 195
      in pulmonary edema, 87
   right, 86, 86f, 212f
      ECG criteria for, 86
      in hypertrophic cardiomyopathy, 199
      in lung disease, 183
      in pulmonary embolus, 189
      in pulmonic stenosis, 215
      in right ventricular hypertrophy, 104
Atrial arrhythmia:
   differential diagnosis of, 267, 268, 293, 295–297
   ectopic tachycardia, 264

Atrial arrhythmia (*Cont.*):
  fibrillation, (*see* Atrial fibrillation)
  flutter, 264, 265, 266f, 267f, 295f, 297
  paroxysmal supraventricular tachycardia,
    259–262, 264f, 294f, 297
  premature complexes, 269–272, 270f, 271f
Atrial enlargement (*see* Atrial abnormality)
Atrial fibrillation, 265–268, 268f, 269f, 296f,
  297
  in aortic stenosis, 203
  in atrial septal defect, 209
  in hypertension, 200
  in hypertrophic cardiomyopathy, 199
  in mitral regurgitation, 205
  in mitral stenosis, 205
  in pericarditis, chronic, 195
Atrial flutter (*see* Atrial arrhythmia)
Atrial infarction, 165
  atrial arrhythmias in, 165
  PR segment in, 165
  P wave in, 165
Atrial septal defect, 207, 209, 211
  anatomic classification of, 207
  atrial fibrillation in, 209
  ECG findings in, 207–211, 208f
  important considerations in, 209, 211
Atrial T wave, 58, 58f
Atrioventricular (AV) block, 299–307
  anterograde, 306
  in AV junctional rhythms, 278
  first degree, 300
  retrograde, 306
  second degree, 300–302
    Mobitz type II, 301, 302f
    Wenckebach phenomenon, 300, 301,
      301f, 311, 315
  third degree (complete), 302
  unidirectional, 306, 318
Atrioventricular (AV) dissociation, 278, 279,
  279f
  longitudinal, in reciprocal complexes, 318
Atrioventricular (AV) junction:
  escape complexes, 274, 302
  pacemaker function, 273
  premature complexes, 274, 276f, 277f
Atrioventricular (AV) junctional
  tachycardia, 277, 278
Atrioventricular (AV) nodal reentry, 259,
  262
Automaticity, 241, 242, 244
AV diagram, 247–255, 250f, 251f, 252f, 253f,
  254f

AV ladder, 247–255
AV node, 8, 10f

Bayes' Theorem, 50
Bifascicular block (*see* Fascicular block,
  bifascicular)
Bigeminy:
  atrial, 309–311, 310f
  ventricular, 309–311, 311f
Bradycardia:
  in AV dissociation, 279f
  in AV junctional escape rhythm, 273, 274
  in complete heart block, 302
  sinus, 258–259
Bundle branch:
  left, 10f, 11
    fascicles of, 119
  right, 10f, 11
Bundle branch block, 105–117
  complete, 105
  definition of, 105
  incomplete, 105
  in hypertension, 200
  in infiltrative cardiomyopathy, 200
  in myocarditis, 199
  left, 105–113, 106f, 108f, 109f, 110f, 112f,
    114f
    in aortic stenosis, 203
    in congestive cardiomyopathy, 197
    ECG criteria for, 105, 107
    important considerations in, 107, 111,
      113
  nonspecific intraventricular block, 117
  right, 106f, 108f, 113, 115–117, 116f, 118f,
    120f, 122f
    differential diagnosis of, 115
    in Ebstein's anomaly, 220
    ECG criteria for, 113, 115
    important considerations in, 115, 117
    in ostium primum defect, 211
    in pulmonary embolus, 189
Bundle of Kent, 131, 261

Calcium ion, 6
  hypercalcemia, 225
  hypocalcemia, 222f, 225
Capture beats, 278
Cardiac cycle, 8, 10f, 11
Cardiomyopathy, 197–200
  congestive, dilated, 197, 198f, 199

Cardiomyopathy (Cont.):
    hypertension, 200
    hypertrophic, 199
        ECG findings in, 199
        left atrial abnormality in, 87, 199
        septal hypertrophy in, 98
    infiltrative, 200
    myocarditis, 199, 200
Carotid sinus pressure, 296–297
    in atrial fibrillation, 267, 296f, 297
    in atrial flutter, 265, 295f, 297
    in ectopic atrial tachycardia, 264
    in paroxysmal supraventricular
        tachycardia, 294f, 297
    precautions, 297
    in sinus tachycardia, 259, 292f, 297
Cell:
    electrical potential difference of, 5
    electrophysiology of, 5–8
    membrane, 5
    negative and positive charges of, 5
    negative and positive poles of, 7
    polarized, 5
    transitional region of, 7
Central nervous system disorders,
        225–226
    ECG findings in, 226
    important considerations in, 226
Central (indifferent) terminal:
    definition of, 24
    of precordial leads, 27
Chloride ion, 6
Coarctation of aorta, 214f, 219
    ECG findings in, 219
Conduction defect (see Bundle branch
    block)
Conduction system, 11
Conductivity, 241, 242
    supernormal, 244
Congenital heart disease,
    specific types of, 207–220
Coronary artery disease, normal ECG in,
    139, 167
    (See also Myocardial infarction;
        Myocardial ischemia)

Deflections:
    intrinsicoid:
        definition of, 98
        delay in left ventricular hypertrophy,
            98, 99

Deflections, intrinsicoid (Cont.):
    delay in right ventricular hypertrophy,
        101
    terminology of electrocardiographic, 41–43
        biphasic (diphasic) QRS complex, 43
        monophasic QRS complex, 43
        P wave, 41
        QRS complex, 41
        Q wave, 41
        R wave, 41
        S wave, 43
        triphasic QRS complex, 43
        T wave, 43
        U wave, 43
Delta wave, 132f, 133, 134, 134f, 136–137
Depolarization, 5, 7
    sequence of left bundle branch block, 105,
        107, 109f
    sequence of normal ventricular conducting
        system, 8, 11
    sequence of right bundle branch block,
        113, 116f
Dextrocardia:
    ECG findings in, 220
    important considerations in, 220
Digitalis, 227–235, 228f, 230f, 232f, 234f
    arrhythmias due to, 229
    digitalis effect, 227
    ECG findings due to, 227
    important considerations in, 227
Diphasic complex, 43
Dipole:
    definition of, 5
    single dipole theory, 7, 8

Ebstein's anomaly, ECG findings in, 219,
    220
Ectopic complexes (see Premature
    complexes)
Einthoven's triangle, concept of, 20
Electrical alternans in pericardial effusion,
    196
Electrical forces [see Vector(s)]
Electrocardiogram:
    absence of normal values for, 48
    approach to the interpretation of, 46, 47
    computerized interpretation of, 49
    confirmation of criteria for, 52, 53
    constitutional influences, 48
    heart rate determination from, 43, 44f,
        249, 249f

Electrocardiogram (*Cont.*):
  intervals of, 45
  measurements, 43–45
    PR interval, 45, 320t
    QRS interval, 45
    QT interval, 45, 321t
    voltage, 43
  newborn, 69
  normal, 57–69, 58f, 59f, 60f, 62f, 64f, 66f, 68f, 70f
    in acute mitral regurgitation, 205
    in aortic stenosis, 201
    in coronary disease, 139
    physiologic influences on, 48
    preadult, 69
    standardization of, 43
    statistical considerations in, 50–52
      Bayes' theorem, 50
      predictive accuracy, 50
      sensitivity, 50
      specificity, 50
    technical considerations in, 48, 49
Electrocardiography, methods of interpretation in, 3
Electrode:
  definition of, 16
  placement of, 20, 27, 28
Electrolyte imbalance, 221–225
  ECG findings: in hypercalcemia, 225
    in hyperkalemia, 221–223
    in hypermagnesemia, 225
    in hypernatremia, 225
    in hypocalcemia, 225
    in hypokalemia, 223, 224
    in hypomagnesemia, 225
    in hyponatremia, 225
Electrophysiology (*see* Cell, electrophysiology of)
Equipotential forces, 8
Escape complexes, 273, 274, 281
  in AV dissociation, 279f
  AV junctional, 273, 274
  in sinus pause, 273, 274
  ventricular, 281
Extremity leads (*see* Leads, bipolar frontal)

Fascicular block, 119–129
  bifascicular block, 119, 127
  combinations of, 125, 127
  definition of, 119

Fascicular block (*Cont.*):
  important considerations in, 127, 129
  left anterior (divisional, hemi-), 108f, 121, 123, 126f, 128f
  left posterior (divisional, hemi-), 108f, 116f, 118f, 123, 125
  mimicking infarction, 129
  due to septal fibrosis, 98
  trifascicular, 127
  types of, 119
Frontal leads (*see* Leads: bipolar frontal, unipolar frontal)
Frontal plane, determination of direction of forces, 23f, 24–26, 25f, 26f
Frontal plane leads, 20
Fusion complexes, 316f, 318
  atrial, 250, 251f, 318
  in atrial parasystole, 314f, 318
  ventricular, 252f, 254, 316f, 318
  in ventricular parasystole, 312f, 315, 318

Galvanometer, 16
Group beating, 309–311, 315

Heart rate:
  determination of, 43, 44f, 249, 249f
  normal, 258, 259
Hemiblock (*see* Fascicular block: left anterior, left posterior)
Hemochromatosis (*see* Cardiomyopathy, infiltrative)
Hexaxial reference system:
  definition of, 21f, 24
  electrical axis and, 45
His bundle, 10f, 11, 119, 299
Hypercalcemia, 225
Hyperkalemia, 221–223
Hypermagnesemia, 225
Hypernatremia, 225
Hypertension:
  ECG findings in, 200
  left atrial abnormality in, 87
  left ventricular hypertrophy in, 93f, 95f, 98
Hypertrophic cardiomyopathy (*see* Cardiomyopathy, hypertrophic)
Hypocalcemia, 225
Hypokalemia, 223, 224

Hypomagnesemia, 225
Hyponatremia, 225

Indifferent terminal (*see* Central terminal)
Infarction (*see* Myocardial infarction)
Injury current, 140
Interference, 253f, 255
Interpolated complex, 282
Intervals of the electrocardiogram, 45
Intraventricular conduction defect (*see* Bundle branch block)
Intrinsicoid deflection (*see* Deflections, intrinsicoid)
Ischemia (*see* Myocardial ischemia)
Isoelectric line:
 definition of, 16
 and phase 4, 5, 7

Juvenile T pattern, 68f, 69

Kent bundle, 131, 261

Lead(s):
 axis, definition of, 16
 bipolar frontal (limb, extremity), 20–27
  location of positive terminal, 20
  mathematical relationship of, 23
 definition of, 16
 precordial (V, chest), 27–31
  central terminal of, 27
  determination of direction of forces, 28–31
  location of positive terminal, 27, 28
  transitional complex of, 29
 projection of electrical forces on, 16
 unipolar (augmented) frontal, 24
  location of positive terminals, 24
  mathematical relationship of, 24
Left anterior fascicular block (*see* Fascicular block, left anterior)
Left atrial abnormality (*see* Atrial abnormality, left)
Left axis deviation (*see* QRS axis, left axis deviation)
Left bundle branch (*see* Bundle branch, left)
Left bundle branch block (*see* Bundle branch block, left)
Left posterior fascicular block (*see* Fascicular block, left posterior)

Left ventricle (*see* Ventricle, left)
Left ventricular hypertrophy (*see* Ventricular hypertrophy, left)
Lown-Ganong-Levine syndrome (*see* Preexcitation)
Lung disease, chronic obstructive, 183–187, 184f
 ECG criteria for, 183, 185
 important considerations in, 185, 187
 QRS vector in, 183, 185
 right atrial abnormality in, 183
 right ventricular hypertrophy in, 185
 SI, II, III pattern in, 185

Membrane resting potential, 5
Mitral regurgitation, 205, 206
 ECG findings in, 205, 206
 left atrial abnormality in, 87
 in ostium primum defect, 211
Mitral stenosis, 102f, 186f, 203, 205
 ECG findings in, 203, 205
 left atrial abnormality in, 87
 right ventricular hypertrophy in, 104
Mitral valve prolapse, 205, 206
 ECG findings in, 205, 206
 WPW in, 136
Mobitz II AV block, 301
Myocardial disease (*see* Cardiomyopathy)
Myocardial infarction, 139–169
 age of, 165, 167, 169
 anatomic extension of, 151, 153
 current of injury in, 140
 ECG criteria for, 140–143
 epicardial, 140
 hyperacute T wave in, 140
 important considerations in, 147, 151
 nontransmural, 153
 normal ECG in, 139
 pseudomyocardial infarction, 149, 182t
 silent, 153
 site of, 153–165
  anterior, 140f, 146f, 147f, 155, 157, 162f, 166f, 168f, 170f, 172f, 174f, 176f
  apical, 140f, 144f, 161, 163, 174f
  atrial, 165
  inferior (diaphragmatic), 140f, 141f, 142f, 150f, 152f, 154f, 156f, 157, 158f, 159, 160f

Myocardial infraction, site of (Cont.):
  posterior, 140f, 142f, 143f, 150f, 152f, 159, 161
  right ventricular, 163
  subendocardial, 163, 164f
  subepicardial, 163
Myocardial ischemia, 169–175, 180f
  due to coronary spasm, 169
  epicardial, 169
  mimics of, 173, 175
  subendocardial, 171
Myocarditis, 199, 200
  ECG findings in, 199, 200

Newborn, ECG changes from newborn to adult, 69
Nomenclature of electrocardiogram, 41–43
Nonspecific intraventricular block, 117
Normal ECG, 57–79
Normal variants of the ECG, early repolarization pattern, 65, 78f

Ostium primum septal defect, 207, 209, 211
Overload pattern:
  diastolic: in aortic regurgitation, 203
    definition of, 203
    important considerations in, 206
    in patent ductus arteriosus, 215
    in ventricular septal defect, 213
  systolic: in aortic stenosis, 203
    definition of, 201, 203
    important considerations in, 206
    in ventricular septal defect, 213

Pacemaker cells (see Sinus node)
Parasystole, 315, 316, 318
  atrial, 314f, 318
  exit block in, 316
  ventricular, 312f, 315
Paroxysmal supraventricular tachycardia (see Atrial arrhythmia)
Patent ductus arteriosus, 213, 215
  ECG findings in, 213, 215
Pause, 269–271
  compensatory, 269, 270, 282
  noncompensatory, 269, 270
  sinus, 273, 274, 306
Pericardial effusion, 196
  ECG criteria for, 196

Pericardial effusion (Cont.):
  electrical alternans in, 196
Pericarditis:
  acute, 191, 192f, 193, 193f, 195
    differential diagnosis, 195
    ECG criteria for, 191, 193
    important considerations in, 195
  chronic, 195, 196
    ECG findings in, 195, 196
Plane:
  frontal, 20
  precordial, 27
Pneumothorax, left 190
  ECG findings in, 190
Potassium ion, 5–7
Potential:
  action, 6
  difference, 5
  resting transmembrane, 5
  threshold, 7
  zero, 7
Precordial leads (see Leads, precordial)
Preexcitation, 131–137, 132f, 134f, 136f
  arrhythmias in, 135, 136
  definition of, 131
  Ebstein's anomaly and, 136
  ECG criteria for, 133, 135
  important considerations in, 136, 137
  Lown-Ganong-Levine syndrome, 136, 137
  repolarization in, 135
Premature complexes:
  atrial, 269–272
  atrioventricular (AV) junctional, 274
  differential diagnosis of, 282, 284
  interpolated ventricular, 282
  in parasystole, 315, 316
  pauses following, 269, 270
  ventricular, 282
PR interval:
  definition of, 11
  measurement of, 45
  normal upper limits, 320t
  prolongation in: aortic regurgitation, 203
    atrial septal defect, 207
    congestive cardiomyopathy, 199
    digitalis, 227
    Ebstein's anomaly, 219
    hyperkalemia, 222
    hypertrophic cardiomyopathy, 199
    hypokalemia, 223
    patent ductus arteriosus, 213
  short in preexcitation, 133

PR segment:
  deviation due to: atrial infarction, 165
    early repolarization pattern, 165
    pericarditis, 193
Pseudoinfarction pattern:
  in central nervous system disorders, 226
  in congestive cardiomyopathy, 199
  in hyperkalemia, 222, 223
  in infiltrative cardiomyopathy, 200
  in myocarditis, 200, 201
  in pulmonary embolus, 189, 190
  various causes of, 182t
  in Wolff-Parkinson-White syndrome, 137
Pulmonary embolus, acute, 187, 188f, 189, 190
  ECG criteria for, 187, 189
  important considerations in, 189, 190
  SI, QIII, TIII pattern in, 187
Pulmonic stenosis, 210f, 215, 217
  ECG findings in, 215
  important considerations in, 217
  right ventricular hypertrophy in, 104
P vector [see Vector(s), P]
P wave:
  in atrial infarction, 165
  in atrial septal defect, 207
  in central nervous system disorders, 226
  definition of, 11, 41, 42f
  in dextrocardia, 220
  in differential diagnosis of atrial arrhythmias, 293
  in hyperkalemia, 222
  in hypertension, 200
  in hypokalemia, 223
  in lung disease, 183
  in mitral regurgitation, 205
  in mitral stenosis, 203
  normal, discussion of, 57, 58
  in pericarditis, chronic, 195
  in pulmonary embolus, 189
  in pulmonic stenosis, 215
  in tetralogy of Fallot, 217
  in ventricular septal defect, 211, 213
  (See also Atrial abnormality)

QRS axis:
  left axis deviation: in aortic regurgitation, 203
    in coarctation of aorta, 219
    in congestive cardiomyopathy, 197

QRS axis, left axis deviation (Cont.):
    definition of, 45
    in hyperkalemia, 222
    in hypertension, 200
    in hypertrophic cardiomyopathy, 199
    in left anterior fascicular block, 121, 123, 127
    in lung disease, 185
    in ostium primum defect, 211
    in pulmonary embolus, 187
  normal range of, 45
  right axis deviation, 45
    in coarctation of aorta, 219
    definition of, 45
    in dextrocardia, 220
    in Ebstein's anomaly, 220
    in hyperkalemia, 222
    in mitral stenosis, 203
    in patent ductus arteriosus, 215
    in pneumothorax, 190
    in pulmonary embolus, 187
    in pulmonic stenosis, 215, 217
    in left posterior fascicular block, 125
    in tetralogy of Fallot, 217
  vertical axis: in mitral regurgitation, 205
    in ventricular septal defect, 213
QRS complex, 58
  anteriorly directed, 104
  definition of, 41
  initial 0.01 s vector, 58, 61
  initial 0.04 s vector, 61, 63
  and phase 0, 7
  terminal 0.02 s vector, 63
QRS interval, 105
  measurement of interval, 45
QRS loop, 15, 33, 36f
  definition of, 15
QRS-T angle:
  definition of, 67
  due to digitalis, 227
  in left bundle branch block, 107
  in left ventricular hypertrophy, 99
  in myocardial ischemia, 169
  normal range of, 67
  in right bundle branch block, 115
  in right ventricular hypertrophy, 101
  in SI, SII, SIII pattern, 117
QRS vectors [see Vector(s), QRS]
QS complex, 43
QT interval:
  correction for heart rate, 45

QT interval (*Cont.*):
  measurement of, 45
  normal values for, 321t
  prolongation: in central nervous system
    disorders, 226
    in hypercalcemia, 225
    in hyperkalemia, 222
    in hypocalcemia, 225
    in hypokalemia, 223
  shortened due to digitalis, 227
Q wave:
  in central nervous system disorders, 226
  in congestive cardiomyopathy, 199
  definition of, 41
  definition of abnormal, 143, 149
  differential diagnosis of abnormal, 173
  in fascicular block, 121
  in hypertrophic cardiomyopathy, 199
  loss of in left bundle branch block, 107
  in myocardial infarction, 141–143, 149
  normal, 61, 141, 142
  septal, 61

Rate (*see* Heart rate)
Reciprocal complexes, 317f, 318
Reentry, AV nodal, 259, 262
Repolarization:
  definition of, 5
  digitalis and early, 227
  early repolarization pattern, 65
  in left bundle branch block, 107
  in left ventricular hypertrophy, 99
  normal sequence of, 11
  in right bundle branch block, 113, 115
  in right ventricular hypertrophy, 101
Right atrial abnormality (*see* Atrial
  abnormality, right)
Right axis deviation (*see* QRS axis, right
  axis deviation)
Right bundle branch (*see* Bundle branch,
  right)
Right bundle branch block (*see* Bundle
  branch block, right)
Right ventricle (*see* Ventricle, right)
Right ventricular hypertrophy (*see*
  Ventricular hypertrophy, right)
RSR' pattern in V_1:
  in atrial septal defect, 207
  in Ebstein's anomaly, 220
  normal due to terminal 0.02 s vector, 63

RSR' pattern in V_1 (*Cont.*):
  in pulmonic stenosis, 215
  in right bundle branch block, 113
R wave:
  definition of, 41
  differential diagnosis of tall R in V_1, 159
  in fascicular block, 121
  in left bundle branch block, 107
  in left ventricular hypertrophy, 98
  in myocardial infarction, 159
  normal, 61, 63
  (*See also* Deflections)
  in posterior infarction, 159
  in right bundle branch block, 113
  in right ventricular hypertrophy, 100, 101
  variation in amplitude, 100

SI, SII, SIII pattern, 117, 119, 124f
  in lung disease, 185
  in right ventricular hypertrophy, 101
Sarcoidosis (*see* Cardiomyopathy,
  infiltrative)
Sinoatrial (SA) block, 302–304, 305f, 306,
  307f
Sinus:
  arrhythmia, 257, 258f
  bradycardia, 258, 259, 261f
  tachycardia, 259, 262f
Sinus node:
  location of, 8, 10f
  pacemaker cells, 7, 242
Sinus pause, 273, 274, 306
Sodium ion, 5, 6
ST segment:
  in aortic regurgitation, 203
  in aortic stenosis, 203
  in central nervous system disorders, 226
  in congestive cardiomyopathy, 197
  definition of, 11, 42f, 65
  differential diagnosis of displacement of,
    149, 173, 175
  in digitalis effect, 227
  early repolarization of, 65
  in hyperkalemia, 222, 223
  in hypertension, 200
  in hypertrophic cardiomyopathy, 199
  in hypocalcemia, 225
  in hypokalemia, 223, 224
  J point of, 65
  in myocardial infarction, 140, 141

ST segment, in myocardial infarction (*Cont.*):
   anterior, 157
   apical, 163
   evolution of, 165, 167
   inferior, 159
   posterior, 159
   right ventricular, 163
   subendocardial, 163
   subepicardial, 163
   in myocardial ischemia, 169
   in myocarditis, 199
   normal, 65, 151
   in pericarditis, 191, 193
   and phase 2, 7
   in pulmonary embolus, 189
   in ventricular aneurysm, 167
ST-T changes:
   in left bundle branch block, 107
   in left ventricular hypertrophy, 99
   in right ventricular hypertrophy, 101
ST vectors [*see* Vector(s), ST]
Supraventricular tachycardia, 259, 261, 262, 297
S wave:
   definition of, 43
   due to left ventricular vector, 89, 98
   normal, 61, 63
   due to right ventricular vector, 100, 101

Tachycardia:
   in atrial fibrillation, 265, 266, 297
   in atrial flutter, 265, 297
   atrioventricular (AV) junctional, 277, 278
   differential diagnosis, 291, 293, 295–297
   ectopic atrial, 264
   paroxysmal supraventricular, 259, 261, 262, 297
   paroxysmal AV junctional, 277, 278
   sinus, 259, 297
   ventricular, 287, 288
Ta wave, 58
Terminology (*see* Deflections)
Tetralogy of Fallot, 217
   ECG findings in, 217
   important considerations in, 217
Threshold potential, 7
Transitional:
   clockwise rotation in lung disease, 185

Transitional (*Cont.*):
   complex, 29, 30
   region, 7
Trifascicular block (*see* Fascicular block)
Trigeminy, 309, 311
Triphasic (RSR') complex, 43
T vectors [*see* Vector(s), T]
T wave:
   in aortic regurgitation, 203
   in aortic stenosis, 203
   in central nervous system disorders, 226
   in coarctation of the aorta, 219
   in congestive cardiomyopathy, 199
   definition of, 43
   differential diagnosis of abnormal, 175
   in digitalis, 227
   in Ebstein's anomaly, 220
   in hyperkalemia, 221, 222
   in hypertension, 200
   in hypertrophic cardiomyopathy, 199
   in hypocalcemia, 225
   in hypokalemia, 223–225
   juvenile pattern, 69
   in myocardial infarction, 140
   in myocardial ischemia, 169, 171
   in myocarditis, 199
   normal, 47f, 65, 67
   in patent ductus arteriosus, 215
   in pericarditis, 193, 195, 196
   in pneumothorax, 190
   in pulmonary embolus, 189
   in pulmonic stenosis, 215
   vector of, 65

Unipolar leads (*see* Leads, unipolar)
U wave:
   in central nervous system disorders, 226
   definition of, 43
   in hypokalemia, 223–225
   inverted, various causes of, 171, 173
   normal, 67
   prominent, various causes of, 225

Vector(s):
   concept of, 13–15
   instantaneous, 13
   P vector: in atrial septal defect, 207
      in dextrocardia, 220
      left atrial, 87

Vector(s), P vector (*Cont.*):
   in lung disease, 183
   normal, 47f, 57
   right atrial, 86
   in ventricular septal defect, 211
  QRS vector: in atrial septal defects, 207, 209
   in fascicular blocks, 121, 123, 125
   in left bundle branch block, 105, 107
   left ventricular, 89
   in lung disease, 183, 185
   mean, 15, 47f, 63
     determination of direction of, 25–27
   in myocardial infarction, 141–143
   in newborn, 69
   normal range of, 45, 63
   in preadult, 69
   in pulmonary embolus, 187
   in right bundle branch block, 113
   right, ventricular, 100
  ST vector: in aortic regurgitation, 203
   in aortic stenosis, 203
   differential diagnosis of abnormal, 149, 151
   in digitalis, 227
   in hypertension, 200
   in hypertrophic cardiomyopathy, 199
   in left bundle branch block, 107
   in left ventricular hypertrophy, 99
   in myocardial infarction, 140, 141
   in myocardial ischemia, 169
   in myocarditis, 199
   in pericarditis, 191, 193
   in pulmonary embolus, 189
   in right bundle branch block, 113, 115
   in right ventricular hypertrophy, 101
   in tetralogy of Fallot, 217
  T vector: in aortic regurgitation, 203
   in aortic stenosis, 203
   in coarctation of aorta, 219
   in digitalis, 227
   in Ebstein's anomaly, 220
   in left ventricular hypertrophy, 99
   in mitral valve prolapse, 205, 206
   in myocardial infarction, 140
   in myocardial ischemia, 169, 171
   in newborn, 69
   normal range of, 47f, 65, 67
   in pericarditis, 193
   in preadult, 69

Vector(s), T vector (*Cont.*):
   in pneumothorax, 190
   in pulmonary embolus, 189
   in pulmonic stenosis, 215
   in right ventricular hypertrophy, 101
   in tetralogy of Fallot, 217
Ventricle(s):
  endocardium of, 11
  epicardium of, 11
  left, 11, 89
  right, 11, 100
Ventricular aneurysm, ST changes in, 167
Ventricular arrhythmia:
  fibrillation, 288, 289f
  flutter, 287f, 288
  pacemaker, 281
  premature complexes, 281, 282, 284f
  standstill, 290
  tachycardia, 286f, 287, 288, 291, 293
Ventricular hypertrophy:
  left, 89, 90f, 92f, 94f, 96t, 98, 99
   in aortic regurgitation, 203
   in aortic stenosis, 201
   in coarctation of aorta, 219
   in congestive cardiomyopathy, 197
   ECG criteria for, 89, 98, 99
   in hypertension, 200
   in hypertrophic cardiomyopathy, 199
   important considerations in, 99
   in mitral regurgitation, 205
   QRS vector of, 89, 98
  right, 97t, 100, 101, 102f, 104, 186f, 208f, 210f, 212f
   in coarctation of aorta, 219
   ECG criteria for, 100, 101, 104
   important considerations in, 104
   in lung disease, 183, 185
   in mitral stenosis, 203
   in patent ductus arteriosus, 215
   in pulmonic stenosis, 215
   right atrial abnormality in, 104
   SI, SII, SIII pattern in, 101
   in tetralogy of Fallot, 217
   types A, B, C, 101
Ventricular septum:
  muscular, 11
  septal defect, 211, 213
   ECG findings in, 211, 213
   important considerations in, 213
Ventricular tachycardia (*see* Ventricular arrhythmia)

Voltage, low:
  in chronic pericarditis, 195
  in congestive cardiomyopathy, 197
  differential diagnosis of, 196
  in left pneumothorax, 190
  in lung disease, 185
  in pericardial effusion, 196

Wandering pacemaker, 257, 258, 260f
Wenckebach phenomenon, 299–301, 304, 311, 315
  AV junctional, 299–301, 301f
  group beating and, 311, 315

Wenckebach phenomenon (*Cont.*):
  sinoatrial, 302–304, 305f, 306, 307f, 311
Wolff-Parkinson-White syndrome, 136
  association with other disorders, 136
  association with paroxysmal supraventricular tachycardia, 261, 262
  delta wave in, 133, 137
  type A, 133
    differential diagnosis of, 137
  type B, 134f, 135
    differential diagnosis of, 137

Zero potential plane, transitional, 8, 29